Utopian and Dystopian Themes in Tolkien's Legendarium

Utopian and Dystopian Themes in Tolkien's Legendarium

Mark Doyle

LEXINGTON BOOKS
Lanham • Boulder • New York • London

Published by Lexington Books
An imprint of The Rowman & Littlefield Publishing Group, Inc.
4501 Forbes Boulevard, Suite 200, Lanham, Maryland 20706
www.rowman.com

6 Tinworth Street, London SE11 5AL

Copyright © 2020 by The Rowman & Littlefield Publishing Group, Inc.

All rights reserved. No part of this book may be reproduced in any form or by any electronic or mechanical means, including information storage and retrieval systems, without written permission from the publisher, except by a reviewer who may quote passages in a review.

British Library Cataloguing in Publication Information Available

Library of Congress Cataloging-in-Publication Data Available

ISBN 978-1-4985-9867-5 (cloth)
ISBN 978-1-4985-9869-9 (pbk)
ISBN 978-1-4985-9868-2 (electronic)

Contents

Acknowledgments	vii
Introduction: Tolkien's Popularity and Its Relationship with His Utopian and Dystopian Themes	1
1 Tolkien and Traditional Utopias and Dystopias	9
2 The Sources of Tolkien's Utopian and Dystopian Vision	43
3 How the Environment Becomes Creation in Tolkien's Societies	77
4 Tolkien's Utopian and Dystopian Mythology	107
5 Tolkien's Utopian and Dystopian Politics	137
Epilogue: The Struggle for Tolkien's Utopian and Dystopian Legacy	175
Bibliography	185
Index	189
About the Author	195

Acknowledgments

I want to thank everyone at Lexington Books for their help and encouragement in completing my book, especially Lindsey Porambo Falk, Jessica Thwaite, Holly Buchanan, Megan Conley, and Melissa McClellan. Writing a book can be a lonely process, but I was lucky that my colleagues at Marion Military Institute provided much needed inspiration and practical assistance. Two of my colleagues from MMI, David Spewak and Rankin Sherling, read drafts of my manuscript and provided useful suggestions to help revise it. Professor Spewak read the entire manuscript, and he also serendipitously organized a writing club at MMI whose meetings kept me on track and accountable. My children's very presence helped me write this book since they gave me an excuse to read *The Hobbit* and *The Lord of the Rings* to them five times (one for each child) over the past twenty years. My older children also read parts of the manuscript and gave sage advice, especially about popular culture and video games. Finally, my most heartfelt thanks goes to my wife who had the unenviable task of reading every word of my manuscript multiple times. No matter how many times she picked it up, she always brought a fresh pair of eyes and her preternatural powers of concentration.

Introduction

Tolkien's Popularity and Its Relationship with His Utopian and Dystopian Themes

My son spent the spring semester his junior year in college in the Central Asian country of Kyrgyzstan. There he met twin sisters Zarina and Alina, who turned out to be die-hard J.R.R. Tolkien fans. They were fans not just in the sense of seeing the Peter Jackson films or even reading *The Lord of the Rings*, but the type of enthusiasts who buy leather-bound special-edition copies of Tolkien works and newly released reference books like *The Atlas of Tolkien* and *The Heroes of Tolkien* (these books were published in 2015 and 2017, respectively). What makes these particular Tolkien enthusiasts so interesting is the contrast between their fervor for Tolkien and their geographical isolation from the centers of cultural and political power. Landlocked Kyrgyzstan is one of the most remote countries in Asia, surrounded by other Turkic former Soviet republics and the most backward part of Western China. Even compared to other second-world countries of the former Soviet Union, Kyrgyzstan is poor and underdeveloped. My son described how he would sometimes meet wandering Westerners who arrived in Kyrgyzstan because it was metaphorically "the end of the road," one of the most isolated places in Asia (much like misanthropic American wanderers often end up in Alaska because it is "the end of the road" in North America). The fact that Tolkien, a quiet English academic who disliked foreign travel, could enthrall fans so different from him, like twenty-first-century Russian-speakers from Kyrgyzstan, shows the remarkable reach and appeal of his narratives. This incredible depth and appeal of Tolkien deserves an explanation and this book is an attempt to provide one. Yet one of the most intimidating parts about writing about Tolkien comes from his fans' vast reserves of knowledge that certainly match or surpass what many "professional" scholars know (including me!).

Evidence of Tolkien's enormous popularity and reach goes beyond even anecdotes like this. Tolkien's works are some of the most read and beloved books of our time, as confirmed by numerous surveys. For instance, a Waterstone Booksellers' 1997 poll named *The Lord of the Rings* "the Book of the Century" in Britain.[1] In another British survey, by the BBC, readers ranked Tolkien's *The Lord of the Rings* as the number one novel written in English, ahead of both classics like *Pride and Prejudice* and *Great Expectations* as well as popular works like *The Hitchhiker's Guide to the Galaxy* and the Harry Potter series.[2] Tolkien's *The Lord of the Rings* also was named as one of the hundred best loved books in the *Great American Read* survey by PBS. This popularity is also borne out by other measures. In 2015, the writer James V. Chapman compiled a list of the ten most read books in the world and Tolkien's *The Lord of the Rings* came in fourth.[3] Even though most of these surveys name *The Lord of the Rings*, other Tolkien works are also extremely popular. For example, Tolkien's *The Hobbit* is one of the most popular children's books of all time. Even Tolkien's lesser known books, like *The Silmarillion*, do well compared to most novels. *The Silmarillion* sold out its first printing of 325,000 books in its first year and so another run of 325,000 books had to be printed. While there are many reasons for the popularity of Tolkien's works, I make the argument in this book that much of Tolkien's appeal comes from how he speaks to the desires and fears of his twentieth- and twenty-first-century readers.

The way that Tolkien inspires and terrifies his vast audience comes not only from creating beautiful landscapes, inspiring heroes, and fearsome villains, but from how he uses utopian and dystopian themes to intensify his audience's longings and fears. I say Tolkien uses utopian and dystopian themes rather than creates utopias and dystopias because in many ways his works differ from classic utopias and dystopias. This does not mean, however, that they are not an effective means of inspiring idealism for a better society or concern for where our current society is headed. Not only that, I argue that Tolkien's approach of creating good, but not "perfect" societies has been more effective in connecting with his audience than most utopian and dystopian literature. Compare the relative popularity of Tolkien's works to classic utopias such as those described in Sir Thomas More's eponymous *Utopia* and Plato's *Republic*. I think many people would travel without hesitation to Middle-earth if given a choice, even though these societies face challenges and dangers. At the same time, there are relatively few "fans" of the more classic utopias and even fewer who would be interested in living in More's Utopia or Plato's Republic. A lot of what makes Tolkien's societies so appealing comes from what problems he ignores and what problems he addresses in creating his fictional world; his works ignore the central concern of most classic utopias—that of creating societies of relative comfort and peace. Indeed, I suspect what makes Tolkien's narratives appear utopian to readers has more to do with his works providing readers with a sense of meaning, rather than relieving them of struggle. In a similar way, Tolkien's dystopian-themed societies, Mordor and Thangorodrim, seem frighteningly familiar even if they appear to be set in some distant medieval or ancient society. Tolkien's evil societies operate in ways that seem recognizable to how evil works in our world. Instead of operating with the totalizing power described in famous dystopias like *1984* and *Brave New World*, evil in Tolkien's malevolent civilizations appears much less all-encompassing and powerful. Similarly, the leaders of Tolkien's bad societies have much less control over them than the leaders in Aldous Huxley's and George Orwell's dystopias. The results of his malevolent societies' efforts are often disastrous, and they repeatedly fail in achieving their goals. This history of failure contrasts with most classic dystopian portrayals that show triumphant and unstoppable dystopian leaders effortlessly enforcing their will on their dystopian subjects. Tolkien allows both his good and bad societies to be inspiring as well as terrifying without making them so "perfect" that they lose their connection to the lived experience of his readers. His positive societies contain many good things our societies lack, and his negative societies incorporate many evil practices that our societies condone. In this way, Tolkien reinvigorates the formulas for utopian and dystopian literature, so that they speak more clearly to his readers' hopes and misgivings about their current culture.

Not everyone agrees that Tolkien's works have much to say about our current society or that they merit close examination at all. Many literary and social critics have argued that Tolkien's works do not have the intellectual complexity to merit any analysis, whether it be about their utopian and dystopian themes or any other subject. Examples of this contempt can be found in contemporaneous reviews of *The Lord of the Rings*. Edmund Wilson famously argued that *The Lord of the Rings* was a poor novel because "Dr. Tolkien has little skill at narrative and no instinct for literary form." Wilson speculated that the problem with *The Lord of the Rings* was that it was a simple fairy tale that got out of hand. He concludes that the reason people like the book is "certain people—especially perhaps in Britain—have a lifelong appetite for juvenile trash."[4] This was and still is a common opinion among certain members of the literary establishment. When *The Lord of the Rings* was named the book of the century, Germaine Greer hyperbolically lamented,

> Ever since I arrived at Cambridge as a student in 1964 and encountered a tribe of fully grown women, wearing puffed sleeves, clutching teddies and babbling excitedly about the doing of hobbits, it has been my nightmare that Tolkien would turn out to be the most influential writer of the twentieth century. The bad dream has been realised.[5]

The central complaint of these literary critics is that J.R.R. Tolkien's works are juvenile, either because they assume that they are written for young people or because they declare the writing itself somehow childish or arrested. Of course, *The Hobbit* is a story that was written for children, but this judgment seems unfair for works like *The Lord of the Rings* and, especially, *The Silmarillion*. Part of this assumption about the childishness of Tolkien's works comes from the fact that most people are introduced to

Middle-earth through books or movies in childhood or adolescence. This association with childhood is one of the reasons some people consider Tolkien's novels simplistic or unsophisticated. Another reason that many critics do not take Tolkien's works seriously is that they are a part of "genre" literature that includes science fiction and fantasy. (Fantasy is a genre that Tolkien almost single-handedly created.) The idea is that such literature by its very genre is not "serious" enough to be called great literature.[6] Finally, Tolkien's popularity is also, ironically, a mark against him based on the assumption of many critics that the accessibility of a work of literature is inversely proportional to its artistic merit. Thus, the fact that various polls have named *The Lord of the Rings* one of the most popular or important books of the twentieth century makes these critics less likely to consider it serious literature (though these critics are not always consistent, as the contemporary popularity of *A Tale of Two Cities* or *The Great Gatsby* does not seem to hurt the classic status of these books). The assumption is that better literature (and art in general) challenges its audience, which makes the more challenging works less popular than art that is less difficult. Perhaps this is why Tolkien has not been canonized or anthologized by the critics who are the gatekeepers of "serious" literature.

What I hope to prove is that Tolkien's legendarium is both worthy of serious intellectual study and that its popularity comes from its ability to enchant, yet challenge, its audience. Tolkien introduces the numinous to his secular audience through his good societies and helps them to see the dangers of utilitarian tendencies through his evil ones.

Despite Tolkien's obvious utopian and dystopian themes, there are key differences between Tolkien's works and most utopian and dystopian narratives. For one thing, he combines characteristics of both utopian and dystopian societies in the same narrative. For another, unlike most utopian and dystopian literature, there is nothing pedagogical about Tolkien's narratives: he does not present arguments, ridicule opponents, or refer in an obvious way to current events and people like most utopian works. He provides no tours of utopian perfection and explanations of trade-offs. Tolkien also shows that there are no winners in dystopian societies and even the most powerful dystopian leaders in Middle-earth, Morgoth and Sauron, are as miserable as their meanest slaves. Tolkien's societies are also more fragile than the typical literary utopia or dystopia, which is portrayed as the final endpoint of human evolution or de-evolution. I argue that these many departures from standard utopian and dystopian conventions are what make his works unusually powerful, and in a strange way, more plausible to his readers than the "standard" utopia and dystopia.

I set out to prove this plausibility and the importance of these utopian and dystopian themes, and how they interact with Tolkien's narratives, from a variety of angles in the following chapters. In chapter 1, I define utopian and dystopian literature in general and describe how Tolkien's works compare to classic examples of utopian and dystopian literature. I show how Tolkien includes many utopian and dystopian themes despite the fact they are set in a mythological past rather than the present or future, like most utopias and dystopias. I also contend that the very differences between Tolkien's narratives and utopias and dystopias actually make the ideals he suggests appear more attainable. Tolkien's works avoid the narrowness, authoritarianism, and tedium that characterize most literary utopias. Similarly, Tolkien's evil societies have a disorder about them that makes them seem more plausible than many literary dystopias that seem preternaturally ordered.

In chapter 2, I show the sources that Tolkien drew upon to develop the utopian and dystopian qualities in Middle-earth. These sources mostly come in three forms: primary medieval documents, Victorian medievalism, and Modernism. The way Tolkien combines these sources makes his legendarium seem both deeply familiar yet strangely alien. They also give Tolkien the ability to introduce, and later help his audience consider, concepts that diverge from their hegemonic beliefs mainly because his narratives enchant the readers who are mostly disenchanted by the increasingly materialistic (in the philosophical sense) philosophy of Modernism and Postmodernism. Tolkien's use of these different sources creates narratives that defy genre characteristics and include elements of epic, romance, and the novel to make a whole a new genre: that of fantasy literature.

In the third chapter, I discuss Tolkien's environmental beliefs and their relationship with past and current environmental movements. In this chapter, I argue that though Tolkien's views about environmental preservation mirror many in the current environmental movement, his reasons were quite different. Most environmental activists are unconsciously Romantic (in the eighteenth- and nineteenth-century movement sense of the word) and view the world as one in which nature and people are separate and incommensurate realms. Tolkien does much to dismantle this binary in his legendarium. He instead puts people at the center of nature and argues that the abuse of people and the abuse of nature come from the same cause: people's inability to accept limits and their desire for power. Therefore, Tolkien's environmental utopianism involves people as much as nature, in contrast to many current environmentalists, whose natural utopias are pristine and untouched by humans. The evil in his societies comes from a desire to exceed the natural limits of Creation. Often, this need arises from a futile desire to go beyond nature and create without God. In this focus on accepting limits rather than separating man from nature, Tolkien shows a more Catholic worldview, rather than a Romantic one.

In chapter 4, I examine how Tolkien uses myth to create his societies. I look at both the most popular contemporary theories about myths and

Tolkien's own sophisticated approach to myth and myth-making from his influential essay "On Fairy-Stories." I argue that one of the reasons that Tolkien was able to create stories that resonated with his readers was his ability to create a modern-day myth that could enchant and inspire his audience. Part of how Tolkien does this comes from the atmosphere generated by his careful and consistent use of details. In this, Tolkien demonstrates his theory of myth, which runs counter to the most popular contemporary theories. While many current explanations for the power of myths assume myths operate through Jungian archetypes (or general themes) rather than specific details and atmosphere, Tolkien argues that myths' power comes from the details of myths and their ability to create a plausible alternative to our current reality. He calls this alternative "a secondary world." Tolkien also rejects the contemporary tendency to use myths instrumentally and in a piecemeal fashion to help people construct their identities; instead, he shows how myths can challenge people to change and how some myths can be so powerful that they even subsume people.

Chapter 5 connects Tolkien's societies to his political philosophy. In this chapter, I examine the various theories about Tolkien's politics including his relationship with anarchism, distributionism, and Toryism. As with most of Tolkien's intellectual tendencies, his politics are mostly orthogonal to those of most of his political contemporaries and current political leaders. I explore the sources of Tolkien's political philosophy found both in his letters and in his legendarium. Tolkien's major political concern was how man's desire to control the world and make it work more efficiently has the opposite effect of causing chaos and waste. Tolkien's anarchistic political beliefs come from the belief that attempting to control people inevitably leads to worse results than allowing them maximum freedom. These assumptions appear in how he constructs his societies and in the way he shows the different types of leadership these societies produce. His good societies hold the individual will of their citizens sacred, while Tolkien's evil societies crush and deform their subjects. Similarly, the leaders of Tolkien's ideal societies are well-rounded servant leaders, while the leaders of his evil realms are narrow, micromanaging tyrants. Once again, Tolkien demonstrates that the vaunted "efficiency" that evil leaders promote has inherent weaknesses that lead to these evil societies' inevitable downfalls.

Finally, my conclusion takes a brief look at the variety of other media that have been based or inspired by Tolkien's legendarium, including movies and video games. I observe that as more works are created based on Tolkien's stories, there is a tendency to make them reflect current, rather than Tolkien's, values. This often means that in movies, characters become more complex in some ways and simpler in others. Thus some evil characters, like Sauron, are "lightened" and made more glamorous; and good characters, like Faramir, are "darkened" and made less moral.

In some cases, antiheroes (and not just flawed heroes) are introduced into Middle-earth. On the other hand, the societies of Middle-earth are made less complicated and more flat. Thus, the Shire never falls under the influence of the evil Saruman and all the characters who do not fit neatly into either the good or bad side of the struggles between Mordor and the free peoples of Middle-earth tend to be eliminated. These changes reflect differences in philosophical assumptions between Tolkien's adaptors and Tolkien himself. The desire for "darker" characters and characters who can transcend moral limits reflects the modern desire to believe in self-fashioning and the separation between the moral and physical worlds. They also reflect the idea that morally mixed characters were somehow more complex than more morally upright ones. Many modern people also believe that power can transform a character and make him more interesting. As I will show, Tolkien believed quite the opposite: that the choice for evil in order to gain power narrows and diminishes a character rather than enlarges him or her. Similarly, contemporary society still has a strong belief in the righteousness of certain political states over others. Once again, Tolkien, who was skeptical of all political power, did much in his legendarium to complicate the idea that goodness resided in certain political organizations or states. Though many people wanted to read his narratives through a lens such as that of the "good" Allies being the equivalent of Gondor and Rohan, while the "bad" Nazis were the equivalent of Mordor, Tolkien never did.

In the end, so long as his original works can be read, the utopian and dystopian themes in Tolkien's legendarium will continue to challenge his readers to imagine a better world and dare them to pay attention to the ways in which it is becoming worse. Whatever deviations popular culture adds to his works, these changes will be temporary because of this ability to learn from Tolkien's original legendarium. As we shall see, Tolkien's utopianism attracts, and his dystopianism terrifies, precisely because Tolkien's depictions of these extremes differ from most modern people's presuppositions. The idea that these differences are somehow simplistic or juvenile often reflects critics' fears of their own assumptions being challenged. I hope this book will prove that even if critics do not agree with the worldview presented in Tolkien's legendarium, this disagreement does not come from the fact that Tolkien's ideas are simplistic, but that they are so radical.

NOTES

1. Giles Folden, "100 Books That Made a Century." *Guardian.* January 19, 1997.
2. "The Big Read: Top 100." *BBC.* September 2, 2014. https://www.bbc.co.uk/arts/bigread/top100.shtml.
3. James Chapman, "10 Most Read Books in the World." *Hubpage.* Last modified March 20, 2015. https://hubpages.com/literature/mostreadbooks.

4. Edmund Wilson, "Oo, Those Awful Orcs," in *The Bit between My Teeth: The Literary Chronicle of 1950* (Toronto: Farrar, Straus, and Giroux, 1965), 326–32.

5. Germaine Greer, "The Book of the Century." *W: The Waterstone Magazine*, Winter/Spring 1997, 2–9.

6. On the other hand, a lot of postmodern criticism has "problematicized" (to use a popular postmodern term) this distinction between serious and popular literature. Still, dissolving this distinction has not helped Tolkien's writing and most other examples of genre literature gain entrance in most literary anthologies and English survey courses. I think another reason for the disdain that Tolkien's works receive from academic critics reflects how his works often fall in the dreaded "middlebrow" territory. Critics who might argue that hip-hop or television sitcoms deserve careful cultural analyses based on postmodern assumptions realize that Tolkien does not neatly fit into the typical cultural analysis template because he is a bit outside popular culture. On the other hand, Tolkien's writing seems too popular for other critics who still view great art as the purview of the avant-garde.

ONE
Tolkien and Traditional Utopias and Dystopias

Tolkien creates good and bad societies in *The Lord of the Rings* and *The Silmarillion* that feel believable. Settings like Gondolin, the Shire, Lothlórien, Rivendell, Thangorodrim, and Mordor all have a verisimilitude about them that makes them seem familiar, yet not derivative. His images of just societies especially create a strange sense of nostalgia. As otherworldly as the Shire and Lothlórien are compared to our current world, they appear, to many readers, like a dimly remembered ancestral home that has been newly rediscovered and reclaimed. Similarly, the blasted wastelands of Tolkien's evil realms recall the all-too-familiar prison camps, barren battlefields, and industrial refuge heaps that mar modern landscapes. This chapter examines how Tolkien creates this sense of familiarity, how he constructs both ideal and abhorrent societies that feel credible, and how he avoids the shallowness that mars much utopian and dystopian literature. What Tolkien creates differs from most literary utopias and dystopias because of his assumptions about what makes the good life and what destroys it. As later chapters will show, Tolkien mined rich veins of intellectual history, including medieval literature, nineteenth-century medievalism, Catholic social thought, the pastoral (and the latent environmental) movement, myths, and localism, among others, to create this complex vision of the nature of good and evil.

Though I speak of Tolkien making his societies seem "believable" to twenty-first-century readers, this language is misleading in at least one sense. Tolkien does not make Middle-earth's good societies plausible by drawing them according to the assumptions of his twentieth (and twenty-first) century readers. He does quite the opposite: he re-enchants his readers so that they accept Middle-earth in all its artistic and philosophical grandeur rather than making his creations small enough to fit the somewhat impoverished and materialistic worldview of most twentieth- and twenty-first-century society. Tolkien does this by relying on his world-building skills to create societies that show either the glories of human potential or the terrors of human degradation on a visceral, rather than just an intellectual, level. The "enchantment" comes from making the ordinary sacred. In this way, he makes his readers believers, rather than his world believable.

Before discussing Tolkien's relationship to utopian and dystopian theories, we must define our terms—a more difficult task than it appears because the terms have several layers of meaning. The obvious definition of a utopia as a "perfect" society (this is the definition that most often appears in dictionaries) makes no sense in terms of the proposed or imagined utopias described in Plato's *Republic*, Thomas More's *Utopia*, or even Jonathan Swift's ironic land of the Houyhnhnms.[1] After all, these utopias contain criminals and punishments, which would not be necessary for a "perfect" place. As James Madison said, "If Men were angels, no government would be necessary." It appears, however, that even in utopias people are not angels, and they still need governing. This suggests a distinction between utopia and paradise, where paradise is a place where evil cannot exist, while utopia is a place where evil is greatly diminished or controlled. Readers also sense that trade-offs exist even in a utopia. B. G. Knepper comments on the conundrum presented in representing a "perfect" society in a literary work:

> If a utopia is to be convincing, it cannot present a perfect society made of fallible human beings. No one believes in such things, suspended disbelief as much as one will. Then, too, as a human society, a new society inevitably retains some aspects of the old society so that in utopia or dystopia there must be a certain amount of trade-off and compromise; increased order and discipline is exchanged for increasing blandness, unrelieved beauty for the highlighting provided by ugliness, and so on.[2]

The best utopias allow readers to accept these trade-offs and suspend their beliefs enough to accept the utopian society as far superior to our society, if not perfect. A better definition than a perfect place, and the definition that I will use for this book, is that utopia is not an ideal "place," but an ideal state and culture (in the broadest senses of those words). My definition focuses on the politics, laws, mores, and social structures of the imagined society. These utopian states have customs and rules that are perfectly designed to restrain individuals from doing evil, as opposed to a perfect society whose inhabitants are incapable of evil. Not only that, but the narratives focus on explaining how utopian society works and "selling" the reader about its benefits. Predictably then, many utopian narratives present their societies with the plots arranged more like a "tour" of the utopian society that highlights its customs and laws rather than a story that depends on a series of progressive events. We see just these type of tours in classic utopias like Thomas More's eponymous narrative, Edward Bellamy's *Looking Backward*, William Morris's *News from Nowhere*, and many others.

Dystopias, as the photo negative of utopias, have the opposite problems of utopias: that of a good thing happening accidentally, like Winston falling in love with Julia in the novel *1984*. Any instance of happiness stops a dystopia from being "pure evil" no matter how temporary or infrequent the pleasure. This brings up a more basic philosophical problem for dystopias; if one has an Augustinian view of evil (which Tolkien did), how can one create an evil society? According to Augustinian theology, evil is not a thing in itself, but a mere privation of the good; therefore, an evil society must be parasitic to the good or it would not exist. These assumptions make it clear that utopias and dystopias depend on a traditional Christian view of the world that recognizes the world that is, in some sense, fallen from its Edenic glory, but also good.[3] Utopias and dystopias both assume that good and evil both belong in the world but that they can be amplified or attenuated by the conditions of the utopia or dystopia. Thus my definition of dystopia is the opposite of utopia: dystopian states have customs and rules that are perfectly designed to encourage individuals to do evil, as opposed to a society whose inhabitants are incapable of good. Once again, a major portion of dystopian works tend to explain "how" the society works (though often in ways more organic to the story than the typical utopia).

Within recent scholarship, Lyman Tower Sergent has offered definitions of both utopias and dystopias that most critics use as a starting point.[4] He defines what he calls a positive utopia as "a non-existent society described in considerable detail and normally located in time and space that the author intended a contemporaneous reader to view as considerably better than the society in which that reader lived." Similarly, he defines a dystopia "a non-existent society described in considerable detail and normally located in time and space that the author intended a contemporaneous reader to view as considerably worse than the society in which that reader lived."[5] The problem with both these definitions is that they are so general that they would encompass not only all of Tolkien's works, but much of science fiction and fantasy literature today. Darko Suvin offers a more complex definition of a literary utopia:

> Utopia is the verbal construction of a particular quasi-human community where sociopolitical institutions, norms, and individual relationships are organized according to a more perfect principle than in the author's community, this construction being based on estrangement arising out of an alternative historical hypothesis.[6]

This definition cuts closer to mine in that his "sociopolitical institutions, norms, and individual relationships" map onto my categories of "state and culture." Suvin's definition departs from mine in his reliance on the concept of "estrangement" as a linchpin of the power of utopias. Estrangement, a principle from Bertolt Brecht, is when the artist attempts to make familiar things seem strange. We see an attempt at estrangement in *Gulliver's Travels*, when Swift describes how houyhnhnms do not have a word for "lie" and instead call a lie *"the thing which was not."* Thus one of the most common of human activities becomes redefined by this utopian society as something both unspeakable and rare. With this insight, when readers return from the narrative to their "real" society, they hopefully appreciate how bizarre the very idea of lying is and become "estranged" from the concept. Tolkien's approach is generally more positive than this. Tolkien's utopian visions gain their power not so much because of estrangement, since what he provides seems familiar rather than alien, but instead as enchantment because he takes everyday life and makes it appear more attractive. On the other hand, Tolkien's evil societies rely much more on estrangement by replicating the worst aspects of our industrial society and using them to threaten the bucolic beauty of Middle-earth.

Of course, utopias and dystopias imply not just imagined societies, but also a genre of literature. In many cases, especially in utopian literature, the work is written in a form akin to a travel narrative where some visitor from the outside (usually the contemporary world of the reader) learns about the society by experiencing it firsthand. *Utopia* set the mold for such narratives, but many other utopian stories follow this structure, including Book IV of *Gulliver's Travels*, Samuel Butler's *Erewhon,* and Edward Bellamy's *Looking Backward.* Dystopian fiction, on the other hand, tends to be more novelistic because there is no contemporary character outside the world of the dystopia to make explicit comparisons (though there is sometimes an outsider character, like John "the savage" in *Brave New World*). This is what we see in dystopias like Aldous Huxley's *Brave New World* and George Orwell's *1984* that create their own self-contained worlds. Another characteristic of most utopian and dystopian narratives is an explicit didactic purpose. They are used to promote certain political or social views in the case of utopias or, in the case of dystopias, warn of potential dangers in the reader's society.

The societies in J.R.R. Tolkien's legendarium are not utopias or dystopias despite the fact they fit many of the criteria of Sergent's and my definitions.[7] Certainly, they are better than our society in providing the freedom to allow for individual flourishing. Despite this, much of Tolkien's narratives differ from the utopian genre. For instance, no traveler from our current world comes to "show" us the workings of Middle-earth society.[8] Tolkien's works also depart from most classic utopian and dystopian literature in that his stories contain both utopian and dystopian societies in the same works (though the mixing of genres has become more popular in the late twentieth and early twenty-first centuries).

In addition, Tolkien's works are much less explicitly didactic than the typical utopian or dystopian narrative; he does not lay out his utopian societies as an example for us to follow directly or use his dystopias to warn us about particular societal trends or movements. Partly this is because the world of *The Silmarillion* and *The Lord of the Rings* represents (loosely) man's imagined past rather than his imagined future, as is the case with most utopian and dystopian literature. More so, however, the practical operations of the dystopian and utopian society are much less at the center of the narrative in Tolkien's works than they are in most utopian and dystopian literature. His focus is more on the characters in the story rather than explaining how his societies actually work, about which he often gives little information. The closest he comes is his descriptions of the Shire, but even here the focus is much sketchier than the typical utopia. His other good cultures, like Lothlórien and Gondolin, and even more so his evil societies, like Thangorodrim and Mordor, are hardly explained at all and are presented more atmospherically rather than programmatically.

These variances make Tolkien's societies different from most of his predecessors and contemporaries' utopias and dystopias. Even so, some of these differences also exist in other utopian and dystopian narratives. For example, Tolkien's inclusion of both utopias and dystopias in the same work is not completely unprecedented if one considers *Gulliver's Travels*, which also contained societies with utopian and dystopian elements. Recent science fiction also provides examples: Ursula Le Guin's *The Dispossessed*, Samuel Delany's *Trouble in Triton*, and Kim Stanley Robinson's *2312*.[9] There is also a precedent for a backward-looking utopia, even if it is set in the future. William Morris's *News from Nowhere* imagines a pastoral, arts-and-crafts England that draws more from a medieval worldview than from Morris's own nineteenth-century industrial society. Similarly, while Tolkien himself would have been the first to insist that his work was not meant to be explicitly didactic, that does not mean that one can—and many do—find implicit lessons about current society in his works or "application" as he would have called it. My contention is that at the heart of Tolkien's societies are elements of our society exaggerated in such a way as to make broader philosophical points rather than the often pointed social criticism of most utopian and dystopian literature. Tolkien's use of conflicting "sides" allows him to examine these broader philosophical points more effectively by including both utopian and dystopian elements in his works at the same time. Further, this combination of utopian and dystopian elements strengthens Tolkien's narratives. The combination makes his stories more effective because the contrast between how his good societies and bad societies act as paragons or warnings highlights the broader philosophical trends that exist in our society without the specificity characteristic of most other forms of speculative fiction that examine more narrow trends or issues.

Beyond considerations of genre, another reason why some might argue (though not me) that Tolkien's legendarium is not truly utopian (or dystopian) is that elf or hobbit societies are not "human" societies, and therefore, do not describe possible human societies. Because of this distinction, one could argue that the reason the Shire and the elf kingdoms are better than our own societies is the inherent "biological" differences between people and these different "species," rather than the utopian nature of their societies and their practices. For example, the reason why elf society values nature comes from the fact that elves are inherently more appreciative of nature. The Shire is peaceful because hobbits are naturally more docile. In a similar way, since the societies of Thangorodrim and Mordor are inhabited primarily by nonhuman orcs, the dystopian nature of those societies comes more from the nature of the inhabitants rather than the society itself. Then, in that case, it might be a mistake to view Tolkien's works as commenting on our current societies by using utopian and dystopian themes since the societies reflect the natures of their nonhuman inhabitants rather than shaping or forming them. Thus, Tolkien's works are more a speculation about how societies might be different with different races than an exploration of human societies.

I think this view of orcs, elves, and hobbits as different "species" and therefore not connected with "humans" who exist today is misleading in several ways and that Tolkien did not want us to view these groups as separate from us as persons. Instead, he wanted us to compare ourselves directly with these groups. Putting these groups into species would be a category error at least in the evolutionary sense that most contemporary people approach the word; for in the world of Middle-earth, the creation of these separate groups was done by special creation of God, or as Tolkien named Him, Eru Ilúvatar. We should not assume that biological evolution and our understanding of species is any part of this world because this world does not have evolution in the same way that ours does. (An even more extreme example how viewing Middle-earth through our assumptions does not make sense comes when one realizes that the world of *The Silmarillion* was flat, not round, though the world of *The Lord of the Rings* is round). Even based on our conception of species, it is not clear how separate a species elves, orcs, and hobbits are from humans. Elves and humans are capable of having children together and do so at least twice in *The Silmarillion*, and Tolkien implies that orcs and humans can mate and suggests characters like Bill Ferny are half orc. Tolkien also suggests that Saruman created the Uruk-hai through cross-breeding orcs and men. One of the central ways of defining species is if they can create fertile offspring, which in all these cases it appears they can. In *The Silmarillion*, Tolkien describes how Morgoth developed orcs (he cannot create anything) by "ruining" elves. Thus, I think viewing orcs and elves as different species is mistaken. Tolkien clearly viewed them all as very different types of "persons" rather than "species" and gave them all aspects of human psychology even if these aspects were in an exaggerated form. For instance, Tolkien discussed how he viewed elves as like men with a "human" nature, though more noble. Part of the difference of elves came from Tolkien imagining how humans would behave if they were immortal. In a similar way, orcs act as humans do, only in a more base way. Tolkien was known to describe modern humans who irked him as "orcs" in a non-metaphorical way. Rather like Robert Louis Stevenson does in *Dr. Jekyll and Mr. Hyde*, Tolkien uses morally distilled characters to examine different aspects of human nature rather than create alien natures. Therefore, Lothlórien and Mordor are meant to show utopian possibilities and dystopian warnings for our own societies as well as show a new fantastical world.

While I do not think Tolkien's societies fit the strict definition of utopias and dystopias, I believe his legendarium is replete with dystopian and utopian themes and, to a certain extent, with utopian and dystopian purposes. This might seem like a contradiction, but the difference between Tolkien's works and almost all literary utopias and dystopias is that his legendarium was not on commenting directly on his own society. His descriptions focused on making his fantasy worlds believable rather than pedagogical. Tolkien's approach of not providing explicit utopian and dystopian models to instruct but instead providing utopian and dystopian themes is very similar to his approach to his Christian faith, which will be discussed in some detail in chapter 2. While both *The Lord of the Rings* and *The Silmarillion* are clearly *not* books of Christian apologetics (unlike the stories of Tolkien's friend C. S. Lewis), they are suffused with Christian themes and atmosphere. In a similar way, while Tolkien's legendarium does not contain utopias and dystopias in the classic sense, it does contain utopian ideals and dystopian warnings. These ideals and warnings appear much more subtly in Tolkien's works, which focus on changing his readers' worldviews rather than getting them to accept a particular political program.

Whatever the definition, dystopias, like *Brave New World, 1984,* or any number of young adult novels, like *The Hunger Games*, appear much more frequently than utopias in the literature of the twentieth and the early twenty-first centuries.[10] Leszek Kolakowski and Krishan Kumar have both noted what they describe as the "death" and "end" of utopia, respectively, in contemporary literature after a high point for utopian narratives in the late nineteenth century. Instead, we see a flourishing of dystopian literature in the twentieth and twenty-first centuries. This makes the enduring appeal of Tolkien's utopian ideals especially a notable exception in his literature even if his works are not strictly utopian.

Much of the current skepticism about utopian projects comes from the many failures to create utopian societies throughout the world. Because of the number of small-scale utopian failures in the nineteenth century, like New Harmony and the Oneida Colony, and the horrifying large-scale utopian projects in the twentieth, such as the communist revolutions in Russia, China, and Cambodia, utopianism has been associated with authoritarianism and economic privation. Ironically, the swiftest path to the most dystopian of modern governments has often come from utopian projects. Because of these horrific failures, the assumption that a society can achieve utopian results or even perform better than the status quo seems unlikely to many contemporary people. This is so true that Kolakowski notes that the adjective "utopian" has become synonymous with unrealizable and impracticable.[11]

More subtly, artists run into aesthetic difficulties in their attempts to create attractive utopian communities. Nicholas Carr's essay "Utopia Is Creepy" explains how utopian characters sometimes unsettle readers of utopian narratives. The behavior (and affect) of the narratives' citizens appears flattened in fictional utopias, and this compressed humanity leads to a disturbing uncanniness. He describes it this way:

> The uncanny valley also exists when it comes to viewing artistic renderings of a future paradise. Utopia is creepy—or at least it looks creepy. That's probably because utopia requires its residents to behave like robots, never displaying or even feeling fear or anger or jealousy, or despair or bitterness or any of those other messy emotions that plague our fallen world.[12]

Carr uses the "uncanny valley" as a metaphor for the emotional narrowness of utopian citizens. The "uncanny valley" refers to a problem faced by computer animators when animating humans. Modern computers have allowed animators to create ever more realistic human forms and movements. The problem occurs when a person viewing these realistic animations subconsciously discerns that the creatures are not human, even though he or she cannot pinpoint exactly what is different about them. This makes animated characters seem both alive and dead at the same time, in other words, zombies. The distance between the conscious and the subconscious judgment of the character creates that eerie feeling: this is the "uncanny" part of the term. This problem does not occur in more crude animations, which are more obviously approximations of the human form and movement, or in caricatures where exaggerated features or attributes mark the animations as unrealistic. The "uncanny" feeling that Carr describes in utopias comes from a similar fear, not a fear of zombies that are alive and not yet alive, but from citizens of Utopia whose lack of "messy" emotions makes them act in ways that are only partially human because they have lost their free will and have become "robotic." Their limited range of emotions makes them seem uncanny, not only because they lack free will, but even more so because they do not seem to miss it. This moral "uncanniness" is brought out brilliantly in the faux-utopian *Brave New World*, where citizens of what turns out to be a dystopia joyfully participate in their own oppression, or in the movie

The Matrix, where characters like Cypher prefer to submit to the slavery of illusion rather than accept the freedom of reality. In this way, these works show how even utopian societies' admirable goals, such as the desire to make its citizens happy, if achieved by dystopian means like the removal of personal autonomy, can make people less than human.

Yet no one is "robotic" in Tolkien's good societies, and their inhabitants have more political freedom than almost anyone in our "real" world. The Shire operates with only the most rudimentary form of government: an amateur and ceremonial mayor, a few part-time "shiriffs," a semi-official thane of the Tooks, and an absentee monarch. The small size and reach of their government reflects the hobbits' ability to resolve most of their problems on their own without recourse to the state. A few agreed-upon traditional rules seem sufficient to resolve almost all conflicts, which tend to revolve around wandering animals, rather than serious crime. Lothlórien's government structure is not clearly described, but it appears equally unstructured, with Galadriel and Celeborn acting as philosopher-kings whose telepathic powers observe and channel their subjects but do not control them. Life at Rivendell seems similarly anarchic (in the political sense), with ample time for story-telling, poetry creation, and crafts but no mention of jobs or labor. Gondolin operates as both an aristocracy and a monarchy, with a structure that depends upon kin relationships to govern the city. The elf kingdoms especially resemble the stateless communist paradise that Marx describes in his *German Ideology* where one can be a farmer in the morning, a fisherman in the afternoon, and a poet at night. With so many choices, one can never be alienated from one's work and treat it like a "job."

This variety in the societies that Tolkien creates and the vagueness about how they work contrast with the explicit narrowness and regimentation that often undergird the structure of most fictional utopian and dystopian societies. Traditional utopian literature, like *The Republic* and *Utopia*, and dystopian literature, like *1984* and *Brave New World*, minimize conflict through circumscribing the actions, and sometimes even the thoughts, of their citizens. These societies depend upon uniformity to create harmony. Tolkien's works are unusual in that they present not one, but many different types of good societies in Middle-earth that vary greatly both externally and internally. Some are agrarian like the Shire, some sylvan like Lothlórien, and some even academic like Elrond's Last Homely House in Rivendell. The physical environments of these societies also differ markedly, from the pastoral Shire, to the arboreal Lothlórien, and finally to the urban Gondolin. Indeed, their very architecture reflects their harmony with the natural environment: the hobbit holes built into rolling hillsides of the Shire, the *flets* of the Lothlórian elves nestled in the living trees, and Gondolin's urban estates constructed by the stones of mountains that surround it. These connections of Tolkien's benevolent societies with their environment highlight how they grew organically from their own soil.

The idea of organic growth also highlights another difference between Tolkien's good societies and most other fictional utopias: their relationships with the past. Tolkien's ideal societies come about through a dynamic combination of tradition and change that contrasts with most modern utopian projects, which assume a connection between utopian societies and revolutionary politics. As Kolakowski argues, modern utopia depends on "the imminent, ultimate revolution not simply as a fortunate step in the succession of historical events but a rupture in the continuity, a total beginning, a new time."[13] In contrast, Tolkien's utopian societies depend on their inhabitants doing what comes naturally to them in freedom and in harmony with their environments, their history, and their traditions, rather than through a violent overthrow of the existing society and the setting up of completely different social relationships. No group is less revolutionary than the hobbits, whose favorite pastimes are to obsess over genealogy and their local history. The peacefulness of the Shire came about because of, and not despite, the notoriously backward-looking and tradition-bound hobbits. Similarly, part of the traditional stability of elven societies comes from the immortality of its inhabitants, which often means that the wisest and most powerful elves, like Galadriel, Círdan, and Elrond, are also the oldest. The past lives literally through these immortal elves who maintain their traditions and the elves' continuity with their past. This continuity contrasts with the tradition of revolutionary change embodied in the French, Russian, and Chinese revolutions that sought to change the fundamental structure of their societies from their calendar, to their living arrangements, to the very clothes they wore. Unlike these revolutionary attempts at utopia, there are no Year Zeros in the good societies of Middle-earth.

This respect for the past and deference to tradition does not mean that these societies remain perfectly static. The fact that hobbits, despite their traditional contempt for adventuring, still produce a Bilbo and a Frodo who both traveled widely and fought in epic battles, suggests that some rules can be broken. Similarly, Elrond's decision to hold a council at Rivendell and Galadriel's relaxation of the strict border controls to allow the fellowship to enter Lothlórien show how even the notoriously insular elves can adapt to new circumstances. The past and tradition are not final arbiters of what is proper in Tolkien's just societies, but the past has a seat at the table, so to speak. As G. K. Chesterton says in his essay "The Ethics of Elfland," "Tradition means giving a vote to most obscure of all classes, our ancestors. It is the democracy of the dead."[14] Indeed, change often comes by paying heed to the mistakes of one's ancestors. The history of the elves, as told in *The Silmarillion*, suggests how the relatively passive stance of the elves in *The Lord of the Rings* reflects the hard lessons the elves learned in the First and Second Ages. The rash actions of elves like

Fëanor and Celebrimbor led to the destruction of most elves and even to the creation of the Ring of Power. Over the generations, the elves have changed from impulsive and proud creatures willing to take foolhardy risks to wise and collected councilors rejecting opportunities to aggrandize themselves. This wisdom that relies on learning from the mistakes of the past allows the benevolent societies of Middle-earth to adapt based on changing circumstances.

Despite the variety of forms they take, Tolkien's good societies have one principle in common—individual freedom—a type of freedom different from "traditional" utopian societies like that of Plato or More. Classic utopian literature like *The Republic* and *Utopia* includes explicitly authoritarian measures to limit the more unpredictable aspects of human nature. Plato insisted that the children of his utopian republic be raised communally so as to restrict people's natural nepotism. His republic also includes severe restrictions on commercial activity so that people's avarice does not interfere with social tranquility. His society is famously ruled by philosopher-kings who know how to control their subjects and guide them in their wisdom and noblesse oblige so that they have the final say in how the republic is run. Most notoriously, Plato bans poets so that the subjects of his utopia would not be exposed to unpredictable emotions. Similarly, the inhabitants of Thomas More's *Utopia* face punishments for unauthorized travel and have severe restrictions placed on their privacy in the name of public good. In contrast, Tolkien's good societies are anarchic (in the political, not chaotic) sense rather than authoritarian. Tolkien admitted that his "political opinions lean more and more to Anarchy (philosophically understood, meaning abolition of control not whiskered men with bombs)."[15] Keeping with this philosophy, the functioning of the government and the economy in Tolkien's ideal societies are minimally directed. Tolkien felt that the government was such a threat that he hated even the use of the word "state" to describe the government. This did not mean that Tolkien rejected all forms of authority, just that he detested authority exercised from afar, which most often devolved into power rather than legitimate authority.[16] It is hard to imagine an imperial bureaucracy or a clique of minor functionaries in Tolkien's good societies (though we do see them in Sharkey's Shire at the end of *The Lord of the Rings*). The emphasis on the ad hoc and organic, rather than the bureaucratic and the imposed, stands in contrast to the centralizing tendencies of both Plato and More. In this way, Tolkien's good societies most closely resemble Morris's similarly anarchic pastoral utopia in his novel *News from Nowhere*.

Another difference between Tolkien's ideal societies and that of many fictional utopias is the relatively little attention given to differences in wealth and prestige. Plato and More both assumed that the danger of economic inequality was one of the major problems that needed to be solved by their utopias. Thus private property is eliminated in both Plato's *Republic* and More's *Utopia*. In the Shire, private property is not only permitted, but differences in wealth are tolerated even if material goods become a source of conflict. The considerable wealth of Bilbo and Frodo Baggins makes them the object of envy and even a conspiracy to deprive them of Bag's End in the end of *The Hobbit* and *The Lord of the Rings*. Still, despite these differences in wealth, the Shire does not have the crushing poverty that exists in most societies in our world. The Shire's combination of private property, lack of severe poverty, the widespread distribution of that property, and its relative prosperity suggests that the Shire is a fictional representation of distributionism.[17]

Tolkien gives no indication that he considers the private ownership of property a problem to be solved. At the same time, he considers acquisitiveness and a desire to own the property of others to be the cause of much pain and trouble. Almost the whole tragedy of *The Silmarillion* comes about from Fëanor and his sons' desire to own the silmarils. Similarly, the dwarves' greed for the treasure under the mountain threatens to tear the free peoples apart at the end of *The Hobbit*. Despite these examples of the dangers of greed, Tolkien draws a distinction between ownership and possessiveness. This distinction was also a central feature of *Beowulf*, a poem that Tolkien spent much of his professional life at Oxford pondering and teaching. *Beowulf* both celebrates the beauty of objects like swords, torques, and mail coats and the joy of owning such fine objects, while at the same time castigating the greed of unjust kings and dragons who hoard these treasures. The ideal king, like Beowulf and Hrothgar, is both rich and generous. The problem comes not from the wealth itself, but from how the wealth is used (or not used). Tolkien's utopian societies celebrate both wealth and generosity, not in the sense of commercial exchange, but in the free sense of gift-giving between a lord and his thane. Interposing a centralized bureaucracy to gather and distribute goods that were not their own runs counter to the spirit and the practice of gift giving. Tolkien makes this point at the end of *The Lord of the Rings* when he describes how Saruman's "gatherers" and "sharers" take away crops from farmers for later distributions, which sometimes never occur. The ones who control the goods are always tempted to create another "hoard," which they can use to control others. Even if the bureaucracy is not corrupt in this obvious way, the act of distribution is fundamentally different from the act of giving.[18] One is a simple payment of services rendered or goods deserved, while the other demonstrates a bond that suggests a relationship rather than simply a transaction. In *Beowulf*, the formal way in which Hrothgar gives Beowulf horses, mail-shirts, rings, and a torque after Beowulf's slaying of Grendel makes the gift complete. It is not just the physical goods that are important, but the speeches, the formal recitation of a litany of Beowulf's deeds, and the way the gifts are processed (in a procession) through the hall make the whole ceremony more akin to a liturgy than a payment. Like military medals for heroism, the treasures gain power more from the intrinsic esteem symbolized by the gifts rather than from the extrinsic value possessed by their worth.

Along with his emphasis on freedom in all its forms, Tolkien further departs from most fictional utopian states in his emphasis on tradition and traditional wisdom. This means more than a respect for the past and history, but rather allowing the past to exist through practices as well as ideas. Hobbits are deeply suspicious of any change and like to stick to the current way of doing things if at all possible. Tom Shippey and Tolkien himself have noted the many ways in which hobbits resemble bourgeois Victorians in their taste for waistcoats, tobacco, pocket handkerchiefs, postal systems, and umbrellas.[19] The other obvious way the hobbits resemble middle-class Victorian country gentlemen is in their extreme social, political, and personal conservatism. To describe someone as "queer," where "queer" means foreign, is the most potent possible insult in the Shire. For the most part, the hobbits' insular approach to life serves them well. They have managed to escape domination and detection for many centuries by maintaining a low profile. Ironically, it is only when the hobbits become heroes in the War of the Ring that the Shire suffers an outside power's depredations through the revenge of Saruman.

In some ways, the elves are even more conservative than hobbits. The elves' immortality leads them to resist change and to preserve the world as it is as much as possible. Thus the enclaves they create like Rivendell and Lothlórien look backward to earlier more idealized societies like Doriath and Beleriand, and even further back to Aman in the Undying Lands. The elves' focus on preserving both the environmental and cultural past of Middle-earth makes them natural preservationists and conservationists because of their symbiotic dependence on the land. As Tolkien points out, the fact that the elves were more closely aligned with the land makes them counterintuitively less "spiritual" than men. In his essay "On Fairy-Stories," Tolkien argues that "it is man who is, in contrast to fairies, supernatural (and often of diminutive stature); whereas they [fairies, and elves as a member of fairyland] are natural, far more natural than he. Such is their doom."[20] Because they cannot naturally die and leave the physical world, the elves are more closely attached to the earth. On the other hand, the "gift" of mortality given to man by Eru Ilúvatar allows man to escape the physical confines of the world and encourages men to look beyond the natural world toward the spiritual. The strength of the elves' bond to the physical world makes them fear change since the changing of the land risks not only alienating elves from their world but from their very selves. Because the elves' minds change little and their bodies not at all, but the land never stops changing, the elves' attempt to preserve their environment becomes more than an attempt to make the world a familiar place, it is also a way for them to stay in touch with their earlier identities.

Besides variety, freedom, and their acceptance of tradition, other aspects of Tolkien's good societies that make them appear more believable are their imperfections and fragility. Of course, even classic utopias have imperfections since they include imperfect people (even though an imperfect utopia sounds oxymoronic). That is why I established that even classic examples of utopian societies allow ways to punish and reform their citizens (which implies some level of deficiency) and that all utopian visions face inherent contradictions in creating a perfect state out of imperfect citizens. Still, Tolkien allows more imperfections. Thus, he allows his hobbits to be small and petty. As one gains understanding of the nature of Middle-earth in *The Lord of the Rings*, one also starts to understand just how provincial and ungrateful the hobbits are. The conditions that allow the hobbits to live in peace are provided by others. Rangers protect their eastern and northern borders and Rohan and Gondor protect their southern flank. Even the current fertility of their land comes from previous inhabitants of Eriador who are unrelated to them. In short, the Shire is not an ideal society in the sense of a planned community like Plato's *Republic* or More's *Utopia*, but a happy accident constructed as much by the hobbits' vices as their virtues (their lack of ambition, love of comfort, their distrust of strangers, etc.) that helps the Shire continue to be a relative backwater. Besides being ungrateful and provincial, hobbits can be petty and small (in ways besides their stature) and we see that some hobbits, like Lobelia Sackville-Baggins, can be mean and greedy. Tolkien's inclusion of small imperfections like arguments, unpleasant neighbors, and mushroom-stealing, while eliminating large-scale oppression, makes the Shire a mirror image of the tightly controlled utopias, like the ones in the *Republic* or *Utopia*, that trade high levels of control for the elimination of even the smallest of interpersonal conflicts.

The elf kingdoms' imperfections derive from a completely different set of deficiencies than the Shire. Lothlórien and Rivendell are places of unearthly beauty, but societies that are living under a constant state of siege as the diminished and diminishing elf kingdoms fade and shrink. The elves' approach to preserving Lothlórien exposes weaknesses in their understanding of the world and their place in it. As I have already mentioned, part of what makes the elves' immortality a tragedy rather than a gift is that it makes them unable to adjust to a natural world that is constantly changing, while they are doomed to remain, in many ways, the same. This manifests itself in the elves' xenophobic reaction to outsiders who attempt to enter into their realms, whether Mirkwood, Lothlórien, or Rivendell. Except for Mordor, there are no more closed borders other than those that lead to elven realms. This is not a new development for the elves and their secrecy and isolation stretches back to the First Age. But even the love for their land is tinged with sadness. Despite this deep love for Middle-earth, the history of the elves makes them exiles in their own lands. Since the Noldor elves belong in the

Undying Lands[21] yet love Middle-earth, the high elves of Middle-earth live in a state of bittersweet exile, desiring both to leave and remain in Middle-earth (hence their fear of, yet desire for, the sea). Ironically, this conflict adds to the aesthetic beauty of places like Lothlórien. Tolkien's elven realms are also more attractive because of the fact that they are under threat and are localized, and that they will soon pass away whatever side wins the War of the Rings. This is because the same magic that infuses the Ruling Ring of Sauron also helps create the Edenic nature of Lothlórien. Either the Ring is destroyed and Lothlórien will fade, or it will survive and make it back to its master, which will mean a more violent destruction of Lothlórien. The Japanese have a word for this most delicate of feelings, *mono no aware*, meaning the heightened sense of the beauty of things that will soon fade away. For many readers, this feeling becomes even more intense because Tolkien's portrayal of places like Lothlórien evokes images from the readers' own childhoods (woods and groves evoked from childhood memories made more poignant by the lost innocence of their pasts) as well as from the mythology of Western culture like Eden, Avalon, and fairyland.

While for different reasons Lothlórien, Rivendell, or the Shire are not paradise, they are also undeniably better than the societies in which we live. For example, no hobbit has ever murdered another in the Shire's entire history (even though we know that at least creatures related to hobbits are capable of killing since we have the example of Smeagol murdering Deagol to obtain the Ring of Power, and that hobbits killed many big people during the cleansing of the Shire). Lothlórien and Rivendell seem similarly peaceful, with no evidence of either crime or police forces to punish criminality. In addition to a lack of violence in the elf kingdoms, even the pressures of time seem to be nonexistent there. When the fellowship recovered after the trauma of the Mines of Moria, time seemed to slow down and "they could not count the days and nights they had passed there."[22]

The difference between Tolkien's good societies and how most utopias are portrayed comes not only from a sense that they are (Tolkien's cultures) subject to loss and decay, but that decay is inevitable. The hidden kingdom of Gondolin is an example of a good society whose undoing came about through the elven desire to preserve the status quo at all costs. The many centuries of Gondolin's isolation lead to a complacency that becomes the city's destruction. From the beginning, Ulmo (a godlike member of the Valar) had warned Turgon, the king of Gondolin, not to "admire too much the work of his hands" and that, at some point, Gondolin would fail. Ulmo goes even further and sends a man, Tuor, to explicitly warn the elves that they must leave Gondolin as well as Middle-earth and return to the West because the city is doomed to fall. But Turgon does not listen and relies on his external security and secrecy to keep Gondolin safe. What Turgon failed to take into account was the fragility of Gondolin society. As it turns out, the fall of Gondolin comes as much from jealousy and complacency inside the city as from Morgoth's evil outside it. The dark elf Maeglin's restlessness to leave the confines of the city and his desire for Idril leads him to betray Gondolin. Turgon's inability to abandon what he has built, his faith in the city's indetectability, and his inability to heed Tuor's warning lead to the city's downfall. By the time the elves realize that their city's destruction was inevitable, Morgoth's armies had already begun to besiege it. Central to the destruction of the city is the particular elvish desire to always keep things the same.

The Shire's quick fall into autocracy shows the hobbits' unique weaknesses as well. Their complacency, cowardice, and excessive deference allow a relatively small number of bullies to take control of the Shire. These oppressors depended on co-opting hobbits to do most of their work for them through an expanded security force of Shirriffs. Hobbits throughout the Shire cooperated with Saruman, including hobbits from the top of hobbit society, like Lotho Sackville-Baggins, and the bottom, like Ted Sandyman. The fact that it only takes a couple of days for the returning hobbits to liberate themselves suggests the hold that Saruman had over the Shire was based more on the weaknesses in hobbit psychology rather than the raw physical power of Saruman's thugs. Once Merry and Pippin provide the necessary courage, or "spark" as Farmer Cotton puts it, the hobbits muster enough numbers to overthrow their oppressors quickly. Still, Saruman's takeover shows how easily the hobbits could be dominated by limited force. This history supports King Elessar's wisdom in banning men from crossing the Brandywine River; there was probably no other way to protect the inherently fragile hobbit society.

The speed at which the Shire fell into autocracy shows Tolkien's ability to write about novel yet believable evil societies. Not surprisingly, just as Tolkien's good societies differ from most classic and modern utopias, his bad societies also differ from most twentieth- and twenty-first-century dystopias. One of the most surprising differences is his attention to the damage evil does to wielders of power rather than to its victims. Mordor and Thangorodrim appear to be hell on earth: barren, joyless, and brutal, but this hell is shared by their masters as well as their slaves. We see how the rulers of these dungeons are as tortured as their subjects in the image of the cowering, limping Morgoth trapped in his iron fortress and the sleepless, lidless eye of Sauron gazing unceasingly like a paranoid panopticon.[23] As Brian Rosebury notes, Tolkien's portrayal of the leaders of these realms deromanticizes the glamour of evil:

> One can imagine a person wishing to be like Wilkie Collins's Count Fosco or Goethe's Mephistopheles, or even conceivably Milton's Satan (though not Dante's); it is one of the triumphs of Tolkien's literary judgment in *The Lord of the Rings* that fully accomplished evil is repre-

sented by states of personality (or unpersonality) which no sane reader could envy.[24]

This disturbing portrait of evil comes from Tolkien's insight that to become wicked is to diminish. Central to the horror of his evil societies is that the destruction of the environment is matched by the destruction of personality. Rosebury notes that Sauron's servants, like the ringwraiths and the Mouth of Sauron, become so reduced by evil that they lose their names and identities. Similarly, Gollum forgets his name after many years of possessing the Ring of Power and only starts to regain some of his personhood when he remembers that he is Smeagol (though when he does so, he often understands his identity only in the third, rather than the first, person). This diminishment goes beyond the psychological to the physical as Gollum's body is stretched by his abnormally long life. Even more radically, the ringwraiths' bodies literally disappear as they lose their very corporeality, and they become disembodied spirits. Acceptance of evil always leads to a loss, even for those who seem to be in control, and the power gained by evil comes at great cost.

Part of that cost manifests itself in particular weaknesses in imagination, in an inability to cede control, and in excessive fractiousness. No one does a better job of delineating these weaknesses in Sauron than W. H. Auden in his classic essay, "The Quest Hero." He notes that "[Sauron's] primary weakness is a lack of imagination, for, while Good can imagine what it would be like to be Evil, Evil cannot imagine what it would be like to be Good." Gandalf and Galadriel understand the temptation to use the Ring, but Sauron cannot imagine anyone willing to forgo that temptation and destroy it. Auden also notes that Sauron's lust for domination, rather than just obedience, leads him to not question Pippin when he had the chance.[25] Sauron failed to question Pippin quickly because he (Sauron) wanted to have total control of the hobbit in Mordor rather than seizing his opportunity to interrogate the hobbit in what he assumed was the Orthanc (it was actually on the Plains of Rohan). Finally, because evil characters rely on self-interest alone, the different factions in the party of evil are always working at cross-purposes based on individual calculation, even when cooperation would be a more effective strategy. Therefore, orcs kill each other over Frodo's mithril coat and Saruman tries to seize the Ring of Power for himself and deny it to Sauron. Because of these miscalculations, coalitions of evil are always unstable because they are inherently self-serving.[26]

In Tolkien's narratives, these weaknesses reflect a deeper philosophical truth about the nature of evil. For Tolkien, the evil of places like Mordor comes not only from moral error, but from a denial of reality itself, which often weakens it as a society. In dystopias like *1984* and *Brave New World*, evil is triumphant because the leaders of these dystopias have absolute and unshakable control over their subjects and their environment. The assumption is that the apparatus of the dystopian society has completely mastered the human psyche and the physical world. These dystopian works imply that this vision of human weakness and corruption is more complete than our naïve, contemporary cant. In Tolkien's Middle-earth, on the other hand, evil, like good, is shown in all its precarious weakness. Evil societies often damage their own capabilities through their inability to control not only their own subjects' wanton and counterproductive destructiveness, but their physical environment as well.

This destruction reflects the contention that evil is a despoliation and an impoverishment, and that the diminishment of persons and landscapes is philosophically connected in Tolkien's evil realms. Evil will always result in destruction because evil cannot be creative in the same sense that good can be. According to Tolkien's beliefs about creativity, humans as created beings can only "subcreate" in cooperation with Eru Ilúvatar (God) and not create themselves. Tolkien defines subcreation as the recognition that persons, as created creatures, cannot fashion a truly new thing ex nihilo, but can only use existing creation within limits. This means attempts to totally dominate nature will destroy rather than create. Ignoring these "given" conditions means trying to create without cooperation with God. Melkor's original evil was the disruption of the music of Eru in *The Silmarillion*, and it is the paradigmatic example of trying to create without cooperation. I say "trying" because these attempts at independent creation eventually fail and create unforeseen negative consequences. This illicit attempt at creation has several characteristics in Middle-earth: speed, efficiency, mechanization, and destruction. In short, evil depends on using shortcuts. Brian Rosebury connects Tolkien's anarchism to his aversion to these "shortcuts," which Rosebury describes as "the actualisation of impious human desires, such as the desire to travel at high speed or have limitless supplies of luxury goods or destroy one's enemies in large numbers."[27] These shortcuts inevitably lead to environmental and personal destruction, which, in the long run, hinders the success of the forces of evil. I suspect that eventually this random destruction will erode the military potency of places like Thangorodrim and Mordor by destroying the resources necessary to maintain the armies and workshops that reside there. Readers can see this danger of diminishing returns when Tolkien gives a glimpse at the economic infrastructure that maintains and supports Mordor in *The Return of the King*. Tolkien describes the area around Mount Doom in this way: "Between them and the smoking mountain, and about it north and south, all seemed ruinous and dead, a desert burned and choked."[28] It is so desolate that Frodo and Sam wonder how Sauron's armies are fed and provisioned. Tolkien explains this mystery,

> Neither he [Sam] nor Frodo knew anything of the great slave-worked fields away south in this wide realm, beyond the fumes of the Mountain by the dark sad waters of Lake Núrnen nor the great roads that ran away east and south to tributary lands, from which soldiers of the Tower brought long wagon-trains of goods and booty and fresh slaves.[29]

The fact that the maintenance of Mordor requires distant resources suggests an ever-widening zone of destruction as the lands fall further under the control of Sauron. Tolkien's portrayal of the border region of Ithilien describes in some detail how the encroaching forces of Mordor destroy borderlands in an ever-widening arc. The need for "fresh slaves" shows how the human resources of Mordor are squandered and need to be constantly replaced. Thus, all the evidence indicates that Sauron's tyrannical economy is not sustainable and that its constant mode of extraction will eventually lead to its collapse in some distant future.

This diminishment and destruction also leads to another striking result: uniformity.[30] The landscapes and creatures of Thangorodrim and Mordor are similarly bleak. The lands, stripped of most natural living things, are dominated by fortresses, mines, and machines. As places of production and defense, these wastelands do their job well, but at the neglect of every other priority. In a similar way, the creatures that inhabit these realms are also one-dimensional, and therefore limited in many ways. The orcs and trolls' fear of the sun, as well as the Ringwraiths' incorporeality, all come from an inability to interact completely with the physical world they hate and fear. Since this fear comes from an inability to control that world, it is not surprising that one of the first things any of these creatures do when faced with the natural world is to mar it into monochrome bleakness.

Widespread destruction is inefficient for the evil societies of Middle-earth not only because it destroys the productivity of the land but because this destruction unleashes other forces that would remain dormant if only forces of darkness could restrain their most destructive impulses. Tom Shippey argues that this destruction for the sake of a strategic object can quickly slip into destruction for its own sake; that the drive for efficiency can become a drive to do things because they *can* be done and that this particularly modern sin leads to even more destruction. Shippey uses Saruman's attempt to make Isengard into a sort of mini-Mordor as an example of how Saruman goes beyond what he needs to do to create his army in the destruction of Fangorn forest:

> The "applicability" [to our modern situation] of this [wanton destruction] is obvious, with Saruman becoming an image of one of the characteristic vices of modernity, though we have no name for it—a kind of restless ingenuity, skill without purpose, bulldozing for the sake of change.[31]

Saruman's minions destroyed the forests around Isengard beyond any military or industrial need, and the destruction was so widespread that the orcs left many trees rotting on the ground. Saruman does not only want to use the forest; he wants to despoil it, despite its lack of strategic value. Think of a politician who uses overwhelming military force to "liberate" a territory controlled by the enemy regardless of the cost: to destroy the village in order to save it. Sometimes, the urge to destroy becomes an objective in and of itself and actually hinders the war effort.

This is not the only way that Saruman resembles an unscrupulous politician. Shippey notes that Saruman is *The Lord of the Rings'* most recognizably "modern" character. In Saruman's arguments, we can recognize his dependence on current popular bromides about efficacy, about the importance of careful political calculation, and about the inevitability of progress. For Saruman, this shortsightedness leads to the awakening of the Ents and the eventual destruction of his military capacity. In a similar way, orcs' penchant for wanton ecological destruction in the forests around Gondor helps convince the Drúedain to help guide the army of the Rohorrim around Mordor's blocking forces to relieve the siege of Gondor. In both cases, the forces of evil assume that these "remnant" inhabitants of the forest were a spent force. Leaders like Sauron and Saruman, who make their calculations based on the assumed military capabilities of their adversaries, are blind to the blowback that comes as a result of their random destruction.

Another weakness that Tolkien identifies in Middle-earth's evil societies is their centralization of will and initiative, which ironically leads to an erosion of power as it is distributed. The realms of Mordor and Thangorodrim depend entirely on the will of their leaders: Sauron and Morgoth. This is demonstrated by the way Sauron's armies melt away after the Ring of Power's destruction in *The Lord of the Rings*, because the servants of Mordor could not operate independently of Sauron's will. This need for centralized control has consequences for the leaders of Middle-earth's evil societies. Morgoth weakens throughout the First Age because he must disperse his power in order to coerce servants to do his will, which is why he is little match for the Valar at the end of the First Age despite starting out as its most powerful member in the beginning of *The Silmarillion*. Similarly, Sauron pours much of his malice and power into the ruling Ring, but the dividing of his power leads to his eventual destruction. Such dilution goes beyond a decrease in physical power; it is a decrease in "life" itself so that Sauron, like Morgoth, also physically diminishes through the ages. In the First Age, Sauron was a shapeshifter who could change into a variety of forms. In the Second Age, his shape was fixed into a beautiful form, and this beauty allowed him to seduce the Númenóreans. In the Third Age, however, he is permanently grotesque and must rely only on fear and intimidation. His continual devolution throughout the First and Second Ages reflects how he has sacrificed the essence of himself to maintain his control over others.

This monomaniacal approach to control through personal domination contrasts with the messy, but more robust, debate of the "good" peoples of Middle-earth whose varied objectives and refusal to dominate others lead to much debate, confusion, and "inefficiency." Allowance for diversity, even as it seems to cause delay and confusion, also allows a form of undiluted power that the evil societies cannot seem to match. While Thangorodrim and Mordor have the equivalent of military captains such as Aragorn, Eomer, and Faramir to lead their armies, they do not have the equivalent of the love between Beren and Lúthien or the selfless devotion of Frodo and Sam in their arsenal, and that turns out to be their greatest weakness.

The elusiveness of control for the evil leaders of Middle-earth is absent in most classic dystopian texts. The centralization of power, which is a weakness in *The Lord of the Rings*, is described instead as a strength in classic dystopias: O'Brien in *1984* and Mustapha Mond in *Brave New World* seem to maintain total control of their subjects through either fear, conditioning, or pleasure. In both these narratives, disobedience seems an impossibility. Still, despite complaints about the one-dimensionality of orcs by some critics of *The Lord of the Rings*, many orcs appear to have more agency than say, Winston Smith does by the end of *1984*. For one thing, orcs are free to hate Sauron, while Winston must not only obey, but love Big Brother. In a similar way, the society of *1984* cripples the emotional life of its citizens by not even allowing them the possibility of certain emotions, like romantic love in most of the "non-barbarian" citizens. Of course, the exceptions are the servants who have completely ceded their will to Sauron, the ringwraiths. Significantly, though, this sort of total control can only come about when Sauron gives up part of his own will to maintain that control. Once again, Tolkien emphasizes that evil is bounded in ways that most classic dystopias do not. Perhaps this is because of the modern (and postmodern) faith in utilitarianism that makes most contemporary people believe in the power of all-encompassing technocratic solutions. But Tolkien's Middle-earth is a fallen world like our own. Perfection is impossible in classic Christian theology because imperfection is bound up in the very reality of the world; both the people and the world feel the effects of original sin. Evil has no more power to cure these imperfections than good.

Another reason why most modern dystopias seem so much more powerful than Tolkien's malevolent societies is the fact that typically they are told from the point of view of the citizen of the dystopia, and there is no alternative to the dystopian society. At least in *The Lord of the Rings* and *The Hobbit*, however, we rarely get an "inside" view of the dystopian places of Middle-earth. The exception is *The Silmarillion* and its stories from the First Age, like *The Children of Húrin*. In this narrative, Morgoth's domination turns almost all of Middle-earth into a dystopian realm (with the exceptions of the hidden elven realms and backwater settlements of men). In terms of raw power, Morgoth is vastly more powerful than the leaders of *We, Brave New World,* or *1984.* With his demigod-like power, he literally changes the shape of reality (fate) to punish Húrin by cursing his children. Still, despite this curse, Tolkien allows his characters an agency that many modern-day dystopias deny their characters. Húrin's decision to defy Morgoth and openly ridicule him suggests an agency foreign to the inhabitants of *1984,* who lack a similar ability to defy Big Brother. Húrin's son Túrin, in his own way, defies Morgoth even as his life is undone by the Dark Lord's power. Despite the fact that Morgoth destroys Húrin's children through his curse, they retain a part of themselves that characters like Winston Smith and Henry Foster happily accede. Just as he reaches back to *Beowulf* to provide a rival psychology to challenge contemporary market-based assumptions about material goods, Tolkien challenges twentieth- and twenty-first-century assumptions about humans' abilities to resist political and social power. These characters' capability to fight on, despite impossible odds, reflects a kind of "Northern courage" that was part of the ethos of pagan Northern Europe. This attitude seems especially alien to contemporary mores, but not to an Anglo-Saxon scholar familiar with the strange combination of courage and pessimism that characterized the worldview of pre-Christian Northern Europe. This fatalism colored all parts of Northern European paganism. According to Norse mythology, the world was doomed to end in an apocalypse called Ragnarök. Ragnarök means the forces of evil and darkness will destroy most of the gods of Asgard and all but two of the people of Middle Earth (the Middle-earth of Norse legend, not Tolkien's Middle-earth). Even though the gods themselves know that their death is preordained, they will play their roles and engage in combat that they know is hopeless. This acceptance of *wyrd* (the Anglo-Saxon term for fate or doom) was expected of mortals as well. Beowulf self-consciously recognizes that he is doomed to eventually fall in combat, yet he accepts his doom nonetheless. Before his battles with Grendel, then Grendel's mother, and finally, the dragon, Beowulf acknowledges the possibility of his defeat and indeed acknowledges that at some point "his number will come up" and he will die. Ironically, this fatalism that assumes doom will come to all means that if fate cannot be changed, the only choice that a man or woman has within the world is to act with courage or not. Túrin's courage gives agency over the part of himself that he can control and denies it to Morgoth. Thus, this attitude of "Northern courage" does not represent a difference in circumstance (Túrin's situation is more hopeless than Winston's fate) but rather a philosophical difference about the meaning of resistance.

Not only are evil leaders unable to control the inner lives of the "good" people of Middle-earth, they have trouble controlling the bad people as well. This fundamental lack of control over the decision-making of their subjects separates Tolkien's evil leaders from the dystopian leaders of most classic dystopian novels. The malevolent societies of Mordor and Thangorodrim are much more chaotic than the equivalent in most twentieth-century dystopian fiction. Orcs' almost constant bickering and jockeying for control differs from the relatively docile behavior of Winston Smith in *1984* or Bernard Marx in *Brave New World*. Orcs often erupt in uncontrolled violence in ways alien to these other dystopias because orc society includes little of the conflict suppression so prized in most recent dystopian literature. Whether through pleasure, like *We* and *Brave New World*, or through brutality, like *1984*, most modern dystopias prioritize control over all else. By contrast, one of the lessons of Tolkien's legendarium is that evil often spirals out of control. Again and again infighting among different factions of orcs leads to opportunities for their victims. The arguments over Merry and Pippin between the Uruk-hai and orcs of Mordor provide the opening for the hobbits to escape into the Fangorn forest. This argument is just a small-scale example of the conflict between Saruman and Sauron, whose mutual machinations hinder them from creating a coordinated strategy to defeat the free peoples of Middle-earth. The civil war at the Tower at the entrance to Mordor similarly opens the path for Frodo and Sam into the plains of Gorgoroth. Finally, Saruman's death comes not from the returning hobbits, but by the hand of his own servant, Grima Wormtongue.

The violence of the orcs ironically highlights a philosophical conundrum at the heart of Tolkien's bad societies that touches on the relationship between evil and free will. Their uncontrolled violence is ironic, because it suggests an agency that cannot exist in a state of pure evil. Among "good" races like elves, men, and dwarfs, individuals have free will to choose either good or evil. Orcs, trolls, and other "evil" races do not seem to have this choice and by their very natures are evil. The evil in the natures means that they are limited because, as I have argued, evil means lesser. According to *The Silmarillion*, orcs were created out of elves by Morgoth "ruining" them (and trolls were created as a "mockery" of ents). The question then becomes whether orcs can truly be responsible for their evil behavior that comes about from their very natures.[32] If orcs were truly only evil, then the evil societies of Middle-earth came about not because of the social structure of places like Mordor, but from the inherent evil of their inhabitants. Thus, orcs do not have to be "conditioned" to accept their society like the people do in *Brave New World* and *1984*, but naturally fit into the dystopian order without struggle. Tolkien himself wrestled with the Christian orthodoxy of this view of orcs in his May 12, 1965, letter to Auden where he obliquely argues that

> with regard to *The Lord of the Rings* I cannot claim to be a sufficient theologian to say whether my notion of orcs is heretical or not. I do not

feel under any obligation to make my story fit with formalized Christian theology, though I actually intended it to be consonant with Christian thought and belief,[33] which is asserted somewhere, Book Five, page 190, where Frodo asserts that orcs are not evil in origin. We believe that, I suppose, of all human kinds and sorts and breeds, though some appear, both as individual and groups to be, by us at any rate, unredeemable.[34]

I think it is a telling indication of Tolkien's discomfort with this subject that his normally lucid prose is a bit confused in this response. On the one hand, he argues that "orcs were not evil in origin" suggesting maybe their condition is similar to what many theologians argue about fallen angels: originally good, but now irretrievably evil and incapable of salvation. Yet in the next sentence, Tolkien suggests that perhaps orcs only "appear" to be unredeemable, thus making them like great human sinners with a small possibility of redemption. Typical of Tolkien, he writes the letter as if he were some impartial observer about the objective facts of orcs, rather than the creator of these fictional creatures that could be fashioned in any way he pleased. This question over the degree and nature of the evil in orcs and especially the fact that they were somehow created out of elves presents a challenge for Tolkien's theodicy, not only in this letter but throughout his legendarium. Tolkien vacillated between a variety of different theories about the origins of orcs at various times, including orcs bred from the earth, orcs that were bred from men instead of elves, orcs (or at least some of them) that were originally from the maiar, and finally orcs that were living automata that derived their will from Morgoth or Sauron.

Yet, in a strange way, Tolkien's permitting orcs to have the ability to quarrel and his choice over what they fought over suggest that the orcs were not completely evil. Even though orcs selfishly focus on injustices that affect themselves, the fact that many of their conflicts focus on fairness suggests some sense of right and wrong, even if it is in a selfish sense. For example, the mixed Uruk-hai and Morgul orc band that carry Pippin and Merry have an argument about cannibalism. The Mordor orc, Grishnákh, accuses Saruman's Uruk-hai warriors of cannibalism after Uglúk, the Uruk-hai commander, calls the Mordor orcs swine. He says, "*Swine* is it? How do you folk like being called *swine* by the muck-rakers of a dirty little wizard? It's orc-flesh they eat, I warrant."[35] This accusation of Uruk-hai cannibalism leads to the drawing of weapons and the killing of some of the Mordor orcs. The obvious question is why would orcs care if they are accused of eating orc-flesh?[36] Earlier in the same scene, the orcs boasted that they will have the opportunity to eat "man-flesh" so the issue is not the eating of sentient beings. Instead, the protests seem to be over eating members of the same type of person or members of the same tribe. This suggests that orcs are capable of making moral distinctions, however strained and limited these distinctions are. The orcs' combat over Frodo's mithril coat also casts an interesting light on the relationship between orcs and desire. In some sense, orcs must have valued the coat as "good," which implies some sort of distinction between good and bad. Maybe "good" because the orcs can ingratiate themselves with their leaders or perhaps it is good in the sense of utility since mithril armor is the hardest armor possible. Yet, once the reader begins to ponder the reasons why orcs quarrel, it is impossible not to start thinking of them as moral beings with moral agency, unlike say, a shark or a cobra. In order for such debates to happen in the first place orcs must have some sense of justice, however rudimentary. They also must have some sort of agency in the most basic sense. The reader sees this agency in the many instances when orcs disobey or disregard orders. So within the lesser scope of their evil nature, orcs do exhibit limited moral agency.

The irony of my litany of ways in which Tolkien's evil societies depart from their "classic" dystopian counterparts is that, in many ways, these differences highlight how classic utopias have key similarities to Tolkien's malevolent societies. Most classic utopian societies are structured like Mordor or Thangorodrim than they are free like the Shire or Lothlórien. Plato's republic and More's utopia assumed the way to eliminate conflict was to create uniformity. One way to do this is to attack the foundations of society that lead to differential outcomes. The most fundamental units of society, like the family, create the most inequality, so it is not surprising that Plato sought to dismantle them. Both More and Plato sought to eliminate differences in wealth as another way to create equality and reduce conflict. We know essentially nothing about the family life of orcs (if they even have any), but the lack of any mention of kin relationships suggests that family plays little part in orc relationships.[37] Most of Morgoth's and Sauron's servants in Thangorodrim and Mordor also live in an economically flattened society. We do not see orcs with great wealth, and their desire to loot seems more driven by the perverse pleasure of destruction than by the desire to obtain goods. Perhaps orcs are greedy, but we only see orcs on campaign and guard duty. Still, we see orcs destroy, but we never get the indication that they loot. We can suspect that greed is at least part of the reason many of the evil men who followed Morgoth and Sauron became allied with them. Yet, we see some evidence of greed among the evil leaders. Morgoth lusted after the silmarils and wore them in his iron crown, but that is the only example of his interest in material objects. Saruman hoards Shire pipe-weed, but does not seem interested in accumulating other forms of wealth. Sauron wants the Ring of Power, but his desire for it is utilitarian rather than aesthetic. Smaug and the trolls in *The Hobbit* are the only evil creatures that we know of that seemed primarily motivated by greed, but they can hardly be described as leaders of a dystopia.

Despite the similarities drawn between classic utopias and Tolkienian evil societies, within the world of Middle-earth, Tolkien's good and bad cultures are almost photo negatives of each other. The contrasts could not be clearer: Tolkien's good societies are free, idiosyncratic, somewhat chaotic, and accepting of limits, while his evil societies are controlled, uniform, disciplined, and contemptuous of restrictions. The one commonality of all Tolkien's societies is their lack of long-term stability. Both seem to have inherent limitations and volatility that make them different from the permanence promised in both classic utopias and dystopias. Based on the rise and fall of these societies and how they have fought for supremacy over Middle-earth, one can see why so many critics have accused Tolkien of Manichaeism.[38] But there is a better explanation for the instability of Tolkien's good and bad societies: that of the counteracting forces of flawed creation and Providence.

The Christian concept of original sin undergirds many of the flaws of both Tolkien's benevolent and malevolent societies. What I mean by this in not only the specific sin of both Adam and Eve in eating of the Tree of the Knowledge of Good and Evil, but more the mythical purpose of that story: an explanation of how people became alienated from Creation, each other, and even themselves. While it does not have this clear mythical moment of alienation like the Bible, Tolkien's legendarium does contain a sense of a fallen world that lost something precious and gained disordered desires, like domination and greed. In *The Silmarillion*, the elves' journey to Middle-earth comes with a series of falls: their decision to leave the Blessed Realm, the kin-slaying at Alqualondë, the abandonment of Fingolofin at the grinding ice, and the oath of Feänor. Richard Z. Gallant argues in his essay "Original Sin in Heorot and Valinor" that all of these "falls" of the elves come from pride and particularly derived from what he calls "Germanic heroism" that leads them to kin-slaying, the classic original sin of most Germanic epics.[39] On the other hand, the Fall of Man happens off-stage in *The Silmarillion* so the reader is unsure of the motive. In both cases, however, earlier actions of men and elves disrupt their relationships with the natural world and the other sentient creatures of Middle-earth. This level of division continues into the Second and Third Ages of Middle-earth. In the Second Age, Númenóreans start off with an almost utopian society on the island of Númenór, but in a retelling of the Atlantis legend for Middle-earth, they end up destroying their civilization in a search for immortality. The road to this destruction comes from a combination of factors: pride, wealth, desire for power, and fear of death. Thus, Númenór, like all these societies in Middle-earth, eventually decays because of inherent human weaknesses.

The flaws of the inheritors of Númenórean culture, the people of Gondor, also reflect their culture's unique relationship with the elves and their predilections. Since Númenórean culture is a bit "elvish," it is not too surprising that it contains some of the same weaknesses in elvish culture. Gandalf describes how the aristocracy of Gondor has become more interested in the genealogy of their ancestors and the beauty of their tombs than in their children and the future of their land. Like the elves, the leaders of Gondor tend to look backward instead of forward, especially when future-oriented action is needed against Mordor. Therefore, they attempt to preserve the past rather than look toward the future. Gondorians also seem more susceptible to despair because of the advanced age of their culture. Both Boromir and Denethor eventually give in to despair while attempting to protect their land. The people of Gondor have more "man-like" faults as well. Specifically, while the elves' focus on beauty and creativity makes them less interested in power of this world, men (even the men of Númenór) are susceptible to the lure of earthly power. The betrayal of Boromir and the animus of Denethor toward Aragorn both arise from a desire to gain or retain power. Boromir's desire for the Ring comes from his legitimate desire to defend his society and an illegitimate desire to gain power for himself. Denethor resents Aragorn as the returned king because his return means that Denethor will cease to be the de facto ruler of Gondor. His inability to see how Aragorn could help defend his city comes from his pride and self-interest.

The West's disunity in the face of Mordor's aggression also reflects their unique flaws. The mutual suspicion of elves, dwarves, and men that inhibits their common defense comes from an alienation built by histories of conflict and their current ignorance. This alienation from one another comes from a variety of causes. The conflicts between elves and dwarves almost always revolve around their mutual desire for material objects: the Silmarils, the Arkenstone, and so on. The conflict between men and elves comes mainly from ignorance: the Men of Rohan, for example, fear Galadriel as a "witch" based on their limited knowledge. In any case, these weaknesses will never be overcome by some utopian arrangement. These weaknesses are built into the warp and woof of Middle-earth. The inherent pessimism reflects Tolkien's own view of the world, which he described as "one long defeat." Whenever a "good" society is created it only has a limited time before corruption sets in; and even when the forces of evil are temporarily defeated, they are never completely destroyed.

Despite his seeming pessimism about his good societies' survival and prosperity in Middle-earth, Tolkien also acknowledges providential forces that seem to be working against the triumph of dystopian societies. The first force is just evil's basic "lack of imagination" described by Auden. Sauron's inability to imagine that the free peoples of Middle-earth would agree to destroy the Ring of Power makes him vulnerable to Frodo's mission. His focus on those who present a military threat to him, like Saruman and Aragorn, opens up a path into the heart of Mordor for Frodo and Sam. The constant in fighting between the different malevolent factions also seriously weakens the party of evil. The conflict between the Uruk-hai and the orcs of Mordor allows Pippin and Merry to escape, the civil war at the Tower at the entrance to Mordor opens the path for Frodo and Sam into the plains of Gorgoroth, and Saruman's death comes not from the returning hobbits, but by the hand of his own servant, Gríma Wormtongue. Sauron's emptying out of Mordor to face the threat of Aragorn's army was the only possible way for Sam and Frodo to make it into Mount Doom. Sauron's eye surveils everywhere outside Mordor, but he neglects to protect his own realm and this allows the hobbits to go to the one place where he could be defeated. Time and again, at key moments, the forces of evil sabotage their own interests by failing to see what the true danger is—not when the people of Middle-earth would choose evil, but when they would attempt to do good. All these various events lead to what Tolkien famously dubbed a "eucatastrophe"—the sudden, unexpected turn of events that brings about a happy ending in a desperate situation that should end in certain defeat. Tolkien described the emotional effect of this turn as so profound that the happy ending "pierces you with a joy that brings tears."[40]

The serendipitous nature of these unforced errors by the agents of Mordor suggests another force is at work in the defeat of Sauron: Providence. Thomas Gasque, in his essay "Tolkien: The Monsters and the Critics," discusses the relationship between Providence and free will in *The Lord of the Rings*. I will quote his argument in some length because Gasque takes the time to explain Tolkien's complex theodicy. He argues,

> philosophically, if the guiding hand [of God] is really to guide effectively, it must have power to control events, yet not so much as to take away from people acting them out of the capacity of moral choice. The latter being fundamental to Tolkien's conception of man (and other rational beings), must be preserved at all costs. So Tolkien cannot allow his cosmic order to be a fixed, mechanistic, unchangeable chain of causes and effects. The order must be built flexibly around creaturely free will and possible personal providential interventions from on high.[41]

God must be able to intervene, but not in such a way as to interfere with free will.[42] The various "accidents" that allow Frodo and Sam to go on so long uncaptured by the forces of Mordor seem plausible enough individually, but, in retrospect, show a pattern. In each case, the actors involved act of their own free will to bring about the will of the Creator. Many of these actions, the fighting between orcs, for example, are objectively evil, but their decisions inadvertently lead to good results: Merry and Pippin's escape and Frodo and Sam's infiltration of Mordor. The good results also do not involve a "miracle" or some action that takes place outside the limits of the physical world for the most part (though miracles do sometimes occur in Middle-earth). This fits with the cosmology Tolkien conceived in *The Silmarillion*. Melkor's attempt to change the music of Eru fails because even though Melkor's vision went against Eru (and was not an example of subcreation), Eru still conforms the discordant notes into a larger theme.[43] In other words, good came out of evil, which is a mainstay of Christian theodicy. Still, this good only comes out of evil in the long run, and it could be a very long run indeed. Finally, doing good, like doing evil, never comes without a cost.

Tolkien's most subtle suggestions of Providence include mixing sadness with beauty, his celebrating freedom, and loving the natural world. All these elements sacralize Middle-earth. This recognition of the sacred colors the decisions and actions of the good characters in Tolkien's narratives by allowing his characters to see beyond their current circumstances. Even if the good characters are not always destined to win, they possess faith enough to try (even when, as in most of the legends of *The Silmarillion*, the good guys almost always lose). Their willingness suggests a belief in at least the possibility of victory, even if it is the final victory that will only come in the Parousia, or a victory represented by a distant beauty that transcends the mortal world. Sam experiences this faith in a final victory when, almost at wit's end, he spies the morning star in the heart of Mordor:

> Far above Ephel Dúath in the West the night-sky was still dim and pale. There, peeping among the cloud-wrack above a dark tor high up in the mountains, Sam saw a white star twinkle for a while. The beauty of it smote his heart, as he looked up out of the forsaken land and hope returned to him. For like a shaft, clear and cold, the thought pierced him that in the end the Shadow was a small and passing thing: there was light and high beauty for ever beyond its reach.[44]

Tolkien's mixture of the desolate landscape's melancholy with the star's loveliness reflects a metaphysical position. With the exception of the star of Elbereth in this passage, Tolkien almost always describes beauty as a temporary and incomplete reflection of Eden. This passage suggests that he views the ugliness of Mordor ("the Shadow") as similarly fleeting. In Tolkien's view, neither his good nor evil societies have the totalizing power conveyed by permanence, and because of this assumption provides room in these societies for the moral agency to do both good and evil. What does have totalizing power are spiritual forces that are beyond the material world, yet are at the same time bound up with it. These spiritual forces are not always found in remote, beautiful entities like this star, but can also exist in more humble objects. Tolkien often describes these objects of the natural world as possessing something more than the material, something transcendent. The elves' lembas bread, cloaks, boats, and even rope are symbolic in that they function not only as physical objects but as sacramental ones: outward signs of spiritual grace. The irony is that because the forces of evil seem totally concerned with the material world, they are not only incapable of taking advantage of its sacramental potential, but because of their adversarial approach to the physical world, they are always destroying and diminishing even its material potential.

In the final analysis, Tolkien's contribution to utopian and dystopian theory is unique in the twentieth century. Rather than attempting to show how the ideal arrangement of material conditions leads to either bliss or despair, he demarcates the limits of utopias and dystopias and their material aspirations altogether. This does not mean there is not a vast gulf between Thangorodrim and Aman or between Mordor and the Shire. Indeed, in many ways, Tolkien's use of utopian and dystopian concepts in his societies is more convincingly beautiful or terrifying in their complexity and finitude than the most modern and classic examples of utopias and dystopias. Part of this terror and beauty comes from Tolkien giving his characters the possibility of choice in the first place. He denies the often anodyne model of a utopia that attempts to create peace by sacrificing all possibility of conflict and change, as well as the orderly model of dystopia that similarly assumes that all-powerful coercion and surveillance will lead to a robotic obedience. Another reason this control proves so elusive is that the characters in Tolkien's works have imperfections and transcendence that work at cross purposes to the cultural and political goals of those in power—whether good or evil. Humans are both too good and too bad for any scheme proposed by the most clever and methodical of utopian or dystopian planners.

With these tragic limitations, how does Tolkien create good societies that seem, at once, plausible and beautiful? Tolkien recognizes how history, conflict, and a tolerance for idiosyncrasy are ironically part of what is needed to make the good possible, rather than what the utopia is designed to eliminate. The attempt to purge these elements from classic utopian visions results in diminishing the utopian citizen's humanity. Instead, Tolkien creates good societies in which the choice to do mostly good seems plausible and almost "natural." Thus, his societies are not cut from their roots, like most revolutionary utopian societies, but are ones that have been allowed to grow over many years (like trees, Tolkien's favorite living thing). Because of this, his ideal societies like the Shire, Rivendell, Lothlórien, and Gondolin all have unique characteristics that reflect their histories, their people, and their frailties. Tolkien's approach to these frailties does the most to separate him from most utopian and dystopian writers. Rather than trying to use the mechanism of the state to eliminate or minimalize these frailties, Tolkien allows his citizens to have a variety of imperfections: to be bores, to be insular, to be petty. He even allows for the inevitability that even the best of fortune will still cause discomfort to some. After Tolkien describes how the golden spring that followed the scouring of the Shire was almost perfect, he adds, "No one was ill, and everyone was pleased, except those who had to mow the grass."[45] He allows that good fortune for most people will still mean discomfort for others in this vale of tears. Beyond the small irritations that Tolkien allows, he also shows that even his best societies will eventually have fatal, as well as venial, flaws, and like Gondolin and Nargothrond, they will fall because of more than small imperfections. Even so, while they exist, they present a world that seems much more humane and human than our own (even if those worlds are inhabited by elves or hobbits). Thus, part of both the beauty and the realism of Tolkien's good societies comes from the possibility that they can be lost. In this sense, his ideal societies are precious because they can be lost and realistic because they inevitably are. Still, concrete, but not revolutionary, steps can be taken to reach a better society. Tolkien's path of an organic, incremental, change combined with maximum freedom seems much more real and achievable as a good "some place" as opposed to utopia's almost perfect "no place."

Perhaps most importantly, Tolkien's good societies seem real because they occupy a middle position between our quotidian reality and paradise. The belief in the existence or even desirability of the beatific vision is something many contemporary people have trouble accepting. In one sense, Tolkien makes this "vision" not a matter of faith, but a bare fact, a place. Because Tolkien made his paradise an actual geographic location, he allows for a "real" place that is transcendent and more fully utopian outside the good societies of Middle-earth to point toward perfection: the West, the Undying Lands. Beyond that, he presents a further paradise, much like the Christian tradition, beyond the circles of the world where mortals are destined to go. The contrast between the perfect West and the good societies of Middle-earth shows that these are neither utopia nor paradise. Yet, in the same way that Tolkien sacralizes seemingly ordinary objects, he lets Middle-earth's benevolent societies also partake in the sacred. Thus, Tolkien's good societies are truly in the "middle" of the sacred and the profane, between Mordor and the West. This sense of being in the middle of both better and worse spiritual possibilities is what many current and past utopias lack. They lack the sacred and only contain the profane and thus cannot be in "Middle-earth." I think this sense of lack is the reason why even secular readers of Tolkien find themselves drawn to the mystical nature of Middle-earth, and why places like Lothlórien and the Shire are closest to fulfilling their dreams of a better society. No one (at least that I know of) writes "the *Utopia* is real!" or "*The Republic* can be true!" on subway walls, but they do write "Frodo lives!" Tolkien speaks to us in a visceral utopian language that we can understand and believe. This belief comes not from accepting the plausibility of a political program or a new set of cultural norms, but from his readers changing their metaphysical approach to the "good."

NOTES

1. I agree with Lyman Tower Sargent when he says in his book, *Dark Horizons*, "I have always argued that utopias are not descriptions of perfect places" (225).
2. B. G. Knepper, "The Coming Race: Hell? Or Paradise Foretasted." in *No Place Else: Explorations in Utopian and Dystopian Fiction*, eds. Eric S. Rabkin, Martin H. Greenberg et al. (Carbondale: Southern Illinois University Press, 1983), 11–32.
3. Thus a Gnostic cannot arrange to have a utopia in this world, since the material world will always be irredeemably evil.
4. Many critics also include a third and fourth term, "anti-utopia" and "critical dystopia," in addition to utopia and dystopia. While there is quite a bit of contention about what qualifies as an anti-utopia, Frederic Jameson argues that anti-utopia is more properly considered the opposite of utopia rather than dystopia since anti-utopia calls into question the possibility or wisdom of creating utopian societies in the first place. For instance, Tom Moylan in *Scraps of Untainted Sky* draws a distinction between Zamyatin's *We*, which he argues includes the possibility of some future utopian place outside the confines Onestate, and Orwell's *1984*, which denies any space outside the control of Oceania. I do not think this distinction works very well in fictional narratives (I think it works much better in nonfiction works) and depends a great deal on the subjective judgment of the critic about vague indications of utopian possibilities outside the texts. This distinction promoted by many Marxist and left-leaning critics mainly serves the purpose of maintaining revolutionary change as a viable option in a culture that seems much more attuned to dystopian fears than revolutionary hopes after political revolutions have failed repeatedly to deliver their utopias.

Moylan describes critical utopias as narratives that appear to be dystopian but offer "some open out to minimal utopian possibilities" or "offer new utopian trajectories." In these narratives, the protagonist has an awakening where he or she realizes the dystopian nature of his or her society and "moves" toward some better place.

5. Lyman Tower Sargent quoted in Tom Moylan, *Scraps of Untainted Sky: Utopia, Dystopia (Cultural Studies)* (Boulder: Westview Press, 2000), 74.
6. Darko Suvin, *Metamorphoses of Science Fiction: On the Poetics and History of a Literary Genre*. ed. Gerry Canavan (Oxford: Peter Lang, 2016), 49.
7. For example, in M. Keith Booker's *Dystopian Literature: A Theory and Research Guide*, Booker includes over sixty-five authors in his extensive guide to dystopian literature, but does not include Tolkien. Since the majority of the works are science fiction, Booker's failure to include Tolkien is not due to the snobbery that many critics express toward "genre fiction." Booker's criteria are also quite expansive, including works like Dostoevsky's *Notes from the Underground* and *Brothers Karamazov* as well as James Joyce's *Dubliners*, which are more dystopian in theme rather than in plot. Booker also includes a much shorter list of eight utopian works. It is telling that Tolkien does not appear in that list either.
8. Though Tolkien at one point experimented with a never completed time-travel novel called *The Lost Road* that would have just such a traveler from our own world.
9. It is not a coincidence that all these works that mix utopian and dystopian elements are science fiction. Science fiction writers are traditionally interested in examining how technology's ability to fulfill our desires leads to both utopian and dystopian possibilities.
10. The notable exception to the dominance that dystopian works have enjoyed in the twentieth and twenty-first centuries is a utopian revival primarily in science fiction that occurred in the 1960s and 1970s. Even at the high point of this revival, however, dystopian literature continued to be the more prominent genre.
11. Leszek Kolakowski, "The Death of Utopia Reconsidered." (Lecture, *The Tanner Lectures on Human Values*, Australian National University, June 22, 1982) *The Semantic Scholar*, 230, dfs.semanticscholar.org/leb5/ccce5c90d.

12. Nicholas Carr, *Utopia Is Creepy and Other Provocations* (New York: W. W. Norton, 2016), 108–9.

13. Kolakowski, "The Death of Utopia Reconsidered," 230.

14. G. K. Chesterton, "The Ethics of Elfland." *Orthodoxy, Page-by-Page Books*, accessed November 28, 2018, https://www.pagebypagebooks.com/Gilbert_K_Chesterton/Orthodoxy/.

15. J.R.R. Tolkien to Christopher Tolkien, November 29, 1943, in *Letters of J.R.R. Tolkien*, ed. Christopher Tolkien (Wilmington: Mariner Books, 2000), 74.

16. I will discuss Tolkien's complex social and political views in chapter 5.

17. The debate over the relationship between Tolkien and distributionism is acrimonious. See Joseph Pearce's argument for the influence of distributionist thought in Tolkien in the blog *The Imaginative Conservative*. See Jay Richards and Jonathan Witt's *The Hobbit Party* for an equally passionate argument denying such an influence. Yannick Imbert's article, "Tolkien's Shire," does a good job of placing Tolkien's argument in the context of the political currents of late nineteenth- and early twentieth-century Britain. Again, I will discuss the relationship between distributionism and Tolkien in chapter 5.

18. One surprising place where the "gift economy" still exists is the internet. Giorel Curren in her book *21st Century Dissent* notes that the very structure and function of the internet was created partly through the free "gift" of software, and by implication, the labor that created it. We can see also this "gift" approach in the various wikis that exist through the uncompensated labor of many people (the most famous of these being *Wikipedia*).

19. Many critics (see Lois Kuznets, "The Hobbit Is Rooted in the Tradition of Classic British Children's Novels," for example) argue that this love of comfort and peace suggests that hobbits are childish, or even stand-ins for the child reader, in the case of Bilbo in *The Hobbit*. This assumption does not fit particularly well with the hobbits' obvious distaste for authority and their obsession with meals being served on time. To me, hobbits embody the cranky conservativeness characteristic of many middle-aged homebodies rather than the fearfulness of an anxious child.

20. J.R.R. Tolkien, "On Fairy-Stories." *Tolkien on Fairy-Stories Expanded Edition, with Commentary and Notes*, eds. Verilyn Fliegler and Douglas A. Anderson (London: HarperCollins, 2008), 28.

21. The land to the east of Middle-earth where the elves can dwell with the Valar.

22. J.R.R. Tolkien, *The Fellowship of the Ring* (New York: Ballantine Books, 1994), 416.

23. There is some debate about whether Sauron is literally a lidless eye in Mordor or whether Sauron has a more human-like or corporeal form and the eye is an illusion or a symbol Sauron creates for himself. Some people argue that Sauron appears as a "vision" of an eye to others. For example, there is some evidence for this illusion theory in this passage from *The Return of the King*: "One moment only it stared out, but as from some great window immeasurably high there stabbed northward a flame of red, the flicker of a piercing Eye; and the shadows were furled again and the terrible *vision* [my italics] was removed" (270). Still, earlier in *The Return of the King* Tolkien mentions the Eye of Sauron several times in a seemingly non-metaphorical fashion. For example, Tolkien describes Sauron as a literal eye in this sentence: "The Dark Power was deep in thought and the Eye turned inward pondering tidings of doubt and danger" (245). In this passage, there is no one to see a "vision" of Sauron and the Eye seems self-referential. Still, it is not unusual for creatures in Tolkien's books to seem to change their physical characteristics over time. Certainly, the Black Riders in *The Fellowship of the Ring* appear markedly different from the Nazgŭl of *The Return of the King*. Similarly, Tolkien himself rewrote Gollum in later versions of *The Hobbit* to fit his revised character in *The Lord of the Rings*.

24. Brian Rosebury, *Tolkien: A Cultural Phenomenon* (London: Palgrave Macmillan, 2003), 47.

25. W. H. Auden, "The Quest Hero." *Tolkien and the Critics* (South Bend, IN: Notre Dame University Press, 1969), 57–58.

26. Auden, "The Quest Hero," 58.
27. Rosebury, *Tolkien: A Cultural Phenomenon*, 180.
28. J.R.R. Tolkien, *The Return of the King* (New York: Ballantine Books, 1994), 213.
29. Tolkien, *The Return of the King*, 213.
30. Rosebury, *Tolkien: A Cultural Phenomenon*, 44–45.
31. Tom Shippey, *J.R.R. Tolkien: Author of the Century* (London, HarperCollins, 2000), 171.
32. This is quickly ceasing to be a hypothetical question in our society. With advances in genetic engineering, for example, it is possible to imagine soldiers being genetically engineered to be more aggressive by some future military.
33. This very Tolkienian statement exemplifies the difficulty of analyzing Tolkien's works from a Christian, or Catholic, perspective. On the one hand, Tolkien insists that his stories should not have "to fit with formalized Christian theology," while, on the other hand, he declares his stories are "intended to be consonant with Christian thought and belief." Tolkien draws a subtle distinction between the strict interpretation of his work as an example of Christian apologetics and the looser interpretation of his work as creating a Christian culture through aesthetic means (i.e., is he a Christian artist or an artist who is a Christian?). I will explore this issue in more detail in chapter 2.
34. Tolkien, *Letters*, 355.
35. J.R.R. Tolkien, *The Two Towers* (New York: Ballantine Books, 1994), 44.
36. This is the place where the Peter Jackson movie version of *The Lord of the Rings* simplifies the novel. Instead of arguing over cannibalism, all the orcs gleefully tear into the flesh and entrails of a fallen orc after Uglúk proclaims, "Meat is back on the menu, boys"—a line that is not found in Tolkien's *The Lord of the Rings*.
37. The one exception is Bolg, who was described as the son of Azog, mentioned both in *The Hobbit* and in the appendices to the *Lord of the Rings*.
38. Manichaeism was a religion that competed with early Christianity and posited a world with two dueling deities: one perfectly good God and one perfectly evil Satan who were in perpetual combat for control over the universe. Evil was associated with darkness and the material world and good was associated with light and spirituality. Manichaeism differs from orthodox Christianity by denying the omnipotence of God (both God and Satan are equal in power) and by denying the goodness of material creation.
39. Richard Z. Gallant, "Original Sin in Heorot and Valinor," *Tolkien Studies* 11, (2014): 109–10.
40. Tolkien, *Letters*, 100.
41. Thomas Gasque, "Tolkien: The Monster and the Critters." *Tolkien and the Critics*, eds. N. D. Isaacs and Rose Abdulnoor Zimbardo (South Bend, IN: Notre Dame University Press, 1969), 14.
42. Grant Sterling, in his essay "The Consolation of Bilbo," suggests another solution to the problem of free will and providential control. He argues that Tolkien's view of the relationship between God as omniscient and free will was similar to the philosopher Boethius. Boethius argued that God was outside time and exists in a single moment that combines all the past and the future. Thus to speak of God knowing, making, or predestining events to happen in the world is to falsely imply that he exists in time rather than outside it.
43. One could argue that Tolkien's creation story has Neo-platonic and Gnostic, as well as Christian, elements. Tolkien's decision to involve the Valar in creation and weave evil into the very fabric of the material world by Melkor partially resembles the idea of the world being fashioned by a Demiurge rather than a Christian God. Obviously, Tolkien departed from the Gnostics, especially in rejecting the idea that the material world is wholly evil.
44. Tolkien, *The Return of the King*, 211.
45. Tolkien, *The Return of the King*, 331.

TWO
The Sources of Tolkien's Utopian and Dystopian Vision

I claimed in chapter 1 that Tolkien makes his ideal and evil societies vivid and believable to the modern reader while most ancient and contemporary utopias and dystopias appear flat and artificial by comparison. In this chapter, I argue that part of this effect comes from Tolkien's use of what I call "Victorian medieval" and Modernist sources. While a great deal of scholarship has already been done tracing the sources of Tolkien's works, especially *The Lord of the Rings* and *The Hobbit*, this chapter will examine how these sources specifically influenced Tolkien's crafting of the prominent utopian and dystopian themes in his works.[1] The idea is not to show a one-to-one correspondence between the sources and events in the narratives, but to demonstrate how Tolkien uses the different philosophical presuppositions of his sources to weave together a series of societies that are at once alien and strangely familiar. The alien nature comes mostly from Tolkien's introduction to his readers of a medieval approach to the world with deep ties to the environment and social relationships that contrast with contemporary people's often more superficial approach to the material world and each other. Tolkien's Victorian medievalism, on the other hand, works by generating a familiar sense of nostalgia both for Victorian culture and the Victorian artists' unique approach to the medieval period. Finally, Tolkien uses Modern and Postmodern tropes to both to show his readers the dangers of current cultural trends and to help then relate to his characters (especially his hobbits).

Tolkien, as the Rawlinson and Bosworth Professor of Anglo-Saxon at Oxford, was steeped in medieval literature of all types and called on this extensive knowledge to broaden and deepen his legendarium. I have already made the claim that Tolkien used *Beowulf* to present a different approach to the exchange of material possessions than our current capitalist exchange-value assumptions. I also argue that this use of medieval tropes and ideas that challenge current metaphysical and ideological assumptions occurs throughout his works. These challenges are especially sharp in three areas: contemporary people's relationship with the physical world, their relationship with each other, and their relationship with society. Through his use of older medieval models, Tolkien approaches issues from outside the current political and cultural axioms of most contemporary people. In each of these areas, Tolkien uses medieval assumptions to challenge current beliefs in order to give his readers insight into their own hegemonic worldviews so that they can see why many aspects of their ideology feel so inadequate. In this way, he exposes the utopian possibilities of the older beliefs to contemporary readers.

One assumption Tolkien challenges is default philosophical materialism (as in the belief that the only things that exist or are important in the world are material) of most twentieth- and twenty-first-century people. In contrast to this materialist assumption, Tolkien assumes the physical world has an almost animistic quality as he imbues objects with sacred, and sometimes soul-like, power. Tolkien starts the *Silmarillion* with a pagan pantheon of gods called the Valar. Eru Ilúvatar gives each of the Valar a certain aspect of the physical world to control: Manwë is the god of the winds and atmosphere, Ulmo is god of the waters, and so on. In this way, the Valar resemble the classical Greek, Roman, and Norse pantheon assigned to different aspects of material reality. The association of deity-like Valar to different parts of the created world personalizes even the most inert parts of the world, like the air, water, and earth. In this way, Tolkien re-enchants the physical world of Middle-earth as a contrast to the "real" world most contemporary people in the West experience that has been steadily desacralized since the Enlightenment. This is just one way that Tolkien crosses the boundaries between the living and the inanimate, the sentient and the aconscious. Tolkien challenges these boundaries through his very diction by describing inanimate objects as if they are alive. He speaks of the "living rock" or how mountains have "roots" not just in poetry, but in the everyday speech of his characters. I have already mentioned how Tolkien sacralizes crafted objects, but he goes beyond hallowing these objects by giving them agency and teleology. Many times in *The Lord of the Rings*, characters speak of the Ring of Power in an almost person-like way, as a creature with a will of its own and a desire to get back to its master (Sauron). In an even more explicit way in *The Silmarillion*, Túrin's sword, Gurthang, speaks at the end of the story and agrees to take the life of its master. He also blurs the lines between plant and animal life, with intermediate creatures like Ents that take on the aspects of both plants and animals. Sometimes this transformation can cross species barriers, such as when the Hourns and Old Man Willow show how trees in Middle-earth can "wake up" and become animal-like.

Tolkien takes this theme of physical objects with agency from Northern myth. Sometimes his borrowings from Northern mythology are quite direct. In the Finnish epic poem *Kalevala*, Kullervo, like Túrin, has a talking black sword that takes the life of its hapless master. Readers of Arthurian legend have also become familiar with inanimate objects that have a will of their own and sacred power, like Excalibur, which had the ability to pick the rightful king; the Holy Grail, which would only choose the most worthy knight; and the Ring of Nibelung, which curses with destruction all who possess it.

The blurring of the lines between what we consider hard metaphysical and taxonomic categories is a common trope in Anglo-Saxon and Northern European literature as well. This happens at the metaphysical scale in Norse mythology where the giant tree Yggdrasil is the Universe. Sacred trees played a prominent role in both Greek mythology (with its sacred groves) and for Germanic tribes (which often had sacred trees and woods as a central part of their villages and territories).[2] In early Anglo-Saxon Christian literature, a personified tree also played a central metaphysical role.[3] In the poem "The Dream of the Rood," the tree used to crucify Christ speaks to a dreaming man and explains itself to him. Sometimes, rather than plants taking on human attributes, the reverse is true. The Green Knight in *Sir Gawain and the Green Knight* appears to be both a knight and the Green Man, a pagan god of rebirth who can, like a plant, be dismembered (by having his head chopped off), but still live, just like a plant can be pruned and then grow back. Including a pagan deity like the Green Man crosses another boundary where a Christian poem is "allowed" to have pagan elements. With characters like Goldberry and Tom Bombadil, a sort of water-nymph and guardian of the forest, Tolkien, like the *Sir Gawain* poet, shows a very medieval propensity not to be threatened by minor pagan deities.

The effect that Tolkien creates with the bending and merging of these supposedly hard categories like animate/inanimate, plant/animal, and Christian/pagan is to challenge the reader's modern and postmodern sensibilities with a more medieval one. Whereas most contemporary people either think in unconscious Cartesian terms that assign dualistic body/soul categories to reality or in purely materialistic terms that assume nothing outside the physical, the medieval approach assumes a spiritual worlds that is both the primary reality and is not separated from the material. Tolkien emphasizes the primacy of the spiritual in *The Silmarillion* when he describes how the physical world is only created after the Music of the Ainur (Tolkien's metaphor for spiritual creation). Thus the physical world both comes after the spiritual world and is dependent on it. One also gets this sense from a great deal of medieval literature. In *Beowulf*, the physical and spiritual worlds intersect in the way scripture and the world intertwine, so Grendel is a relative of Cain and Beowulf kills Grendel's mother with a pre-flood sword of the giants (no doubt owned by a Nephilim). As he goes to meet the pagan god of the Green Man and the Green Man's wife, the sorceress Morgan le Fay, Gawain of *Sir Gawain and the Green Knight* carries the red-cross shield of Christianity. Not only does the physical world reflect the spiritual, but spiritual deficiencies become physically embodied. Therefore, God punishes Gawain physically with a cut on the neck for his lack of faith.

By sacralizing the material, Tolkien gives the physical world a depth and resonance that many feel they have lost in the modern and postmodern world. The rapid economic and social changes that have transformed the world in the twentieth and twenty-first centuries have left many people confused and insecure. Perhaps even more troubling to many people, the philosophical revolutions of the last three centuries have thinned the thick sense of meaning that characterized the pre-industrial world (for both good and ill). Many Enlightenment, Romantic, and Modernist thinkers were much more effective in their wholesale rejection of traditions of the past than they were in finding new intellectual structures to replace them.[4] What has often replaced narratives that present a life with meaning and purpose are ideologies that have systemically stripped life of its teleology, from purposeless evolution to Nietzschean will-to-power. This left many people adrift and longing for a sense of rootedness. If anything, this sense of social isolation and atomization that started in the Modern Era has increased in the Postmodern Era. Many thinkers, like Zygmunt Bauman, have noted how rapid social and material change has brought about an even more frenetic form of cultural and social displacement he calls "liquid modernity." According to Bauman, people in the late Modern and Postmodern era have become ever more "nomadic" in terms of their ideological beliefs and this has allowed them to escape social strictures, but at the same time, have become alienated from supportive social structures.[5] On a deeper level, elements of technological progress have encouraged a technocratic view of people as resources to be manipulated rather than the medieval view of people as creatures made in the image of God. Roman Guardini describes how this new view of man makes an individual a "mass man," whom he defines as "the man who is absorbed by technology and rational abstraction."[6] According to Guardini, man becomes part of the standardized, normalized (as in the normal curve) part of the machinery of society which leads to a "loss of personality" and "the steady fading away of that sense of uniqueness with which man had viewed his own existence."[7] It is against this backdrop of an ever thinner view of persons and the material world that Tolkien's more spiritually robust Middle-earth finds so much aesthetic purchase among his twentieth- and twenty-first-century readers.

Another aspect of the medieval worldview that many contemporary readers likely find attractive is its "thicker" social ties. Even so, these ties depend on one aspect that many of Tolkien's critics found the most objectionable about his legendarium: the relative rigidity of Middle-earth's social and gender hierarchy. People hold their positions because of their hereditary caste, whether it is Aragorn as heir to Isildur, Théoden as a king of Rohan, or even Frodo as the master of Sam. Throughout his legendarium, natural deference is given to those of a higher class by those below them. At the same time, many of these hierarchical relationships are deep and longstanding and based on lifetimes of interaction. Other relationships are based on lord/vassal oaths that are made by the agreement of both parties. Pippin pledges his service to Denethor, and Merry does the same to Théoden. The loyalty required, and the solemnity of these oaths, go well beyond the more common employee/boss model that dominates current professional relationships. Instead of being a monetary contract, these lord/vassal relationships are more akin to adoptions. All these powerful relationships that go beyond the self-interested capitalist model are both attractive and frightening to many contemporary people.[8] I mentioned how contemporary people long to be less atomistic yet appreciate being able to escape the strictures of more traditional societies. The characters in Tolkien's Middle-earth wholeheartedly engage in these entangling and constraining relationships in a way that appears both reckless and refreshing to many modern readers.[9]

Tolkien also includes ways that characters can transcend hierarchies, but these ways of transcending have medieval qualities to them as well. As I mentioned earlier, the characters in Middle-earth have a strict hierarchy. For instance, Gandalf as a Maiar ranks above Aragorn as a king, who ranks above Frodo as a commoner freeholder, who ranks above Sam as a servant. Even so, there is more than one hierarchy at work. By the end of the story, because Frodo as ringbearer has saved Middle-earth, he transcends the other mortal characters no matter their nobility. In a similar way, Éowyn transcends the gender hierarchy and becomes the only possible warrior who could kill the Witch-king of Angmar because of the prophecy that he could not be killed by the hand of a man. This setting up of strict hierarchies and allowing them to be broken or transcended should seem familiar to those who study medieval narratives. These hierarchies can be overturned in part because there were more than one set of them in the medieval world. Dante's *The Divine Comedy* illustrates this phenomenon well. Hell, Purgatory, and Paradise are set up with a familiar form of medieval hierarchy, but it is a hierarchy of holiness, separate from the hierarchy of the world, so that there are popes and kings in Hell yet peasants in Heaven. This spiritual hierarchy can upset power arrangements of the earthly world as well, such that a sixteen-year-old peasant girl, Joan of Arc, can wield a divine mandate to lead armies, relieve a siege, and crown a king in fourteenth-century France.

Tolkien not only used medieval models in his approach to the physical and social world of Middle-earth, he also used a more general medieval attitude about reality to create his legendarium: an attitude that approaches difference with a syncretic rather than an exclusionary instinct.

Tolkien approaches his source material from a catholic (in the sense of universal, though also in the sense of medieval Roman Catholic) perspective. Therefore, Tolkien uses a medieval syncretic approach to his legendarium. Often (though not always) the medieval church's approach to pagan customs would be to see if they could find the "good" in a pagan practice and belief rather than look for the "bad" (from the point of view of Catholic theology). If the church deemed the pagan custom harmless, it would be incorporated into the church or ignored. Thus, Christmas trees, Easter eggs, and shamrocks started off as pagan symbols, yet became incorporated into Christian life in medieval Europe. Even pagan religious practices, like dancing around the maypole, were mostly left alone for hundreds of years during the Middle Ages once shorn of their religious meaning (only to be suppressed after the Protestant ascendancy in many European countries).

Tolkien copied the most extreme example of medieval tolerance for outside ideologies in that he created Christian works without explicit references to the Christian religion. Just as medieval scholars did not always see hard breaks between physical categories like animate and inanimate, plant and animal, Tolkien's medieval models did not see paganism and Christianity as completely opposed to one another.[10] This allowed medieval scholars to promiscuously mix what, in the modern mind, should be separate genres.[11] Medieval pagan/Christian hybrids, like *Beowulf* and *Sir Gawain and the Green Knight,* gave Tolkien a model of how to create a Christian work, not only with pagan elements, but with little reference to specific Christian practices in *The Lord of the Rings* and *The Silmarillion*.

Tolkien had two reasons why he did not want to explicitly mention Christianity. First, he created his legendarium to be a pre-Christian one. Second, Tolkien's aesthetic standards demanded that his "secondary world" (the world created by art) be different enough from our "primary world" (the real world) so that readers would not be distracted by this resemblance. Tolkien argued in his essay "On Fairy-Stories" that if too many elements of what he calls the "primary world" enter into his created "secondary world" disbelief arises and "the spell has been broken; the magic, or rather art, has failed."[12] Tolkien's creation of liturgical practices that were too obvious and too contingent on the primary world is just such a spell-breaking phenomenon that Tolkien wanted to avoid at all costs. Despite this lack of reference to Christianity and his insistence that his works were pre-Christian, Tolkien still maintained that *The Lord of the Rings* was a Christian work:

> *The Lord of the Rings* is of course a fundamentally religious and Catholic work; unconsciously so at first, but consciously at the revision. That is why I have not put in, or have cut out, practically all references to anything like 'religion' to cults or to practices in the imaginary world.

For the religious element is absorbed into the story and the symbolism.[13]

The irony here is that Tolkien argues that because his work is "fundamentally Catholic" he removes any references to "religion." He is referring to *The Lord of the Rings*, but he also excises most references to religion in *The Silmarillion* as well, except for the generally theistic and pagan ones. I interpret this departure not as evidence that Tolkien, the Roman Catholic daily communicant, did not take worship seriously, but that he took it so seriously that he did not want to trivialize it. For Tolkien, the Mass was not a human-created ritual, but a divinely ordained sacrifice that transcended any other human activity. The idea of creating a facsimile of such a sacrifice for Middle-earth or other elements of Christian liturgy was blasphemous. Such a facsimile would also interfere with Tolkien's artistic aims. Because Tolkien took Christianity so seriously, his theological approach to Middle-earth resembles that of the Christian *Beowulf* poet Tolkien admired. Like Tolkien, the *Beowulf* poet fails to mention any liturgy except when the backsliding Danes swore oaths and offered sacrifices at pagan shrines. God rules the Middle-earth of *Beowulf*, but He appears to be much more a pre-Christian one; Tolkien chose to make his Middle-earth pre-Christian as well or perhaps with the Valar, semi-pagan. Still, I would argue that the differences between the pagan and Christian worldviews are smaller than the differences between assumptions of an enchanted or sacred worldview and the default materialist worldview that most people, even many nominal Christians, have today. Tolkien's and the author of *Beowulf*'s relationship with religion contrasts with a more iconoclastic approach that flourished among Catholics, and especially Protestants, after the Reformation that emphasized doctrinal purity and exclusion of non-Christian beliefs.[14]

The most complete investigation of the relationship between the pagan and Christian elements of Tolkien's work from a philosophical point of view has been done by Claudio A. Testi in his essay "Tolkien's Work: Is It Christian or Pagan?" In it, Testi posits that Tolkien's legendarium has three characteristics. First, he argues that Tolkien's stories take place in what he calls the "natural world," by which he means that the "knowledge, choices, and actions of his characters result only from their inherent natural abilities, with no specific reference to any form of supernatural Faith or Biblical Revelation." Second, he contends that despite not referencing these supernatural elements, Tolkien's legendarium is "in harmony with the supernatural plane of the Christian Revelation." Finally, he argues that the two premises lead to the conclusion that "we can consider Tolkien's work as an expression of Catholic culture."[15] Even though my approach is historical and Testi's approach is logical, we both end up with a similar conclusion: that Tolkien's works end up culturally Christian and Catholic even though they describe a pagan world. Testi argues that his logical approach makes the most sense since Tolkien's anachronisms and deliberate separation of his legendarium from European history make an historical (or, as he says, "chronological") approach untenable.[16] This is true except the "history" I describe is more literary history than historical events. Tolkien used medieval literature as a model, rather than medieval or ancient history. We can see this in the way that narratives like *Beowulf* or *Sir Gawain and the Green Knight* share pagan and Christian elements as well as the anachronisms just as Tolkien's legendarium does. This also does not preclude Tolkien blending more contemporary literary models into his legendarium.

This narrow view of doctrinal purity over a more catholic approach has survived well into our Modern and Postmodern world. John Holmes, in his article "'Like Heathen Kings': Religion as Palimpsest in Tolkien's Fiction," speculates that Tolkien's approach to myth is a way to combat this narrowness. Holmes notes the irony that many current thinkers actively misread medieval texts and ideas as fundamentalist attacks on pagan sources while many modern thinkers dismiss medieval texts using much more "fundamentalist" readings.

> Thus, while apologists for modernism see the Christian assimilation of heathen culture as a bigoted destruction of a rival religion, Tolkien suspects that the real bigotry is in the narrow fundamentalist form of modernism, and sees instead in medieval minstrelsy a Christian art that preserves what comes before it in the same way that mythmakers always have.[17]

Part of the reason why many medieval thinkers did not feel threatened by pagan legends like Greek and Roman mythology and *Beowulf* comes from the assumption that these religions were a preparation for Christianity rather than a rival to it. Holmes notes that many medieval thinkers', like Bernardus Silvestris, "approach to Pagan beliefs was not to prove them untrue, but to reveal the allegorical meaning of whatever truth they exhibited." In other words, the medieval approach focuses on finding what is true and related about texts, whereas our modern approach often focuses on ferreting out what is in error and making distinctions between texts.[18]

One can see how Tolkien's combination of medieval influences in his legendarium speaks to many people unsettled by the culture of the twentieth and twenty-first centuries. The way Tolkien uses medieval approaches to the material and natural world reenchants them and restores a sense of beauty and purpose that has been lost in contemporary philosophies that emphasize a mechanistic and purposeless worldview. Tolkien's more catholic view of both medieval Paganism and Christianity contrasts with the more discriminating and narrowing tendencies of the modern world that seek to police ideological purity. While most aspects of Tolkien's work appeal to what many feel has been lost in the modern world, one aspect of his work more resembles the contemporary world than the medieval one: his decision to downplay the ritualistic aspect of the Middle Ages. The lack of ritual in his legendarium fits in well with the increasingly "spiritual, not religious" thrust of Western culture in the last fifty years.

The ironic upshot of Tolkien's incorporation of medieval influences in his legendarium is that he creates several good societies using a culture that many of his contemporaries and later generations have considered particularly primitive and rigid. Though in another sense, using the medieval period as a source for utopian fantasies seems familiar. The localism and "primitiveness" of the Middle Ages lends itself particularly well to pastoral and Edenic fantasies of a simpler time. As we shall see, the Romantics and the Victorians had already mined this rich vein of nostalgia in the eighteenth and nineteenth centuries. What makes Tolkien's approach to the utopian potential for the Middle Ages different from most is his use of the social complexity of the medieval period to give his good societies a social and spiritual resonance that contrasts with the feelings of alienation and anomie that plague many contemporary people. Tolkien creates a dense web of social and physical connections between his characters, their place in society, and even within the history of Middle-earth. Physical objects, like Merry's sword, are imbued with the sacredness I spoke of earlier, but also have a historical and relational aspect to them that is at once medieval and utopian. For example, Merry obtained a sword from a haunted barrow in an incident that almost cost his life and the lives of his hobbit companions. So part of the value of the object for Merry is relational. He obtained the sword with his companions during a moment of danger that will be one of the many trying experiences that draw the hobbits together. In another sense, the sword has a value based on its history; it was created by the men of Westernesse to destroy the servants of Sauron. Moreover, it was forged not only to fight Sauron's creatures, but Tolkien writes that it was created by a smith of Arthedain specifically to kill the Witch-king of Angmar. Merry uses that same sword to strike the leg of the Lord of the Nazgûl at the Battle of the Pelennor Fields and break the spell of the Witch-king. The fact the sword was made for that purpose and was able to fulfill that purpose suggests something about the relationship between teleology and *The Lord of the Rings*—namely that in this world, things, as well as people, have purposes. The finding of sacred swords, like Excalibur or Joan of Arc's sword behind the altar at the Church of Saint Catherine at Fierbois, says something about the metaphysical beliefs of the audience that accepts them by presenting a world that is believably teleological. The audience's acceptance of the sword's teleology and Merry's place in its teleology not only reinforces the object's purpose, but implicates the audience in this alien metaphysical worldview. That Tolkien's readers come to accept this teleology speaks to their own lack of purpose and creates the desire for a different world where physical objects can be part of a providential plan. How can the typical modern person have the same rich relationship with their mass-produced, manufactured possessions that Merry has with his one-of-a-kind sword that has so many additional dimensions? This is only one of the thousands of rich associations that Tolkien provides for his reader that speak to the specific deficit in meaning that many people experience in the twentieth and twenty-first centuries. It is through these associations and connections that Tolkien generates utopian possibilities, not out of the traditional objects of utopian desire, physical comfort or ease (which many of his first-world readers already have in abundance), but by creating a world that feels deeper and more purposeful.

This attraction to the medieval has a much longer history than Tolkien's legendarium.[19] From the late eighteenth-century Romantic and Gothic movements to the Edwardian period, an undercurrent of admiration for medieval society has attracted thinkers as diverse as John Keats, Thomas Carlyle, John Henry Newman, Dante Gabriel Rossetti, Alfred Tennyson, Walter Pater, William Morris, and Oscar Wilde.[20] Many, in the Victorian period, were especially enamored with the medieval world, which manifested itself in the period's architecture, literature, arts, liturgy, and even in its political and social movements. Still, the particular cultural and political situation of the Victorians influenced how their interest and attraction to the Middle Ages manifested itself, so it would be a mistake to assume the Victorians had a "neutral" view of the period untainted by their own presuppositions and politics (as it would be a mistake to view our own view of the period as innocent of any temporal imperialism). That is why I have classified "Victorian medievalism" as a separate category from medievalism itself in this chapter. I also argue that Tolkien's own cultural and academic background suggests that he would have come into contact with this particular form of medievalism and indeed this form was probably his earliest entry into the medieval world. Victorian medievalism also had its own utopian pretensions that reflect what the Victorians wanted to emphasize and ignore about the medieval period.

Tolkien, whose childhood began in the Victorian era, had many personal connections to the period and the leading figures of Victorian medievalism. Of course, the most important Victorian medievalist influence in Tolkien's life was his mother, Mabel Tolkien, who lived her entire short life in the Victorian era. Her journey from a Baptist upbringing to the Catholic Church was similar to one many people of a traditional intellectual or aesthetic bent took in the mid- to late nineteenth century. While there is no clear indication why Mabel Tolkien converted, she certainly did not convert for reasons of convenience or social pressure, since all the family and social pressure would be for her to remain a Baptist. Indeed, she converted after the death of her husband when she was relying on her extended family to help support her and her sons. Not long after her conversion all the financial support that she desperately needed was withdrawn in retaliation for her conversion. Thus, her conversion must have been made out of deep personal conviction. This journey to the Catholic Church, often at great personal and financial cost, was a well-worn path for many British seekers in an anti-Catholic society that often considered Catholicism anti-British and maybe even subversive. Still, intellectuals like Cardinal John Henry Newman and Gerard Manley Hopkins felt compelled to make that journey. That Mabel Tolkien was willing to take that step says something about her: she was independent, she prioritized her convictions over her comfort, and she was willing to earnestly follow the truth of her beliefs, whatever the consequences. This pursuit of what was right and following one's convictions despite the jeopardizing of personal relationships was not just a characteristic of Victorian Catholic converts: the willingness of many Victorians to join a variety of unpopular groups besides the Catholic Church, including the Pre-Raphaelite Brotherhood, the Socialist Party, and various evangelical churches, came from a similar insistence on following one's convictions no matter the cost.

I would argue that the emphasis Victorians placed on debating first principles and acting on them has a medieval tinge to it, similar to the way Thomas Aquinas felt a need to prove from first principles everything within the Catholic doctrine, starting with the existence of God (without depending on revelation to clinch the argument). Indeed, the importance of the "earnestness" of the search connects the Victorians with more medieval modes of thinking.[21] It is not a coincidence that the popular caricature of the rigid, doctrinaire, moralistic Victorian bears more than a passing resemblance to a similar caricature of the medieval scholar. From almost the start of his life, Tolkien was part of a church that rooted much of its existence in the Middle Ages at a time when many Victorians questioned how to get back to their roots.

Unsurprisingly after his mother's conversion, she and her small family ended up at the Birmingham Oratory. This church that Tolkien grew up spending a great deal of time in and that was as much a center of his social and family life as a place of worship was a church founded by Cardinal Newman. Not only was the Birmingham Oratory a center for reviving Catholicism in nineteenth- and early twentieth-century Britain, it was itself an institution founded by the religious revival brought about by Victorian medievalism. Newman eventually left the current Church of England because he decided that the ancient Church of England was the current Catholic Church (after Newman accounted for doctrinal developments). The assumption of most in the Oxford Movement was that the medieval church in England somehow was closer to a restored (as in a less Protestant) Church of England than to Rome. They imagined that both Rome and Geneva (John Calvin's Protestantism) had moved away from a moderate "middle" position that was the Church of England that represented "true" Christianity. Still, the guiding principle was that medieval Christianity was the proper form that nineteenth-century Britain was deviating from; the only question was whether High Church Anglicanism or Roman Catholicism was closer to the proper form. Within Anglican services, a stronger emphasis on ritual, "smells and bells," vestments, and even reinstitution of Catholic sacraments and practices—like confession and celibacy—made them appear more "Catholic." Not coincidentally, these practices were basically a return to medievalism after the Protestant Reformation; the question was whether the return would be Roman Catholic or Anglo-Catholic. Tolkien was born into the Roman Catholic side of this debate, but this debate was essentially a Victorian one about how to incorporate medieval spiritual beliefs into the nineteenth-century world.

The debate about the relationship of the medieval church and whether it was "Catholic" or "proto-Protestant" was going on since the Reformation (as well as the debate about whether ancient Christianity was more Protestant or Catholic). Still, the Tractarian movement was unusual in that the focus was less on using the Medieval church to bolster the proselytizing claims of either Protestant or Catholics, but to restore true medieval practices. Thus, it emphasized reviving the actual liturgical and devotional practices of the medieval period. Many Protestants objected to these practices as papist accretions to the pure Christianity of the apostles.

Even so, this religious debate was a subset of the overall Victorian debate about medievalism, which encompassed more than religion but also attempted to incorporate medieval ideas into art, architecture, and even social and political movements. The Pre-Raphaelite artistic movement looked to the Middle Ages for artistic inspiration. Augustus Pugin was instrumental in reviving Gothic architecture in nineteenth-century Britain and arguing that this architecture reflected the superior values of medieval institutions.[22] Thomas Carlyle in *Past and Present* uses a medieval monastery as a positive example of leadership as opposed to the relatively corrupt way nineteenth-century leaders were chosen and trained. Even in arts like furniture making and household decor, William Morris looked toward medieval ideals of individual craftsmanship and guilds and rejected the mass-produced goods that came to dominate the market in late nineteenth-century Britain. Across a variety of disciplines and political affiliations, respect for medieval society was an important (if minority) viewpoint among the British intelligentsia.

Just as the church Tolkien belonged to was a central focus of the medieval revival, the university where Tolkien spent most of his academic career, Oxford University, was famous as a leading intellectual center of Victorian medievalism. It was at Oriel College Oxford that Cardinal Newman penned his famous Tracts that helped start the Oxford movement in the Church of England, which attempted to return the Anglican Church to its more medieval roots. Oxford, as one of the oldest universities in the world, was a place where the medieval and the twentieth-century world intersected in terms of architecture, tradition, and even educational methods.

Victorian medievalism was both a reaction to the many changes that occurred in the Victorian period and a positive program to imagine a future based on different assumptions than the current Victorian ideology. I have already argued that the Modern and Postmodern periods were times of unprecedented social change and upheaval. I think one could argue that the Victorian era in Britain was a period of greater material changes than any other period before or since. Britain started the period in the 1830s as a rising, primarily agricultural, and aristocratic society with limited technology and ended the period in the early 1900s as a declining industrial, democratic, and technologically oriented one (and one of the first in most of these categories). Certainly, part of the attraction of the medieval period for many Victorians was that it was a return to a simpler, more predictable time. But that was not the only reason. Certainly, many of the Victorian ecclesiastical reformers, like Edward Pusey, wanted to return to a more complex theology and liturgy. Similarly, one could argue that medieval ethics, social structures, and community relations were more, not less, complex than their nineteenth-century counterparts (that is what I argue makes them "thicker") and that the social atomization that accelerated in the twentieth and twenty-first centuries started in the nineteenth. So many of the attractions of medieval society that appeal to contemporary people also appealed to the Victorians. Still, Victorians could more readily accept the structural rigidity of medieval society since remnants of medieval social structures existed (though in a vastly weakened and decaying form) in nineteenth-century Britain. We can see this illustrated in Trollopian Barchester where medieval institutions like Hiram's Hospital still existed, and in Thackerian London where a person's hereditary title still carried social weight with those in "trade" whatever the title-holder's economic status. The market economy had not yet completely replaced all markers as the almost exclusive measure of cultural power (as it has today).

A lot of evidence suggests that Tolkien was influenced by both Victorian thought and Victorian medievalism in particular. Some of the earliest influences he remembers are Victorian ones. As a child, *The Red Fairy Book* (1890) by Andrew Lang had a profound influence on his imagination. Especially exciting for the young Tolkien were the stories about and illustrations of dragons. His interest in fairy tales and the popularity of providing them as reading matter for children was very much a product of Victorian culture. Later in his childhood, Tolkien also read George MacDonald's bestselling *The Princess and the Goblins* (1872), another Victorian narrative set in a vaguely medieval era with kings and castles that includes dastardly goblins who live underground. The influence of and access to fairy tales came at an especially high point in Tolkien's childhood during the late Victorian period.[23]

One underappreciated aspect of the Victorian medieval revival was the influence it had on the genre of Victorian romance, which ran through authors as disparate as Sir Walter Scott, Rider Haggard, and Robert Louis Stevenson. When one thinks of Victorian novels, the dominant genre of realistic novels with serious social commentary, like those written by Elizabeth Gaskell, Charles Dickens, Anthony Trollope, and Thomas Hardy, come to mind. Still, there was an undercurrent of less critically acclaimed stories that were wildly popular: the Romances. These works had much in common with medieval narratives, often including a focus on a quest, an emphasis on plot over character, and a focus on ancient artifacts. Rider Haggard's bestseller *She* included all these elements of romance: the story focuses on a journey to a mythical land of the Amahagger, where in "an empire of the imagination" magic still exists. Like many romances, the characters are more cardboard cutouts than real people, including the impossibly handsome, anodyne Leo Vincey, as well as simian but brilliant Horace Holly. Finally, the narrative contains an artifact called the "Sherd of Amenartes," a sort of Rosetta Stone artifact with ancient and modern languages, which links the quest narrative to a more romantic, enchanting past. These types of romances were very popular in the Victorian period but since they are not nearly as often anthologized as the realist novels, not many people associate them with the Victorians. They also map much more closely to traditional epic literature than the modern novel, and certainly, characters like Beowulf or Achilles are written with less psychological complexity than most characters in realist novels. Rather than exploring their inner psychological feelings, much of their character is revealed by their actions or "externalized" by the epic poet. For example, Beowulf, as the ideal Germanic hero and king, does not present the reader with much moral complexity, so his external struggles against monsters and fate itself become the central question, rather than Beowulf as an individual.[24] This does not mean that this externalization cannot create complexity—how Achilles acts in response to the perceived slight to his honor at the beginning of *The Iliad* and then to the death of Patroclus shows the complex relationship between individual honor and personal relationships even if we do not receive insights into Achilles' inner thoughts. In a similar way, we are not privy to the inner thoughts of Haggard's characters, but the symbolic resonance of *She* spoke to many Victorians and Edwardians as varied as Andrew Lang and Sigmund Freud. Much of the modern criticism of Tolkien can be based on genre confusion, where many critics complain that Tolkien's narratives do not follow the rules of the realist or contemporary novels and therefore they are deemed juvenile or escapist (or both) by these same critics. Instead, part of what Tolkien does in his narratives continues the direct line from ancient and medieval epics to Victorian romances.

Some critics have argued that Tolkien's books owe more to the Edwardian period than the Victorian. Jared Lobdell, in his book *The World of the Rings*, argues that the structure of Tolkien's *The Lord of the Rings* was especially influenced and resembles what he calls "an adventure story in the Edwardian mode."[25] He notes how many characteristics of Edwardian adventure stories—their lack of characterization, their focus on a "band of brothers," their structure as a story of "there and back again," and finally their Tory/aristocratic point of view—are all similar to *The Lord of the Rings*.[26] He also argues that part of the reason that many in the literary community did not receive the novel well was that they did not understand that it was part of this genre.

We can see this Victorian and Edwardian influence especially clearly in Tolkien's first published poems and his early prose work, *The Book of Lost Tales*. The inspiration for his poem "Kôr: In a City Lost and Dead" is a scene from Rider Haggard's *She* that describes the abandoned city of a lost civilization. Similarly, much of Tolkien's early fairy poetry resembles the late Victorian mania for the folk supernatural. Finally, Tolkien's earliest descriptions of elves (or gnomes, as he sometimes called them) suggest that they resemble the childlike small creatures found in Victorian illustrations and in J. M. Barrie's *Peter Pan*. Of course, many of these Victorian sources only serve as a jumping-off point for Tolkien's imaginative re-creation of the source material. John Garth, in *Tolkien and the Great War*, discusses how Tolkien changes Haggard's more "nihilistic" view of the city as a place where the inhabitants were undone by their hubris to a more complex one where the city's grandeur has value even in the absence of its inhabitants and therefore the tone is more "conciliatory" than nihilistic.[27] Tolkien would also quickly come to regret the diminutive and childlike elves of his early, more Victorian, work and decide to make his elves into tall, stately creatures in his later legendarium. This is a common move for Tolkien; to take elements rather directly in his early work then slowly transform the material over decades with his many revisions and rewritings. Still, one can sense even in these later works remnants of these Victorian romantic influences.

Despite this, another aspect of Tolkien's legendarium departs from these romance and epic models and creates his own genre. Tolkien's stories are different from Victorian romances in the way he layered more complex characterization and especially enormous amounts of world-building detail on this Romance-based model to give *The Lord of the Rings* and *The Silmarillion* a seeming verisimilitude absent in earlier narratives. He also mixed complex and simple characterization so that his narratives contained elements of both romance and realism. Brian Rosbury and Tom Shippey have noted that Tolkien's craftsmanship in prose with elements like dialogue and description makes, at least *The Lord of the Rings*, appear to have a novelistic rather than an epic or mythological quality to it in many places. Another "realistic" aspect of Tolkien's work is the way technical aspects of his prose match the way mythological and legendary narratives of the past have been handed down to modern readers. In *The Silmarillion*, Tolkien makes his stories "seem" old by making them seem like isolated, translated pieces of some much larger group of oral legends and narratives, just as epics like *The Iliad* and *The Odyssey* appear to us. Tolkien also uses this sense of some larger body of legend in his various allusions in *The Lord of the Rings* to give his narrative a sort of antiquarian patina that contributes to its authenticity. Still, combined with these elements are others that seem wholly out of sympathy with the modern novel. While characters like Frodo and Gollum have the three-dimensional quality favored by most modern novelists, other characters like Aragorn and Sauron appear much more like the two-dimensional characters that appear in ancient and medieval literature, as well as Victorian romances. Even in *The Silmarillion* a similar pattern occurs where some characters like Fëanor and Túrin feel more complex in a way that is reminiscent of popular modern narratives, while others like Beren or Tuor appear simpler, like more ancient models. This hybridizing of ancient and contemporary approaches to characterization no doubt partially accounts for the bifurcated critical reaction that accompanied *The Lord of the Rings* and *The Silmarillion*. Critics who complain Tolkien was "simplistic" or "juvenile" usually focus on these simpler characters. Layered on this disdain for simple characters and action-oriented plots is the fact that Tolkien's most simple characters were often the most evil ones, which goes against the "sympathy with the devil" approach to evil that has been especially popular since the Romantic era. Whereas most modern authors provide ever more complex motivations for their evil characters, Tolkien does not feel a need to explain evil in the same way he needs to explore how one becomes good in an evil world. As I mentioned, one of Tolkien's philosophical assumptions is that evil is by nature more simple and limited than good; therefore Tolkien is less interested in explaining it.

Another aspect of Tolkien's use of Victorian medieval tropes is the way his dystopian turn relies on the specific ways that Victorian medievalism was a reaction to the Victorian worship of progress. The hegemonic belief among most British Victorian cultural leaders was that the world was becoming a progressively better place and that Britain was leading the way. Events like the Great Exhibition in 1851 and Queen Victoria's Diamond Jubilee in 1897 celebrated British industrial and imperial might. Victorian medievalism, like many antiquarian and fundamentalist movements, came about in response to this Whig view of history that dominated Victorian ideology. The most obvious target of Victorian medievalism was the unrestrained capitalism and philosophical utilitarianism that dominated the intellectual life of the period with thinkers such as Adam

Smith, David Ricardo, and Jeremy Bentham.[28] In *The Lord of the Rings*, utilitarian arguments almost always appear in the mouths of the series' villains, like Saruman. Beyond words, even the imagery of *The Lord of the Rings* draws on utilitarian concepts. It is not a coincidence that the Eye of Sauron bears more than a passing resemblance to Jeremy Bentham's Panopticon. Bentham imagined a prison where a single watchman could watch any prisoner without the prisoner knowing whether he or she was being observed. In very Mordor-like language, Bentham argued that the Panopticon prison was "a mill for grinding rogues honest."[29] This threat of constant surveillance and control bears a striking resemblance to Sauron's approach to control. This form of control is also the worst and most dehumanizing aspect of Mordor. When the Witch-king threatens Éowyn, the most terrible fate he can conjure for her is that "he [the Nazgûl] will not slay thee in thy turn. He will bear thee away to the houses of lamentation, beyond all darkness, where thy flesh shall be devoured, and thy shriveled mind be left naked to the Lidless Eye" (141).[30] To be surveilled, diminished, and controlled unceasingly (hence, the lidless eye) is the worst possible fate.

Like his medieval sources, Tolkien's Victorian medieval sources contribute to his success at generating believable societies. They form a bridge between Tolkien's Modernist tropes and his reintroduction of a medieval point of view. The concerns that the Victorians first identified with the industrial world—its inhumane scale, its tendency to isolate, and its reliance on the crudest forms of self-interest to ensure conformity—are answered by Tolkien's utopian vision to counter just these Victorian tendencies. In Tolkien's good societies, the scale tends to be small and human-centered, whether in the small farming hamlets of the Shire or the cozy feasting halls of Rivendell.[31] Tolkien's story celebrates the bonds between people, often connecting people of different races, like the friendship between Gimli and Legolas despite the traditional hostility between elves and dwarves. Finally, the whole plot of *The Lord of the Rings* and many of the plots in *The Silmarillion* model the reasons to take action even if the hedonic calculus suggests that inaction is the best course. Frodo's (and Gandalf's) hopeless quest to destroy the Ring of Power is based on a "fool's hope" just as the elves' hope to defeat Morgoth in the First Age is predicated on ignoring the impossible odds.

This particular attack on Victorian utilitarian morality is central to Tolkien's utopian and dystopian ethos in Middle-earth and one that leading voices in Victorian medievalism had already made. Thomas Carlyle in *Sartor Resartus* and *Past and Present* laments the utilitarian assumptions of his capitalist society and especially the idea that a material calculus should outweigh spiritual factors in deciding how a society should be organized. William Morris's advocacy of the Arts and Crafts movement and his distaste for industrialization were a rejection of the idea that the most efficient way to achieve a product (i.e., the way with the least cost) was therefore the "best" way. In a similar way, John Ruskin's "art for art's sake" movement depended on the denial of the didactic (and thus utilitarian) function of art that was so prominent in Victorian thinking. Thus, though Tolkien rejected the dominant Victorian ideology of progress and utility, his rejection was influenced by a specifically Victorian type of rejection.

If we look at *The Silmarillion* and *The Lord of the Rings* we can see that both his good and bad societies depended on Victorian models. Certainly, Tolkien's view of leadership seems to align well with Carlyle's "great man theory of leadership," which posits that great leaders are born, not made, and that, as Carlyle argued, "The history of the world is but the biography of great men." In terms of characters like Saruman and Gandalf, these leaders, as Maiar, possess a wisdom and a power of persuasion that are different from men or the other races of Middle-earth. Even human characters, like Aragorn, by virtue of their genetic inheritance seem to have natural abilities to lead and influence other men. Tolkien did have a nuanced view of these characters, and both allowed that characters with this inheritance might fail (like Isildur) or that others without this inheritance might show leadership (like Frodo and Sam). He also gives Aragorn a long apprenticeship as a ranger and leader of Gondor to develop these traits, so Tolkien does not totally discount the influence of the environment.[32] Certainly, Tolkien also suggests that the history of Middle-earth depends upon the actions of individuals rather than impersonal sociological forces beyond their control (though these individuals need not always be "great men"). In a similar way, the relationship between the "good" people in Middle-earth and what they manufacture is more in line with the ideas of Morris and Ruskin than the standard approach to "products" in the modern world. Whether it is ale brewed by hobbits in the Shire or the ropes or clothes woven by elves in Lothlórien, a high premium is placed on craftsmanship and little is placed on efficiency. In a similar way, the dwarves' approach to metalwork and jewelry-making or the general approach to the creation of poetry is almost entirely noncommercial, especially at the highest levels, and these arts are clearly practiced for their own sake rather than for any utility they could provide.

While Tolkien's utopianism draws from the countercultural forces of Victorian medievalism, his dystopian inspiration seems to draw from the more main currents of Victorian progress and utilitarianism. I have already mentioned that Sauron, as the great eye, reflects the Benthamite obsession with control. Mordor appears to be as much a place of industry as any premodern place could be with its endless workshops, blasted landscapes, fouled rivers, and polluted skies. One wonders how much of Tolkien's Mordor imagery comes from his childhood memories of his home in Birmingham, which was one of the leading industrial centers of the world during his time there. Certainly, the smoke belching out of

Mount Doom is an echo of the industrial smoke and coal dust that coated much of industrial Northern England during the turn of the twentieth century.

Despite my setting up Modernism and Postmodernism as a foil to Tolkien's more medieval and Victorian medieval worldview, I do think (and many critics have also noted) that there are Modernist influences in Tolkien's writings. I would argue that what is particularly interesting about Tolkien's Modernist influences are the ways that they have distinct geographies in Tolkien's world because, for Tolkien, Modernism often means dystopian and therefore his Modernist affect almost always occurs in his hearts of darkness, Thangorodrim and Mordor. Interestingly enough, this also suggests that they have a chronology where the most "modern" (meaning "contemporary," rather than the artistic and literary movement) places in Middle-earth are also the most evil and dysfunctional.

These places are also "modern" in the sense that they represent the Modernist Movement with its wholesale rejection of tradition, its validation of irrationality, and its love of gigantism. From the beginning of *The Silmarillion*, Melkor's grandiose rebellion echoes the similar rebellion that categorizes the Modernist (or Romantic) genius who rejects the status quo for his or her own vision of the truth. Indeed, even the description of the type of music that Melkor creates in order to defy Eru Ilúvatar seems reminiscent of Stravinsky or Bruckner. Tolkien writes in the beginning of *The Silmarillion*,

> Some of these thoughts he (Melkor) now wove into his music, and straight-way discord rose about him, and many that sang nigh him grew despondent, and their thought was disturbed and their music faltered but some began to attune their music to his rather than the thought which they had at first. Then the discord of Melkor spread ever wider, and the melodies which had been heard before floundered in a sea of turbulent sound.[33]

Tolkien describes Melkor's music as cacophonous and the reaction of his audience as bifurcated. One group is discouraged and another group tries to harmonize with the new melody. It is a reaction reminiscent of Stravinsky's Paris performance of *The Rite of Spring* or the critical reaction to Picasso's Cubist paintings. First, comes a wholesale rejection of the traditions of melody or representational art and then comes a sorting into disparate groups depending on the reaction. Whether the group is one that sympathizes with the rebellion or the one that does not, discord is the result.

This suspicion of rebellion is one aspect of Tolkien's work that not only separates him from the Moderns but also from the Romantics with whom Tolkien otherwise had much in common. This goes back to Tolkien's understanding of the relationship of creativity and art that is much humbler than the often Promethean visions of both the Moderns and the Romantics. Elements of the Byronic hero, the brooding hero willing to transcend moral barriers, nursing some sort of secret sin eating away at him, and exhibiting some special excellence or abilities that put him above the common man (and he nearly always is a man in Romantic narratives) do sometimes appear in Tolkien, but often in a villain rather than a hero. As I mentioned, Morgoth, like Satan, is the ultimate rebel against Eru. Denethor and his son Boromir similarly transcend boundaries to protect Gondor in Denethor's use of the palantír and Boromir's attempt to seize the Ring of Power. Their violations of the moral order end up destroying both characters and jeopardizing the free peoples of Middle-earth. The paradigmatic Byronic character in *The Silmarillion* is Fëanor, whose pride and possessiveness of the silmarils lead the elves of the First Age to untold suffering. Túrin is the exception to this negative portrayal of Byronic heroes in that much of his suffering comes about because of the combination of the curse of Morgoth and Túrin's own prideful behavior. Still, acts of rebellion in Middle-earth nearly always cause the destruction of heroes and the suffering of others. This is quite separate from the personal strength or excellence of the hero. Non-Byronic characters like Gandalf and Aragorn are often personally excellent without being Byronic.

The contrast to the Byronic hero that Tolkien provides are characters who despite their personal weaknesses triumph over the strong. The most obvious examples of these "weak" heroes are the hobbits who, despite their small stature and rustic ways, manage to defeat a powerful dragon and the even more powerful Sauron to save Middle-earth. In *The Silmarillion*, this role of weakness is often played by men in contrast to the stronger elves. So it ends up that the man, Beren, with the help of the elf Luthien, manages to steal a silmaril from the very crown of Morgoth. This feat is accomplished even though the elves have been unable to do it throughout the long First Age, despite the elves' vast armies and superior wisdom.

Still, Tolkien does not treat all aspects of modernity and Modernism as evil. I have already mentioned that Tolkien does not shun all aspects of the modern world in his works (though there are different degrees of modernity depending on the work, with *The Hobbit* and *The Lord of the Rings* including much more modern references and even diction compared to *The Silmarillion*). Hobbits especially are as much products of the Victorian and Edwardian eras as the medieval. A careful reader will note a series of anachronisms in the Shire that do not occur in the rest of Middle-earth: smoking, waistcoats, pocket-handkerchiefs, umbrellas, and even postal services. I mentioned in chapter 1 that this allows the reader an entrance into Middle-earth through the eyes of a creature that is closer culturally to us than most of the more "epic" denizens of Middle-earth.

The use of hobbits as stand-ins for "modern" people goes beyond superficial anachronism and includes Modern aspects to these characters and even Tolkien's approach to his narrative. Roger Sale, in his essay "Tolkien and Frodo Baggins," argues that *The Lord of the Rings* is "at its best modern literature" and that "Frodo is a modern, his landscape, his challenge, and his heroism all distinctively belonging to no earlier century [than the twentieth]."[34] One can see how the actively hostile nature of Mordor resembles the pitiless nature of classic Modern literature, as in T. S. Eliot's *The Wasteland* or Joseph Conrad's *Heart of Darkness*. Beyond this obvious similarity, Sale focuses extensively on how Frodo is a "modern" hero who is lonely, lost, frightened, willing, and compassionate," unlike more traditional heroes who are powerful, strong leaders. Sale goes on to make the argument that the successful part of the book is this Modernist element and that the rest of the novel fails because of its "literariness," which stems from Tolkien's inablity to write successfully about "Gandalf and elves, and of ancient men" because Tolkien had only read about them in books.

While I disagree with much of Sale's analysis, I do think that there is a kernel of truth in Tolkien's use of Modernist tropes to deepen and complicate his narrative. Unlike Sale, I do not think that archaic elements in Tolkien's books are any more "literary" than his more modern touches. Great artists can transcend their own identities and present realities they have never experienced. I would even argue that Tolkien's imagination is powerful enough that he was able to experience Middle-earth as clearly as he did other "real" places. In any case, throughout Tolkien's work, he is an "and" artist rather than an "either/or" one. Tolkien is often effective in recasting people's assumptions about the nature of reality by showing positive medieval examples of a gift-giving culture or heroism (or our relationship with the environment that I will argue in chapter 3) that contrast with most people's modern assumptions. I also question whether Frodo's heroism is a uniquely "modern" one. His description of Frodo as "lonely, lost, frightened, willing, and compassionate" would seem to apply equally to Christ before his Passion (except for the "lost"), who is certainly not a "Modern" hero, so pre-twentieth-century people would definitely be able to relate to this form of sacrificial heroism.

Even so, I would argue that there are ways in which Tolkien's heroes do sometimes appear as Modern heroes living in a modern world. Frodo's hopeless journey through Mordor and his moral failure to destroy the ring at the Cracks of Doom reflect the dystopian turn that characterized many Modern works. His quest is the central one of the book; and his weakness and failure depends on a crisis in virtue absent in the self-assured heroes of the past—including most of Tolkien's own heroes in *The Silmarillion*. The distinction between failure caused by circumstance and failure caused by lack of will or virtue makes the way Frodo succumbs to temptation at the Crack of Doom feel particularly Modern.

Frodo's giving in to temptation comes in two stages. First, Frodo loses his ability to make decisions or even care about himself and cedes almost all this responsibility to Sam. Frodo's loss of will is so profound that at the final stage of the journey through Mordor, Sam has to carry Frodo up the slopes of Mount Doom. Second, Frodo's will is overcome by his desire for the Ring of Power so that when Frodo does act, he acts willfully and sinfully. Frodo has become at first enervated and enslaved by a force outside himself and then, when he acts, Frodo gives in to his selfish desires. When Beowulf is killed by the dragon or Achilles dies of an arrow to the heel, the hero fails because of a circumstance rather than a failure of the character's own heroism. Even in classical tragedy where a tragic flaw is often central, the failure is not of will, but much more likely the opposite, a failure caused by hubris. In Tolkien's own tragedies, like the "Children of Húrin" or the *Allakabeth*, lack of virtue is not the central problem, but the excess of will—whether individual or group—is what causes the problem. What makes Frodo's failure so Modern is that his problem is a failure of will, or to be more accurate, that Frodo is alienated from his own will in a particularly modern (and I would argue postmodern) way. Frodo's problem is not that his excessive will causes him to overstep social or divine boundaries (a common plot of many tragedies), but that his will has become overwhelmed by powerful forces outside his control, a common theme of many Modern dramas. In this way, Frodo reflects the pathetic (in the non-pejorative sense of the word, to be pitied) and vacillating heroes of Modernism like J. Alfred Prufrock and Stephen Daedalus. Also like these Modernist heroes, Frodo eventually becomes so alienated from his society, and Middle-earth itself, that he becomes an exile when he leaves for the West.

But before he becomes alienated from his society, he becomes alienated even from himself: the Sméagol/Gollum split foreshadows how Frodo's personality is coming apart throughout *The Lord of the Rings* much like the typical antihero in Modernist narratives. Before his failure at the dénouement of the novel, Frodo has started to exhibit many of the characteristics we have seen in Gollum. Frodo has lost his ability to remember the Shire and with the loss of memory comes a loss of identity. Gollum, in his more advanced stage of forgetting, even forgets his own name. Frodo's violent reaction at Sam's offer to carry the Ring in the entrance to Mordor shows how Frodo has started to become possessive of the Ring in ways reminiscent of Gollum. Along with this splitting, we see a hollowing out of Frodo, another characteristic of Modern antiheroes like Eliot's hollow men or Conrad's morally empty Kurtz. In place of the memories that helped to create Frodo's identity comes a desire for the Ring. At the slopes of Mount Doom Frodo has forgotten the green grass and cool water of the Shire and can only see a "Ring of Fire" or, in other words, the Ring of Power. Therefore, the "hollowing" consists of replacing the greater with the smaller to make Frodo in some way less than he was, just as

Kurtz replaced his idealistic desire for the improvement of the Congolese natives with his avarice for ivory. The horror of *The Heart of Darkness* comes when Marlow finds Kurtz at the center of the journey, not as some epic hero, but as an empty and broken man who has been subsumed by his environment and its "unspeakable rites" rather than rising above them. Similarly, Frodo becomes more and more subsumed into the environment until he, too, becomes a creature of Mordor and fails to do the right thing at the most important moral juncture of his life.

Sharin Schroeder also notes the fact that Tolkien gives his "monsters" a voice, which she believes reflects Modern rather than medieval values.[35] Tolkien lets the orcs, Gollum, and Smaug speak to us whereas Grendel, his mother, the dragon, and other monsters of medieval epics remain silent. More importantly, Tolkien focuses on the internal struggle between good and evil, as well as the external one. This is a particularly Modern obsession.

Not only was Tolkien influenced by Modernism, but Tolkien participated in one of the most defining events of the Modernist era, World War I. That war had an enormous effect on Tolkien and the creation of *The Lord of the Rings* and *The Silmarillion*. The relationship between the First World War and the Modernist movement is more complicated than it might seem at first. The cynicism and radicalism of Modernism preceded World War I so the assumption that the movement's rejection of traditional values stems from the veterans' experiences in World War I is not warranted.[36] Instead, the brutality and wastefulness of the war seemed to confirm many of the criticisms of Western civilization that preceded the war. It also led to making Modernism, which started out as an avant-garde movement, into a movement that appealed to a much wider swath of the population. As we shall also see, Tolkien's turn toward a particular kind of fantasy as his artistic reaction to the war put him in a minority of many World War I veterans. Rather than precipitating a wholesale rejection of the traditional cultural and military values, World War I led Tolkien to a rejection of the modern conditions that led to the way the war was conducted and a turn toward fantasy as a consolation as well as a challenge to the changes brought about by the war.

Tolkien started writing *The Book of Lost Tales*, which would later become the genesis for *The Silmarillion*, when he was recovering from trench fever after spending several months at the front. Many critics have noted the connection between Tolkien's legendarium and his World War I experience. Janet Brennan Croft notes that Tolkien was not the only military veteran of World War I (or World War II) to turn to fantasy after their wartime experiences. She specifically mentions both C. S. Lewis in *The Chronicles of Narnia* and David Jones in *Parenthesis* as authors who "mythologize" their wartime experiences much in the same way as Tolkien.[37] One way this mythologizing occurs comes from how Tolkien incorporated elements of the martial culture of World War I into *The Lord of the*

Rings. For example, Tolkien has acknowledged that Sam's character was modeled after many of the enlisted soldiers he served with in World War I. In his letter to J. H. Cotton Minchin, Tolkien confirms that "my 'Samwise' is indeed largely a reflection of the English soldier—grafted from the village-boys of early days, the memory of the privates and my batman that I knew in the 1914 War, and recognized as far superior to myself."[38] Croft notes how Tolkien incorporates the same type of understatement used by soldiers in World War I into the dialogue in *The Lord of the Rings*. For example, after Pippin and Merry's capture by the orcs, Merry greets Pippin with "So you have come on this expedition, too? Where do we bed and breakfast?"[39] Croft then compares Merry's understatement to a similar example from a World War I officer who described the conditions of trench life as "'darned unpleasant' and ceaseless rain as 'a certain dampness.'"[40] Of course, dramatic understatement, or litotes, is also a characteristic of Anglo-Saxon literature. For example, the *Beowulf* poet describes the bottomless pool where Grendel's mother dwells as an uncanny supernatural place so terrifying that a pursued deer will choose to be torn apart by the dogs chasing it rather than to dive into its depths. Yet the poet ends the description with the litotes, "That is no good place." This suggests that the rigors of the soldiering life have created a propensity for ironic understatements in soldiers throughout history.

While soldiers in different historical periods might have employed irony about their personal discomfort, they have been less tolerant of irony about the heroic ideal until rather recently. One innovation of Modernity, and especially Modernity after World War I, that Tolkien mostly avoids is the ironic tone that many Modernist writers take toward war heroism. The bitterness, the self-loathing, and the sense of betrayal that many writers felt as the "lost generation" after World War I seems to have bypassed Tolkien. Unlike World War I veterans such as Wilfred Owen and Siegfried Sassoon, Tolkien wrote about heroic warfare and self-sacrifice without a hint of sarcasm. In particular, the rejection of traditional concepts like chivalry and patriotism that figures prominently in works from World War I poets and novelists does not appear in Tolkien's works (though he is adept at writing about the costs and horrors of combat). The complicated part about evaluating the effect of World War I on the canonical literature of World War I is to decipher to what extent the war caused the rejection of traditional values or to what extent that war was viewed through the lens of an artistic establishment that had already rejected those values. If one's only exposure to World War I literature is Wilfred Owen's "Dulce et Decorum Est" or Erich Maria Remarque's *All Quiet on the Western Front* one is likely to get a distorted view of the effect of and the attitudes toward the war by many of its participants. Hew Strachan's *The First World War* argues that the common view of the war as a pointless monstrosity that destroyed the idealism of a generation is too simple. As he says,

> In the 1920s there had been many interpretations of the war; thereafter one [the one that argued the war shattered illusions] increasingly dominated all the others. It created a barrier between our understanding of the war and that of those who fought in it. Even those who survived came to see it in terms different from those which they embraced at the time.[41]

We shall see that many of Tolkien's reactions to the war do not follow the template set out by the most well-known poets and novelists of World War I. Instead of turning to irony and realism, Tolkien turned to earnestness and fantasy; instead of being disillusioned by the war, he became fired with a new sense of the importance of his idealistic mission.

Even though Tolkien's reaction to the folly of World War I is different, one can certainly trace changes in his early writing based on his wartime experience. John Garth's meticulous book, *Tolkien and the Great War*, examines Tolkien's writing before, during, and after his service in World War I. He argues that in many ways the world war was a catalyst for hardening the youthful enthusiasm that many young people have for accomplishing great things into an obligation to accomplish the artistic task that Tolkien, as a prewar boy, only vaguely envisioned. As a teenager, Tolkien became part of the TCBS (Tea Club and Barrovian Society) in King Edward's School with like-minded intellectual boys. Garth describes its transformation from a lighthearted adolescent debating society to an idealistic group bent on combating the cynicism and cleverness of early twentieth-century Britain as "the immortal four." The death of two of the four members and the horrors of World War I motivated Tolkien to start working on this idealistic vision. Of course, the vision itself was not completely unchanged by the war. Garth notes that Melko (the character that would later become Melkor, or his other name, Morgoth) appears only after Tolkien's wartime experiences and prophetically before the many dictators of the twentieth century.[42] Garth notes that the war did not change Tolkien and TCBS's idealistic mission, but provided a darker backdrop from which to express it. In many ways, Tolkien reverses the canonical World War I narrative of innocence lost. Garth argues that "his characters set out, more often than not, from a point of something like [Northrop] Frye's 'ironic' mode, in bondage, frustration, or absurdity, but they break free of those conditions, and so become heroes."[43] Tolkien thus reverses the narrative of wartime disenchantment that was part of the larger sense of ideological disenchantment championed by Modernist thinkers.

Therefore, Tolkien's way of integrating his wartime experience differed from many of his contemporaries. Instead of rejecting the traditional ideal of soldiering and military heroism, Tolkien seems to have rejected the modern version of "mass war." As often is the case when he seeks to criticize contemporary mores, Tolkien used Thangorodrim and Mordor to illustrate some aspect of Modernity that he found particularly objectionable. Croft notes that orcs' tactics and behavior resemble the conscript armies of World War I rather than medieval ones. The orcs' love of tunneling and machines resembles trench warfare rather than the pitched battles of the medieval period. Not surprisingly, one of the first tasks the orcs do at the siege of Minas Tirith is to construct a giant trench around the entire city. Like modern societies at war, the forces of evil often seek technological solutions to military problems. Thus, Saruman attempts to use gunpowder to blow up the walls of Helm's Deep. Morgoth and Sauron's willingness to sacrifice their soldiers recklessly also resembles the mass casualty tactics used at the Somme and Ypres. Like in these battles, wave upon wave of infantry assaults are thrown upon fortified positions regardless of the cost. In general, the viewing of men-at-arms as disposable "military assets" or part of a machine of war feels more contemporary than medieval. In describing "Grond," Sauron's massive battering ram designed to breach the gates of Minas Tirith, Kevin Black points out,

> Grond is a massive machine, and orcs swarm around it to keep it running, making it almost seem alive. But though it depends on orc labor to operate, the orcs are considered to be the most expendable parts of the mechanism, and are wasted and replaced without any consideration. The good of the machine is held as all important, and the value of life is completely degraded in comparison.[44]

Individual soldiers are viewed as just another asset for military planners like Saruman and Sauron and not necessarily the most valuable one.

Croft points out that Morgoth and Sauron exemplify another feature of "mass war" that came about during World War I: that of the "chateau general."[45] The chateau generals were general officers who removed themselves from the dangers and discomfort of the frontline battles to chateaus far behind the trenches. There were practical reasons why general officers were located far from the front: new techniques in communications and intelligence allowed generals access to vast amounts of information that only could be processed away from the front; the relatively static nature of trench warfare encouraged the creation of permanent staff headquarters with ever increasing infrastructure; and the incredible scale of World War I meant that visiting discrete parts of the battlefield yielded less strategic information than it had in the past. The World War I chateau generals' isolation from their troops contrasted with earlier generals who needed to be close to the front lines in order to access the strategic situation of their armies. Both Morgoth and Sauron behave very much like these World War I chateau generals. Morgoth cowers throughout the First Age in his underground palace of Thangorodrim and directs his troops from a distance (except once, when he could not refuse the challenge of Fingolfin to single combat and still retain the loyalty of his followers). Sauron is similarly static. Immobile in his tower at Mordor, Sauron directs his armies from well behind the front lines. Croft contrasts Sauron's behind the lines modern-war leadership strategy with Aragorn and Gandalf's "lead from-the-front" leadership that was much more characteristic of the medieval and ancient military leaders.

Tolkien's narratives illustrate the practical and moral problems of this chateau general phenomenon.[46] One can see that many of Sauron's strategic blunders come from his distance from the sources of his intelligence, while Aragorn and Gandalf's on-the-ground leadership both helps create and exploits surprises like Aragorn's bringing a relief army in the ships of the Corsairs to clinch the Battle of Pelennor Fields. Sauron again and again behaves in a predictable manner, allowing his enemies to outmaneuver him. Once again, evil turns out to be not only bad but stupid, and this stupidity is closely associated with Modernist assumptions. One could argue that the same issues played out in World War I where many behind-the-front generals ordered absurd attacks, which they might not have with more local knowledge. Beyond these practical considerations clearly Tolkien thinks that this lead-from-behind method of leadership is wrong in addition to being ineffective. Besides the obvious reason that leaders ask their subordinates to sacrifice in ways they are not willing to do, Tolkien's objection comes from these leaders' abdication of responsibility based on "efficiency." As I will describe in some detail in chapter 5, Tolkien especially did not like moral decisions (like the relationship between soldiers and their leaders) to be decided by measures like "efficiency." He argues that such decisions often lead to inhumane (and inhuman) results, like leaders living in relative comfort in chateaus, while their followers live in squalor in trenches. Such conditions are not offset by improved centralization and intelligence gathering.

So what is the relationship between these Modernist themes and Tolkien's effectiveness in using utopian and dystopian themes for his twentieth- and twenty-first-century readers? Tolkien's negative use of Modernist themes—such as association of rebelliousness with evil and his connection of the attributes of mass war to his evil societies—shows his traditionalist, and even reactionary, leanings. This does not mean that disobedience is always wrong in Middle-earth, but rebellion is less validated than it typically is in most twentieth-century literature. Just as Tolkien often uses medieval and Victorian medieval themes to suggest ways that contemporary life is more shallow and unsatisfying than in the past, he also uses Modernist themes to more explicitly demonstrate the dangers of our current way of life. He thus discredits the assumptions of the heroic rebel or the necessity of total war by mapping these attributes to the most dysfunctional characters and societies in his novel. Thangorodrim and Mordor, with their distant leaders and mass war tactics, should be uncomfortably familiar to most readers as practices of our own society. They seem especially connected to Tolkien's society at the turn of the twentieth century and the beginning of the Great War. He uses the darker aspects of what Guardini calls "mass society" to suggest how they can be leading us to an ever more inhuman way to organize ourselves.

On the other hand, Tolkien also includes "modern" and "Modernistic" characteristics in some of his most beloved characters, like Bilbo and Frodo. Thus, it cannot be argued that he is a total reactionary who rejects all contemporary life for some antiquarian fantasy. Frodo's struggles especially are the struggles that many modern (and Modern) people have with addiction, alienation, and self-loathing. Thus Tolkien provides characters that his twentieth- and twenty-first-century readers can understand and relate to. Certainly, Tolkien allows for his characters to have weaknesses and even moral failings, yet still be good characters. These weaknesses show that even in his "good" societies people can lose their way and are in need of redemption. This belief in the need for second chances also seems more contemporary than the more rigid standards of traditional societies. Once again upon closer examination, Tolkien's works appear more complex than the simple reactionary caricatures that his critics sometimes present.

Throughout this chapter I have reviewed three sources of inspiration for Tolkien's legendarium: the medieval, the Victorian medieval, and the Modern. The first and third sources have been especially well researched and explored by critics. My additional contribution to this research has focused on how these sources contributed to Tolkien's creation and use of utopian and dystopian themes. Tolkien often used medieval sources to suggest the utopian possibilities in creating a world where complex and thicker spiritual as well as personal relationships predominate instead of the increasingly materialistic and isolated relationships of our twenty-first-century society. Tolkien uses Victorian medieval sources to both sharpen his critique of the modern world and provide a familiar entry point into the world of fantasy. What Tolkien saw as dystopian in the twentieth-century world was already being challenged by the Victorian medievalist in the nineteenth century, especially the utilitarian mind-set that measures all actions by a simple good-minus-bad calculus and does not recognize that "victimless" crimes can lead to negative externalities that cannot easily be measured. He, like the Victorian medievalists, saw the value in a more communal and spiritual life and rejected the benefits of industrialization and mass production for the satisfaction of arts and crafts. Finally, Tolkien used Modernist thought as the primary reflection of the evils of the modern world, both socially and materially. Even so, he also includes characters with modern, Modernist, and Victorian characteristics in *The Hobbit* and *The Lord of the Rings* in order to provide an entry point for his readers into the world of Middle-earth.[47]

What makes Tolkien's use of these three types of sources so effective is not just their presence in his narrative, but the way he has these strands *interact* with each other to create the utopian and dystopian qualities in *The Hobbit* and *The Lord of the Rings*. Tolkien starts by creating a familiar medieval world, a world that is already familiar because it is a Victorian medieval world that has been built over many decades in the nineteenth century and is part of many of his readers' cultural memories. It is also familiar because it is a world inhabited by non-threatening Victorian bachelors, in other words, hobbits. In it, the reader already recognizes the comforts often denied by the modern world: a sense of place, grand yet human architecture, and an appreciation for one's handiwork. Tolkien then introduces more alien and more truly "medieval" concepts that resonate like echoes of long-lost stories. These are more challenging to accept than Victorian medieval ideas because they challenge Tolkien's contemporary readers to accept limitations. The medieval world contains more rigid class and gender categories, it demands fidelity to one's superiors, and it ignores the calculus of efficiency as the most important guide to action. It also demands a heroism that is little appreciated in the twentieth and twenty-first centuries. Not surprisingly, much of the criticism of Tolkien's works comes from these medieval elements. Yet it is out of these elements that Tolkien constructs the most utopian parts of his narratives, including a strong sense of purpose, a desire for heroism, and an appreciation for the value of mutual sacrifice. Poised against these utopian elements are the dystopian themes apparent in Thangorodrim and Mordor that express in the most atavistic form all the disquiet people feel about the trajectory of twentieth- and twenty-first-century society. In these societies that exaggerate the worst aspect of Modernism and contemporary society, we see citizens treated as cannon fodder by distant rulers who make decisions based on amoral self-interest. Tolkien gives us a vision of what it is to be on the receiving end of the types of total wars that dominated the twentieth century. Yet not all the elements of Modernism are cast as negative in *The Lord of the Rings.* For example, Frodo, the hero of *The Lord of the Rings*, is less a content Victorian bourgeois (like Bilbo) than a modern man of the early twentieth century struggling with a world in which his identity is threatened by division and erasure. Tolkien's masterful balancing of these different strains in his narratives helps create the powerful sense of both identification and nostalgia that characterizes *The Hobbit* and *The Lord of the Rings*.

Tolkien's approach to *The Silmarillion* provides a contrast to this interweaving of different narrative strategies. Tolkien focuses on the medieval, and to a lesser extent, the Modernist, sources to create in *The Silmarillion* a narrative that has a sprawling, mythological, and sometimes Biblical quality to it, while he eschews most Victorian and Modernist novelistic conventions that we see in *The Hobbit* and *The Lord of the Rings*. Like those novels, Tolkien associates the medieval qualities in *The Silmarillion* with utopia and Modernist elements with dystopia, but he fails to include the characterization typical of Victorian and Modern novels. There are no hobbits who act as stand-ins for contemporary readers, and Tolkien thrusts those readers into an alien world with a lot more in common with epics like *The Odyssey* or *Beowulf* than a typical novel. Not surprisingly because of its more alien structure and purpose, *The Silmarillion* has always had a smaller audience than *The Lord of the Rings* or *The Hobbit*.[48]

NOTES

1. For example, see Christopher Synder's excellent *The Making of Middle-earth*, which tracks down a vast number of Tolkien sources and references for his entire legendarium.

2. Tacitus in *Germania* says that Germanic tribesmen "consecrate woods and groves and they apply the name of gods to that mysterious presence which they see only with the eye of devotion."

3. This is an example of Catholic syncretism. Northern pagan societies often worshiped sacred trees and plants, yet the Church rather than attempting to suppress all forms of this worship allows this impulse to be incorporated into Christian context through practices like allowing people to decorate their homes with Christmas trees and wreaths.

4. In a similar way, Marx was much better at diagnosing the disruptive economic effects of the market economy, that is, "all that is solid melts into air," than he was at coming up with effective solutions or predictions about what was to come.

5. In this sentence, I am glossing over the debate about whether our current period is a brand-new one, the "Postmodern" period, or whether it is part of the same period as the early twentieth century, the late "Modern" period (or even more controversially Bruno Latour's contention that we have never been Modern). I am using Postmodern to describe a time period from the mid- to late twentieth century to the present day, as much as a movement.

6. Roman Guardini, *The End of the Modern World* (Wilmington: ISI Books, 2001), 76.

7. Guardini, *The End of the Modern World*, 79.

8. Not coincidentally, practically the only places where this model of deep and committed oaths and relationships occurs in contemporary society are the clergy and the military. Unsurprisingly, these are the professions that many contemporary people both admire and fear more than any other.

9. Readers can see an analogous recklessness in the gusto with which medieval romances occur, such as Lancelot and Guinevere, Tristan and Iseult, and Paolo and Francesca, which contrast with the staid and cautious manner in which many twenty-first-century romances are portrayed and conducted. Even in terms of the written language in which courtship was conducted, someone comparing, say, a Petrarchan love sonnet with the dialogue from a contemporary novel will be struck by the relative emotional audacity of the medieval language compared to the more anodyne contemporary speech.

10. Of course, the Roman Catholic Church's relationship with the pagan world was a complicated one and dependent on local circumstances, so that this syncretic approach was not always followed. This is especially true in the official narratives of the Church where a more combative tone predominates. One can see this especially in the hagiography of saints and martyrs, where the theme of defiance against the pagan world predominates and pagan rites are denounced, temples destroyed, and sacred trees cut down, etc.

11. One can see contemporary people's discomfort at the hybrid nature of these medieval texts in the way some scholars have attempted to uncover the "real" pagan source material of poems like *Beowulf*. Predictably, Tolkien hated these attempts to "purify" the poem of its Christian elements in order to make the poem fit more clearly into modern categories.

12. J.R.R. Tolkien, "On Fairy-Stories." *Tolkien on Fairy-Stories Expanded Edition, with Commentary and Notes*, eds. Verilyn Fliegler and Douglas A. Anderson (London: HarperCollins, 2008), 50.

13. J.R.R. Tolkien to Robert Murray, December 2, 1953, in *The Letters of J.R.R. Tolkien*, ed. Christopher Tolkien (Boston: Houghton Mifflin Harcourt, 2000), 191.

14. The irony is that in the popular imagination, medieval thought, especially medieval religious thought, is associated with irrational orthodoxy and lack of intellectual freedom. Yet in many ways medieval thinkers (especially the earliest ones) were more willing to tolerate and even incorporate benign aspects of other cultures. After all, it was medieval scholars who preserved a "purely" pagan literature through the painstaking copying of manuscripts. Most of these were classical pagan works of Greece and Rome, but early Christian poet Snorri Sturluson also preserved Northern pagan legends. Indeed, much of what we know about pagan myths comes from preservation efforts of the Catholic Church (as well as Orthodox and Muslim scholars). Ironically, the efforts popularly associated with medieval oppression like the Spanish Inquisition and the witch trials actually took place in the Early Modern period after the Renaissance had supposedly begun liberating people from their medieval superstitions.

15. Claudio A. Testi, "Tolkien's Work: Is it Christian or Pagan? A Proposal for a Synthetic Approach," *Tolkien Studies* 10 (2013): 10.

16. Testi, "Tolkien's Work," 11.

17. John Holmes, "'Like Heathen Kings': Religion as a Palimpsest in Tolkien's Fiction," in *The Ring and the Cross: Christianity and the Lord of the Rings*, ed. Paul E. Kerry (Madison, NJ: Farleigh Dickinson University Press, 213), 123–24.

18. This difference in approach between medieval writers as well as modern and postmodern critics is no more obvious than in Catherine Madsen's essay, "'Light from an Invisible Lamp': Natural Religion in *The Lord of the Rings*." In it, Madsen argues that *The Lord of the Rings* is not a Christian narrative and that even its theistic qualities are so vague as to be relatively unimportant. In her analysis, she unwittingly highlights the difference between more modern and postmodern approaches to myths as opposed to Tolkien as well as medieval approaches to myths. She notes, "The critics who have undertaken to 'prove' the book's [*The Lord of the Rings*] Christianity have used some interesting methods; they have mined it for Christian content with the same ingenuity their spiritual forbears used to find foreshadowing of Jesus among the law and the prophets." I would hope that current Christians would also find foreshadowing of Jesus in Isaiah's "suffering servant" and in Deuteronomy's exhortation to "love your God with all your heart." As Augustine said, "See not to believe, but believe so that thou may see." In any case, Madsen's skeptical approach that assumes a "Christian or not" approach to *The Lord of the Rings* is exactly the crux of what makes the more medieval/Tolkienian "both/and" attitude so different. The more catholic view looks for commonality and assumes compatibility rather than searches for difference and demands ideological purity.

19. This denigration of all things medieval goes back to Renaissance thinkers disparaging high medieval architecture as "Gothic" (or barbarian) or Edward Gibbon's transparent preference for late pagan Rome to the early Christian one. One could argue that some of the Romantic and Victorian admiration of the medieval was a reaction to the dismissive opinions of many Renaissance and Enlightenment thinkers.

20. One always has to keep in mind that there were Victorian thinkers who were just as adamantly anti-medieval. The most obvious ones are Charles Dickens and Mark Twain.

21. This is an earnestness that seems ripe for mockery in less serious times, as Oscar Wilde does to Victorians in *The Importance of Being Earnest* and Monty Python does to medieval people in *Monty Python and the Holy Grail*.

22. One can get a visual idea of the importance of Victorian medievalism by looking at Britain's current Houses of Parliament, which "look" medieval but were completed in 1870.

23. Fairy tales were somewhat restricted during the early Victorian period because of Evangelical and, to a certain extent, Gradgrindian utilitarian concerns about their sloth-inducing effects on young children. Ironically in contemporary society, fears about the reactionary ideology of some fairy tales especially in regard in gender once again are making fairy tales unpopular in some quarters.

24. Revealingly, the 2007 3D motion-capture movie *Beowulf* changed the original narrative to create just the sort of moral complexity favored in contemporary narratives and missing from the medieval poem. In the movie, Grendel's mother seduces Beowulf and gives birth to their "child" who is the dragon whom he must defeat. Thus, Beowulf is a much more morally ambiguous character than in the original, and his heroic battle with the dragon is an attempt to redeem his weakness.

Similarly, in her novel *A Mere Wife*, Maria Dahvana Headley aggressively attempts to rehabilitate Grendel's mother by making her a victim of the patriarchy. Headley argues that one of the reasons she wrote the novel is to rectify a mistranslation perpetuated by male scholars, including Tolkien, of *Beowulf*. These scholars describe Grendel's mother as "hag-like" when Headley argues that the word to describe her should be "formidable."

25. Jared Lobdell, *The World of the Rings* (Chicago: Open Court Publishing, 2004), 14. As a Victorianist, I find Lobdell's desire to describe late Victorian novels as "Edwardian" a bit disconcerting. For example, he repeatedly calls Rider Haggard's novel *She* "Edwardian" even though it was published in 1886, fifteen years before Edward ascended the throne. Some authors who died before the Edwardian era began, like Robert Louis Stevenson, become honorary Edwardians in Lobdell's *The World of the Rings*.

26. Lobdell, *The World of the Rings*, 19–20.

27. John Garth, *Tolkien and the Great War: The Threshold of Middle-earth* (Wilmington: Mariner Books, 2005), 79–80.

28. I don't want to suggest that utilitarianism was the only social force existing during the Victorian period. It was a complex time. This was also a time of renewed religious revival, especially Evangelical Christian revival. Still, the utilitarian approach to public policy had an enormous influence among Britain's ruling classes (as it does in our own), and this influence is what Tolkien particularly attacks in the characteristics of his legendarium's evil societies, especially Mordor.

29. Jeremy Bentham, *The Works. Volume 10, Memoirs Part 1 and Correspondence.* "Online Library" (London: Arkross Press, 2015), https://oll.libertyfund.org/.

30. J.R.R. Tolkien, *The Return of the King* (New York: Ballantine Books, 1994), 114.

31. The creation of monumental architecture is usually (though not always) a signal of a moral decline in "good" societies in Middle-earth. The dwarf kingdoms, for example, were not exactly "evil" when they built the Mines of Moria or the Kingdom under the Mountain, but this monumental architecture does come just before the fall of these cities at least partially brought about by the notorious greed of the dwarves. Similarly, the downfall of Númenór coincided with the Númenóreans building a giant temple, Armenelos the Golden, to worship Morgoth. The Gondorians' decision to build giant towers also ended up being a mistake because they ended up in the hands of the enemy, with Minas Ithil falling to Sauron and becoming Minas Morgul and the Orthanc falling to Saruman. Tolkien connects the hubris of these projects to their inhuman scale and the moral decline they represent.

32. This is in contrast to other fantasy and science fiction works in which inheritance seems to be all important. The most obvious example is Frank Herbert's *Dune* series, where inherited traits completely dominate the destinies of the characters.

33. J.R.R. Tolkien, *The Silmarillion,* ed. Christopher Tolkien (London: Ballantine Books, 1999), 5.

34. Robert Sale, "Tolkien and Frodo Baggins," in *Tolkien and the Critics*, ed. Neil David Isaacs (South Bend, IN: University of Notre Dame Press, 1968), 31, 58.

35. Sharin Schroeder, "Tolkien and the Modern," in *Approaches for Teaching Tolkien's* The Lord of the Rings *and Other Works*, ed. Leslie A. Donovan (New York: Modern Language Association, 2015), 129.

36. The rejection of traditional, non-abstract painting through artistic movements like German Expressionism and Cubism occurred in the first decade of the twentieth century before World War I. Stravinsky's cacophonous *Rite of Spring* was written just before the start of the war.

37. Janet Brennan Croft, *War in the Works of J.R.R. Tolkien* (Santa Barbara: Praeger, 2004), 40.

38. Tolkien, *The Letters of J.R.R. Tolkien*, 264.

39. J.R.R. Tolkien, *The Two Towers* (New York: Ballantine Books, 1994), 64.

40. Croft, quoted from Fussell, 41.

41. Hew Strachan, *The First World War* (London: Penguin Books, 2005), 339.

42. John Garth, *Tolkien and the Great War: The Threshold of Middle-earth* (Wilmington: Mariner Books, 2005), 223.

43. Garth, *Tolkien and the Great War*, 305.

44. Kevin Black, "The Battle against Modernity in J.R.R. Tolkien's *The Lord of the Rings*" (Senior Thesis, Princeton, 1995).

45. Croft, *War in the Works of J.R.R. Tolkien*, 79.

46. There is quite a bit of debate about whether the term "chateau general" is accurate. Some historians argue that the stereotype of the World War I general far from the front, living in luxury and indifferent to the sacrifices of the common soldiers is an unfair caricature. Still, the physical separation of the generals from their troops was a real phenomenon; the question is whether the lack of constant contact with the front led the generals to have a greater tolerance for the enormous casualties of World War I.

47. *The Silmarillion*, which does not have these more contemporary hobbit characters, is, not surprisingly, considered much less accessible to contemporary readers than *The Hobbit* and *The Lord of the Rings*.

48. *The Lord of the Rings* and *The Hobbit* have sold approximately 150 million and 100 million copies, respectively, ranking them among the best-selling novels of all time. The exact sales figures for *The Silmarillion* are not known, but they are certainly orders of magnitude smaller than Tolkien's more accessible works.

THREE
How the Environment Becomes Creation in Tolkien's Societies

In *The Silmarillion* and *The Lord of the Rings*, J.R.R. Tolkien presents his good and evil societies as landscapes first, and societies second. When Frodo removes his blindfold and first glances at Lothlórien, he sees the beauty of its mallorn trees and elanor flowers. When he stares down the plains of Mordor, he sees the desolation of its slag heaps and volcanic ash. In *The Silmarillion*, like the Bible, the world starts as an Edenic landscape first and only gains people later. Not coincidentally, one of Melkor's (later Morgoth's) first acts of violence in this new world is an attack on its environment when he destroys the trees of Valinor (he had already destroyed the two lamps of the Valar). This focus on nature first highlights Tolkien's view that a society's relationship with the natural world serves as a shorthand for the moral health of its inhabitants. The reader comes to see throughout Middle-earth that the degradation of nature coincides with the oppression of people.

This chapter compares Tolkien's utopian and dystopian thought to the assumptions and ideology of the modern environmental movement. I will do a brief survey of the philosophical origins of the environmental movement, starting with the Romantic Movement and conservationists' attempts to preserve the natural world that began in the nineteenth century. This chapter will show that though some of Tolkien's environmental beliefs have some similarities to current approaches to the environment, his environmental vision comes from a philosophical approach that derived from his Catholic faith and its continuous teaching from the medieval period to the twentieth century. Tolkien rejects the adversarial approach that many environmentalists take toward people and civilization. Instead, he focuses his ire on contemporary people's inability to accept limits in their exploitation of nature and other people. Tolkien illustrates the relationship between accepting limits and denying them through his benevolent and malevolent societies' relationships with the natural world.

A fair amount of criticism has already examined Tolkien's relationship with environmentalism. Matthew Dickerson and Jonathan Evans's *Ents, Elves and Eriador: The Environmental Vision of J.R.R. Tolkien* takes an eco-critical approach to *The Silmarillion* and *The Lord of the Rings* and argues that Tolkien was not an "environmentalist" in most contemporary senses of the word because he had an "environmental vision" that depended on a religious model of the natural world in which people should be "stewards" of the earth, neither subordinate to it nor abusive masters of it. They also discuss the various forms Tolkien's environmental vision took: from the agricultural hobbit stewardship, to the arboreal elvish approach, to the "pure" wilderness preference of the ents. In his book, *The Ecological Augury in the Works of JRR Tolkien,* Liam Campbell shows how Tolkien's work is an "augury" or an omen of future ecological destruction if the warnings provided by Tolkien are not heeded. In this sense, Campbell argues that contrary to some critics, Tolkien's works are not "escapist" in that they concentrate on the real possibility of future ecological disaster and thus are focused on one of the most important issues of the contemporary world.

Like Dickerson and Evans, my approach examines the connection between Tolkien's religious beliefs and his love of nature, but it also links it to Tolkien's broader philosophy about the nature of creation (and Creation) and our relationship to it. My contention is that Tolkien's approach to the environment, like his approach to many aspects of contemporary mores, has some similarities in his objectives and passions to the environmental movement but is orthogonal to the philosophy that gave rise to modern environmentalism. Rather, like the difference between Tolkien's more medieval approach to paganism and Christianity, Tolkien's approach to the natural world is much less absolute than most environmentalists and their opponents in the twentieth- and twenty-first-century Western World. Perhaps even more importantly, the motives for his appreciation and love of nature are quite different from most current environmentalists'.

There have been several different approaches to nature in the environmental movement throughout its relatively short history. The brief sketch provided here will only touch on the broadest strains of the very complex environmental movement, but they are some of the most influential threads. The earliest environmentalists were conservationists like Sir James Ranald Martin and Alexander Gibson in British India and John Muir and Theodore Roosevelt in the United States. They sought to preserve natural places so that they could be enjoyed, and many of them (especially the Americans) saw wild places as a way to make individuals closer to God by experiencing Him through nature. Often these early conservationists were also hunters, so the preservation of game was a central concern. Throughout the Western world and the British Empire in the late nineteenth and early twentieth centuries, respectively, governments started to set aside land for natural parks and nature preserves based on these conservation principles. Because early environmental pioneers focused on the preservation of nature for the use of people, they differ from most of their successors in the environmental movement who saw technology as the primary threat to the natural world. For example, in the environmental movement of the 1960s, books such as Rachel Carson's *Silent Spring* emphasized the fragility of nature and the dangers of pesticides, and later, nuclear power. Thus, the focus of the movement was expanded from preserving wild places to preventing damage to the wider environment from encroaching technology. These environmentalists often saw industrialized society itself as a problem and sought ways to limit or curb its pollution. There was also a split between those who wanted to use and preserve wild places for recreation, especially hunting and fishing, versus those in the environmental movement who saw managing natural parks as "unnatural." Later in the 1970s, groups like Greenpeace and Earth First! started to shift the debate away from conserving nature to a privileging of nature over civilization. Instead of focusing on preserving nature for the appreciation of current and future generations or limiting what they saw as dangerous technology, some in this new environmental movement saw humanity itself as the primary threat to the natural world and started to view industry and technology as the symptoms, rather than the cause, of environmental destruction. At the most radical end of the spectrum are movements like the Voluntary Human Extinction Movement, which currently assumes that humans are, according to its founder, Les U. Knight, "incompatible with the biosphere" and therefore we should voluntarily exit it.[1] Thus, the primary shift was from a view of nature's value based on what it can provide for people (beauty, rest, communion with God), to a view of nature's value based on a vision of nature untouched by humans.[2] Books like *The World without Us* by Alan Weisman provide fantasies of a human-free world reverting back to a wilder, and, by implication, better state. Still, despite the well-defined philosophical differences of these various strains of the environmental movement, they all held on to the Romantic notion that nature's value comes from its separation from civilization or, in its most extreme form, humanity itself.

Tolkien has a quite different approach to nature. First, he rejects the assumption that nature is almost exclusively good and allows nature to be dangerous and evil. Interestingly, despite many criticisms that Tolkien is morally "simplistic," his approach to the hostility of nature is, in some ways, more sophisticated than the popular Romantic notion (as in the eighteenth- and nineteenth-century movement) that nature is good and pure and civilization is evil and corrupt. Tolkien provides examples in creatures like Old Man Willow from the Old Forest and Huorns from the Fangorn Forest that represent "natural" evil (as in from nature) and corruption (despite the fact that Tolkien's favorite living organisms were trees). Old Man Willow's evil is especially noteworthy for a number of reasons. One is his age; Old Man Willow existed from a time when the Fangorn Forest and the Old Forest where connected in the First Age. This makes him one of the oldest living creatures in Middle-earth and therefore shows that evil came independently of the fall of Melkor into Morgoth. Old Man Willow also does not just attack the hobbits on a whim, he plans to kill them with malice aforethought (only to be thwarted by Tom Bombadil). According to Christian theology, sin must include both knowledge of wrong and purposeful action, and it appears that Old Man Willow can sin. Therefore, Tolkien gives nature the potential to be evil in all senses of the word. Tolkien also populates Middle-earth with werewolves in the First Age and evil wolves in the Third who suggest the terror humans felt for the natural world before it was conquered and tamed (for most of us) within the past few centuries. Because Tolkien allows the division between good and evil to be reflected in the natural world as well as in its rational creatures, he resists the temptation many current environmentalists have of viewing nature as almost exclusively benign.

Second, Tolkien does not view people as an environmental problem to be solved. We can see this in the way that Tolkien is consistently pro-natal throughout his legendarium. One of the symptoms of a declining civilization in Tolkien's Middle-earth is its lack of interest in children. Tolkien shows how depopulation leads to the decline of Númenór in both its Northern Kingdom of Arnor and Southern Kingdom of Gondor. As Frodo and his companions move from Bree to Rivendell, they view the empty "wastes" and the ruins of the kingdom of Arnor, like the old fortress at Weathertop, as examples of decay. In this case, depopulation and the region's returning to nature become a sign of its decline, not a sign of environmental improvement. Similarly, Tolkien also notes how parts of Minas Tirith had become depopulated and specifically mentions the lack of children in the city as evidence of how far the people of Gondor have fallen from their earlier glory.[3] As I mentioned before, Gandalf discusses the Gondorian obsession with tracing genealogy and their indifference to furthering their own line as evidence of Gondor's decline. This orientation toward the past rather than the future is almost always a sign of decadence in Middle-earth. Tolkien also expresses the opposite view: describing the birth of children as a good thing in itself. One of the blessings of the "golden" year of 1420 after the defeat of Sauron and Saruman is the bumper crop of children that the Shire produces that year. Not coincidentally, Sam, in many ways the moral hero of *The Lord of the Rings*, is the father of thirteen children.

Nothing can be further from current mainstream environmentalism than this pro-natal stance. Population control and anti-natal policies have been central to the environmental movement from the mid-twentieth century. Malthusian assumptions about the dangers of population growth have been a staple of the environmental movement in books, like Paul Ehrlich's *The Population Bomb*, and nongovernmental analyses, like *The Limits of Growth*. Zero-population-growth groups, like the non-profit Optimum Population Trust, list environmental concerns as the central reason for their push to limit births. Of course, it would be strange to import a modern concern, like the expanding population, to Tolkien's scarcely populated Middle-earth, but at the extreme end of the environmental movement any number of people degrades nature. Therefore, Tolkien's belief that children are a blessing denies this simple assumption that nature equals good and people equal bad.

Despite the many ways Tolkien's ideas run contrary to the current environmental movement, in other ways, Tolkien's critique seems very similar to it. Treebeard and the ents provide a maximalist position for preserving the wilderness in its most pristine form. Treebeard does not want any sort of "development" (in the modern sense) of his forest and does not base the trees' value on their utility. Tolkien presents Saruman's destruction of the nature in the Shire as a mirror image of Treebeard's valuing trees for their intrinsic worth. For instance, Saruman destroys the trees on Bagshot Row with no compunction because the trees have no value to him. He destroys the trees around Isengard to fuel his war machine. So on the one extreme, we have Treebeard who views trees as valuable in the same sense that we would view persons as valuable. At the other extreme, we have Saruman who views trees as only worthwhile for their immediate use value or perhaps as a way to spitefully attack his enemies. Then there is the value that elves have for nature that has both an intrinsic value and a use value. Tolkien allows different characters to espouse all these views. Therefore a minority of Tolkien's characters do speak of the natural world as primary and incompatible with human interference and view human destruction as its most important danger, just as many current environmentalists believe.

Another way Tolkien's approach is similar to modern environmentalists is his attack on those who wantonly destroy the natural world. Whether or not the natural world is always good, the forces of evil in Middle-earth are always antagonistic to it. So while Tolkien does not view nature as simplistically "good" and people "bad," he does view all those who destroy nature as universally evil. It is no coincidence that in places where evil triumphs, like Thangorodrim and Mordor, almost all living things are completely eradicated and the ones that remain, like Mordor's stunted thorn trees or the biting flies, are compromised and twisted by the abnormal ecology of the wastelands where they live. One of the characteristics of these evil societies is their relative uniformity.

Unlike the good societies of Middle-earth that can come in a variety of different natural forms—wilderness, pastoral, agricultural, and even cavernous—evil tends to create monochrome environments that are unbalanced and inefficient except as vehicles for domination and control.

So if Tolkien's approach differs from the majority of modern environmentalists, but he clearly values nature, what exactly is the difference between his approach and that of most modern environmentalists? While most environmentalists view nature with a Romantic (as in the movement) dualistic lens, Tolkien approaches nature as part of God's creation, which puts man's obligation to it in the context of being a responsible part of nature rather than a force that is outside it. Even most of the earliest conservationists approached nature from a fundamentally different perspective than Tolkien. Early conservationists like John Muir saw nature as essential to the spiritual development of people, yet even this approach presupposes that "wild" places owe their power to the fact that they are separate from "civilization" and, by implication, people. Later environmentalists moved from the presupposition that lack of nature is bad for people and therefore we should provide more of it, to nature being the good itself, regardless of what it does for people. A short step from this reasoning leads some environmentalists to assume that people are bad because they are not good for nature, rather than nature is good because it is good for people. All this reasoning depends on a dualistic view that man and nature are somehow separate. This was a common view of Enlightenment thinkers like Thomas Hobbes, who saw man as giving up his "state of nature" to the government, or John Locke, who describes how men must give up "natural freedom" to secure their lives and property. Generally, these Enlightenment thinkers had a jaundiced view of people in their natural state and tended to privilege civilization over nature. Ironically, the Romantics, starting with Jean-Jacques Rousseau, accepted this duality but wanted to reverse what was considered good and what was considered bad in the binary. They, too, saw this separation of man from nature as a loss of freedom or "mind-forg'd manacles," to use William Blake's term, but instead of accepting this as an acceptable trade-off for security, they wanted to return to an anarchic state of nature. This is one of the many inversions that the Romantics privileged in response to the Age of Reason: they privileged childhood over adulthood, innocence over sophistication, emotion over reason. Note, however, that these are *inversions*, which means the binaries remain intact. The Romantics mostly accepted the same categories as their Enlightenment predecessors; they implicitly assumed that the categories of nature and civilization were inherently separate. As often is the case with Tolkien, he challenges the very centrality of these categories that are so hegemonic that most contemporary people do not even see them.

Other modern thinkers have also challenged these categories. In his essay "Conservation Is Good Work," Wendell Berry insists on using the term "Creation" rather than environment to make just this point. He argues that

> "Environment" means that which surrounds or encircles us; it means a world separate from ourselves, outside us. The real state of things, of course, is far more complex and intimate and interesting than that. The world environs us, that is around us, is also within us. We are made of it; we eat, drink, and breathe it; it is bone of our bone and flesh of our flesh.[4]

Berry notes how our language separates us from the natural world through its very jargon. Not surprisingly, he chooses the most personal Biblical imagery, that of Adam and Eve being "one flesh," to make our relationship with the environmental marital rather than transactional.

In the first book of *The Silmarillion*, Tolkien similarly challenges the current separation of persons from nature when he describes the creation of the world at the mythological beginning of Middle-earth. Like the traditional Judeo-Christian view of Creation, Eru Ilúvatar creates the world ex nihilo: out of nothing. Tolkien uses the metaphor of an elaborate piece of music to show the creation of Eä, or the universe. A key part of this creation is that almost all the persons created in this world were a part of nature.[5] Thus Tolkien describes both men and elves as "awakening" into already existing creation in which they are an organic part. In this way Tolkien makes it clear that both the "First-Born" elves and "Second-Born" men were part of the initial creation of the world through the music of Eru and the Valar rather than created separately. Indeed, the Valar were surprised both by the creation of the universe and by the appearance of both men and elves. Because the created world and its rational creatures spring from the same source, Tolkien implies that "civilization," or people congregating together in large numbers, is not somehow "unnatural," but just another part of nature.

Tolkien also uses elves as examples of how civilization and nature are not naturally at loggerheads. For instance, elves live both in Middle-earth and Valinor and make the natural world more beautiful and more complete than it would be otherwise. In both *The Silmarillion* and *The Lord of the Rings*, elves provide the example of how to live within nature, even while modifying it, without dominating or destroying it. Whether it is the elves of Nargothrond, Gondolin, or Doriath, in the First Age; or Lothlórien, Mirkwood, and Rivendell in the Third, the elves manage to build communities that incorporate and enhance the natural world, rather than destroy it. Lothlórien provides the best example here with the elves literally living with the trees and providing yet another case of Tolkien subverting the boundaries between nature and civilization. Hobbits seem to serve a similar purpose of presenting a society with a healthy relationship with nature, even if they are more agricultural and less arboreal than elves. Hobbit holes, built into the sides of hills, provide a model of integrating rational creatures with the natural world without degrading it.

Other creatures provide a more negative example. For instance, as in our world, men have a familiar ambivalent connection with nature. In the First Age, many of the men ally themselves with Morgoth and participate in the destruction of Middle-earth. In the Second Age especially, Tolkien notes how men's search for power and wealth can damage nature, especially when it leads to wide-scale deforestation of, first, the island of Númenór, and then large parts of Middle-earth. The most negative examples are orcs and other creatures of Sauron, which seem to enjoy destruction for its own sake. By exaggerating both the stewardship of the elves and the wanton destruction of the orcs, Tolkien highlights the different paths individuals and societies can take in relation to the natural world.

Tolkien's creation story is very similar to the traditional Judeo-Christian one, but its differences highlight his unique approach to the natural world and its relationship with people. The universe, Eä, is created out of nothing, and God is totally sovereign over it just like the biblical creation story. Neither of these elements are true of most creation stories (such as the creation story in Greek mythology), which posit the universe being created out of already existing material and by a non-omnipotent deity or deities.[6] This difference has metaphysical implications because Tolkien's and the Judeo-Christian creation stories suggest that time and the universe are progressive and teleological rather than cyclical and purposeless (like many polytheistic and other religions). The fact that Tolkien has the music created first before Eä comes into existence also corresponds with a Christian sense that the world is controlled by Providence rather than the random forces of fate. Finally, Eru Ilúvatar makes the world "good" from the beginning, which again matches Christian theology that saw the created world as basically good, in contrast to many rivals to orthodox Christianity such as Manicheanism, Gnosticism, and some forms of Neo-Platonism, which saw the material world as deficient or, in some cases, evil.[7]

Despite these overarching similarities between Tolkien's creation and the Judeo-Christian creation story, there are significant differences that provide some insight into the way Tolkien viewed the natural world. There are no equivalent to the Valar in the Christian creation story (though there are tantalizing references to the "gods" and "sons of gods" in Genesis 6:1–4). What is especially striking is that these Valar take part in the act of creation itself. Not only that, but Melkor weaves evil within the very essence of creation (though Eru Ilúvatar makes a greater good out of this evil). This is different from a creation tainted by the Fall of Man because that means evil is a natural part of creation. Of course, one of the most striking differences between Tolkien's creation story and the Judeo-Christian one is that God creates other rational species, elves, in addition to men. Therefore men, as second-born creatures, are, in some ways, less important than the first-born elves, so much so that Tolkien's earliest mythology focuses exclusively on them. This fact leads to the most important difference between Tolkien's creation story and that of Scripture. In *The Silmarillion*, God does not create man as an act of special creation with a special mission, but instead elves and men simply "awaken" like a seed that has germinated. Missing as well is the language of man's lordship over creation, which is central to the Genesis creation story. Tolkien also makes the elves, through their immortality and natural inclinations, especially attached to the natural world (but even the men of Middle-earth, despite eventually leaving the world, are more attached to it than the humans of our world because they were created as part of it).

The differences between Tolkien's creation narrative and the scriptural one have metaphysical implications for Middle-earth.[8] One of the most important implications involves the nature of evil. Melkor's participation in creation binds evil up with the world (at least in the short term); thus parts of the natural world can be inherently evil in ways different from the traditional view of Christianity. Creatures like Ungoliant were not created directly like the Valar and the Maiar, but mysteriously "descended from the darkness that lies about Arda" and therefore appear out of the natural world themselves.[9] Ungoliant, like her descendant Shelob, are evil but not part of the hierarchy of evil that includes Morgoth and Sauron. Thus, evil creatures exist as a part of creation, but also outside the "principalities and powers" of fallen angels that exist in the Bible. Because there is more than one type of rational creature in Middle-earth, it is not clear that one group is indeed the master of creation who is formed in the image of God. Indeed, since *The Silmarillion* is primarily a history of the elves, it appears they are, in some sense, closer to God. Even in the Second and Third Ages, when the elves dwindle and start to recede more into the background of Middle-earth, they always possess more wisdom and creativity than the men of Middle-earth. And indeed, the model they provide of ecological stewardship is certainly different from the "dominion" model that at least some forms of Christianity take toward the natural world. Therefore, the absence of men as a "special creation" and a lack of a sense that they were designed to have "dominion" over nature marks a pretty significant departure from Christian theology. Add to that the addition of the godlike Valar and their more obvious dominion over aspects of the natural world, and we can see how Tolkien constructs Middle-earth so that its rational creatures have a more direct connection to it and experience less temptation to see themselves as above nature.

What this closer relationship means is that Tolkien, for much of his legendarium, collapses the binary between civilization and the natural world. The *most* civilized creatures in Middle-earth are the elves, and they are the *most* in tune with the natural world. In contrast, creatures like orcs and trolls are the least civilized and the most alienated from nature (both their own and the natural world). In all the places elves inhabit, they enhance, rather than degrade, nature. Tolkien also shows how nature can be respected in a variety of habitats, including ones that have been modified by people. The "good" places of Middle-earth include a variety of landscapes—from pure wilderness to agricultural lands and even cities. For Tolkien, these human-modified environments can still count as "natural" because elves, hobbits, and men are still part of nature. Tolkien suggests naturalness of these agricultural environments in Middle-earth by creating intermediate creatures like the entwives, who were put on earth by the Vala Yavanna to care for plants like fruit trees, meadows, and vegetables. Entwives protect and sustain agricultural crops just as the ents protect the great forests, which suggests that farms are just as "natural" as forests. Still, their separation from the ents suggests a metaphorical separation of the nature in the wilderness from the nature of agriculture. Even so, as often is the case with Tolkien's complex mythology, he also presents intermediate creatures, like Boern from *The Hobbit*, who inhabits the space between man and beast and between the farm and the wilderness. Not only is Boern a skin-changer who is both man and bear, he is also both a wild animal and an animal herder who produces honey, cream, and mead on his farm. Throughout his legendarium, Tolkien subverts the modern binary of civilization versus nature or man versus the wilderness to show how rational creatures can live with and even modify nature responsibly.

Not only does he disrupt this binary by creating intermediate creatures, both beast and human, Tolkien also presents animals as independent subjects rather than objects. Eleanor R. Simpson, in the article "The Evolution of J.R.R. Tolkien's Portrayal of Nature," argues that Tolkien's portrayal of animals becomes increasingly anti-speciesist from *The Hobbit* to *The Lord of the Rings*. Simpson points out the most obvious example of this development in the fox that spots the hobbits on their way out of the Shire in *The Fellowship of the Ring*. She notes that Tolkien gives the awake and speculating fox "dominance" in the relationship by presenting the sleeping hobbits as objects of the fox's musings.[10] This is one of the many examples where animals are at least given equal consideration to the people in Tolkien's legendarium. For example, Gandalf always must request, never demand, that eagles carry him or others, and he also receives consent from Shadowfax before he rides the horse.

The way Tolkien constructs the mythology of his legendarium has philosophical and moral implications that he explores throughout his works. Instead of the assumption of the moral superiority of nature over civilization that has been a central assumption of the environmental movement since its genesis in the Romantic Movement, Tolkien's central assumption depends on understanding a rational creature's place in creation and how that both places limits on what that creature should morally do with the natural world and also allows him or her to subcreate (to use Tolkien's word) in cooperation with nature to enhance the natural world and make objects of great beauty and utility. People acting on both of these assumptions—nature's superiority or accepting the limits of subcreation—can lead to similar actions in many (though certainly not all) cases, but the metaphysical assumptions are quite different. The former depends on the dualistic thinking that comes naturally to most modern and postmodern people. The latter recognizes rational creatures as part of nature and that the temptation of these creatures to transcend the natural world is where most of the evil comes from rather than anything inherent in civilization or people themselves. We can see this from the beginning of *The Silmarillion* where Morgoth's original sin was his refusal to accept the fact he was a part of nature rather than above it. This arrogance manifested itself in his futile desire to find the "flame imperishable" and create life without Eru Ilúvatar.

Aulë desired to do the same thing but, in a scene from *The Silmarillion* reminiscent of the sacrifice of Abraham, was willing to destroy his own creation in obedience to Eru. The difference in motive is key to why Eru allowed Aulë to fashion dwarves as independent, rational creatures. When Eru first questions Aulë about why he created creatures "beyond thy power and authority," Eru accuses Aulë of making dwarves so that he could dominate them. Aulë's reply that "I did not desire such lordship. I desired things other than I am, to love and teach them so that they too might perceive the beauty of Eä" convinces Eru that these creatures were created out of love rather a desire for power.[11] Because of the purity of Aulë's motives, Eru breathes his sacred fire into the dwarves and animates them as independent creatures. This desire to dominate and control differentiates legitimate forms of creativity and power from illegitimate forms. Ironically this illegitimate control is not only illicit, but also inefficient. Morgoth, and later Sauron, attempt to make their own creatures, but they can only make damaged mockeries of Eru's original creatures. Morgoth and Sauron also ironically subvert the purpose of creation itself. In their very quest to dominate their minions, Morgoth and Sauron do the opposite of what Aulë desired. Aulë's original dwarves could only act as Aulë directed them and had no will of their own when they were first created. When Eru makes them independent creatures with their own free will rather than automatons, the transformation delights Aulë. In contrast, Morgoth and Sauron sought to reverse this process by taking independent creatures with their own free wills and making them into automatons. They fail at even this and these evil creatures are fractious and conflicted. Once again evil by its very nature substitutes the lesser for the greater.

These stories serve as a metaphor for Tolkien's view of creativity and its relationship with Creation. The way that creativity can enhance rather than destroy nature and its creatures is by keeping it within the bounds of Creation; Tolkien defines this as subcreation. Subcreation recognizes that we cannot create anything outside of creation and that we are aware of limits so that our creativity does not damage the world God created. Or to be more precise, creativity ceases to "create" when the desire to "go beyond thy power and authority" comes from a desire to control. This leads to damage instead of creativity, even if the result temporarily gives us some of what we desire.

This philosophical focus on respecting limits is not, of course, exclusive to Tolkien, and it is part of a larger philosophical approach that involves more than limiting environmental destruction. The Catholic Church historically has been one such voice for accepting limits (for both good and ill).[12] If one looks at *The Inferno*, the premier example of high medieval Catholic theology, the damned often end up in Hell for transgressing boundaries in ways that are not only acceptable in the postmodern world, but are celebrated by it. These transgressions are not just sexual ones like Paolo and Francesca's adultery or Brunetto Latini's sodomy, but Odysseus, whose rebelliousness violated the rules of war and thus earned him, as a false councilor, one of the lowest places in Dante's Hell. Even stranger to our contemporary mores is how God damns Odysseus for his desire to explore the world. Dante creates a whole new story for Odysseus in *The Inferno* that differs from the events in *The Odyssey*. In Dante's story, Odysseus never returns to Ithaca, but instead decides to sail beyond the Pillars of Hercules to the ends of the world. The journey ends disastrously when Odysseus dies as his ship flounders on the rocks before Mount Purgatory. Critical opinion is split about whether Dante considered this voyage itself a sin. I think there is no doubt that he did, and I consider it a clear example of what is celebrated in our society, but considered a sin in the medieval world—that of transcending boundaries by going beyond God-given limits. The fascinating part about this poem is how Dante has Odysseus give a rousing speech about being unafraid to follow virtue and knowledge. Thus, Dante casts Odysseus's act in the most heroic light possible, yet still characterizes it as a sin.[13] There is also some debate about whether Latini's sin was really sodomy (he was a married father of several children) or whether Dante was using sodomy as a metaphor for an intellectual sin so that Latini's transgression was a stylistic or philosophical perversion rather than a sexual one. The irony is that in modern society perhaps the only value more important than sexual freedom is intellectual freedom. The idea that one can sin intellectually does not even make sense to many modern people. For the medieval Dante, however, some of the most serious sins are intellectual, and maintaining intellectual boundaries aids in maintaining moral ones. If we turn to *The Silmarillion*, we see that Melkor's (before he became Morgoth) attempts to hijack the "song" of creation and to find the sacred fire to create his own creatures are, in essence, sins of the intellect. Morgoth uses his mind and creativity to do something that is forbidden to him. Ironically, the creative artist Tolkien argues that the desire to create can be the greatest sin if it is not kept within limits.

The contention that intellect and creativity can be sinful because they transgress ethical boundaries is both a live question in our society and one that many people answer negatively based on the Enlightenment tradition.[14] Over and over, since the beginning of the Enlightenment, narratives have been created to explore the dangers of pursuing intellectual projects that transgress moral limits. Johann Goethe's *Faust*, Mary Shelley's *Frankenstein,* and even current films like *Splice* or *Ex Machina* explore what happens when people cross ethical boundaries in search of new creations and creativity. Nearly universally in the narratives, these transgressions result in negative consequences. The perennial nature of these works points to the fact that crossing moral boundaries in pursuit of knowledge has been a continuing cultural concern of the Western world for the past several centuries. Despite these concerns, our society has difficulty accepting limits or even acknowledging them, especially if they challenge individual freedom. For example, the use of live embryos in medical research would have been unheard of even a few decades ago, but now is routine in many parts of the world (including the United States).[15]

Failure to accept limits is especially difficult in humanity's attempts to control the natural world. Since the Enlightenment, people have found it difficult to argue for limits because the very language most of us use depends on the principles of reason and utility; these principles naturally tend to erode ethical prohibitions. Arguments about the limits of genetic engineering, for example, are mostly fought on utilitarian grounds in the Enlightenment tradition. This leads to the pushing of boundaries and then the eventual obliteration of them since a "greater good" justifies almost anything (say, atomic bombs or workers' paradises) if the outcome is assumed to be a large enough improvement over the status quo. If genetic engineering leads to greater crop yields or bigger cows, we will accept it. Negatives like monoculture agriculture or decline in the variety of livestock will not be a big enough negative if food is cheaper. Efficiency (usually measured by dollars saved) becomes an irresistible force for change. The upshot of this philosophical approach becomes that if it can be done, it likely will be done, unless overwhelming negatives can be found because of this bias toward removing barriers. Barriers are expensive.[16]

Tolkien uses the language of prohibition in his legendarium to protect the environment rather than arguing that the environment should be protected because of self-interested or aesthetic reasons. Tolkien's mythology is replete with boundaries: the forbidding of the Valar to create life, the bar on the Númenóreans from reaching the undying lands, even the ban of men from the Shire. Boundaries would also seem to play a large part in the environmental movement; after all, much of the public policy proposed by the environmental movement revolves around bans of various kinds: bans of chemicals like DDT, the elimination of nuclear power, restrictions on the use of genetically engineered crops.[17] Even though there is a similarity in the outcome, there is a big difference between the reasoning that Tolkien uses versus the reasoning that most environmental groups use to come to these limits. Sometimes the environmental movement approaches limits from a utilitarian, Enlightenment perspective, and at other times from a more innocent, Romantic perspective. The utilitarian prospective argues for bans and limitations based on the preponderance of harm, such as the argument in Rachel Carson's *Silent Spring*. The more Romantic argument depends on protecting the goodness and purity of the wilderness from the corrupting influence of civilization. Thus these bans are about protecting people's physical health and/or protecting the wilderness from human contamination. Interestingly, the language used in these environmental arguments often appears similar to that of religious prohibitions. Thus, people are told to eat "clean" food without genetic modifications or antibiotics just like the Torah tells Jews not to eat unclean animals, like pigs. Not surprisingly, Tolkien's bans have neither of these motivations. Tolkien's bans are less about physical harm or purity and more about the damage that transgressing these boundaries does to the essence of the transgressor. I mentioned how Eru Ilúvatar fears that Aulë created dwarves in order to dominate them. The ban on creation preserves the Valar from evil. Similarly, the ban of the Valar that forbade the Númenóreans from sailing to the West was meant to protect them from the physical harm that would come from mortals trying to live in the undying lands (humans living in the West would actually have shorter lifespans, despite many Númenóreans believing they would become immortal there), but, more importantly, the ban was meant to protect them from *wanting* what was, in essence, not good for them spiritually. Tolkien's focus was always on the moral, rather than physical, damage that came from dominating the environment. To trade immortality in the next world for immortality in this world is a classic example of giving up the greater for the lesser, to quote the Bible: "For what does it profit a man, to gain the whole world and forfeit his life?" (Mark 8:36). Similarly, the ban from the Shire was not meant to keep the hobbits "pure" (as I mentioned, the hobbits' provincialism is a vice and therefore should not be protected), but to protect the "big people" from the temptation of bullying those who are smaller than them.

While it might appear that the similarity between the limit-setting in Tolkien's works and the Catholic Church was primarily between the medieval church and Tolkien's legendarium, the pre-twenty-first-century Catholic Church of Tolkien's lifetime also believed in setting limits for business and industry. What distinguishes the church's approach to determining these limits is how it ignores efficiency and utility, the dominant Enlightenment values of our time. The utilitarian argument between capitalism and market economies on the one hand, and socialism and control by the government on the other, that has been going on throughout the nineteenth and twentieth centuries has predictably been debated in terms of utility: which produces the best result materially? For the most part, it appears that the market economy (or, at least, a mixed economy) has won, but the Catholic Church has consistently argued that boundaries must be set, even if they interfere with the efficiency of the market. Pope Leo XIII's encyclical *Rerum Novarum* (*Of the New Things*), written in 1891, discusses one such limit when he argues that "working for gain is creditable, not shameful to a man; since it enables him to earn a honorable livelihood; but to misuse men as though they were things in the pursuit of gain or to value them solely for their physical powers—that is truly shameful and inhuman." Note that Pope Leo starts with the principle of allowing a market economy, "working for gain is credible, not shameful," but then goes on to set a limit, "to misuse men as though they were things."[18] Allowing for freedom and then setting a limit is something that Pope Leo does throughout *Rerum Novarum*. Most interpreters of the encyclical in the past and today view it through the lens of the major competing ideologies of the day: capitalism and socialism. Many see the encyclical as a sort of "middle way" between laissez-faire capitalism and governmental control of the means of production. Militants from both the left and the right can find solace in different parts of the encyclical, but viewing it from either perspective misses how the encyclical operates from completely different philosophical assumptions of both capitalist apologists *and* socialist promoters. The major concern of the encyclical is not the capitalist concerns about efficiency (measured by profits) or socialist demands for equality, but a concern for the dignity of humans who are used as objects. Pope Pius XI in his 1931 encyclical *Quadragesimo Anno* (*In the Fortieth Year*) speaks of these dangers of dehumanization of labor in even more forceful language:

> And thus bodily labor, which Divine Providence decreed to be performed, even after original sin, for the good at once of man's body and soul, is being everywhere changed into an instrument of perversion; for dead matter comes forth from the factory ennobled, while men there are corrupted and degraded.[19]

Pope Pius complains that the management of many factories treats workers "like mere tools" rather than human beings. This focus on the subjective worth of individuals is based on a similar philosophical premise to Tolkien's concern for the environment. *Rerum Novarum, Quadragesimo Anno,* and Tolkien's works see the danger in the modern approaches of both unrestrained capitalism and unrestrained creativity in that they ignore the subjective value of creation and instead focus on the immediate use value of nature and individuals.

While these encyclicals focus on labor relations rather than the environment, writings by later popes made this connection between the treatment of nature and individuals more explicit. John Paul II's address on World Day of Peace in 1990 argues,

> The most profound and serious indication of the moral implications underlying the ecological problem is the lack of RESPECT FOR LIFE evident in many patterns of environmental pollution. Often, the interests of production prevail over concern for the dignity of workers, while economic interests take priority over the good of individuals and even entire peoples. In these cases, pollution or environmental destruction is the result of an unnatural and reductionist vision which at times leads to a genuine contempt for man.[20]

Here, Pope John Paul II also refuses to accept the duality of nature and civilization. He argues that the contempt for the environment and the contempt for man are part of the same "unnatural and reductionist vision." His diagnosis that "economic interests take priority over the good of individuals" once again is a language of limits, since to take the good of individuals into account would necessarily limit these "economic interests" rather than reducing humanity as merely a means to make money. Pope John Paul II refuses to separate people from environment into competing realms and argues instead that what is bad for the environment is bad for people as well.

Pope Francis, in his recent encyclical *Laudato Si (Praise Be to You)*, draws similar connections between the evil done to the environment and the evil done to individuals. Indeed, common phrases used throughout the encyclical emphasize this connection. He argues, "A true ecological approach *always* becomes a social approach"; "he [Saint Francis of Assisi] shows us just how inseparable the bond is between concern for nature, justice for the poor, commitment to society . . . "; and "here [in the global economic system] we see how environmental deterioration and human ethical degradation are closely linked."[21] Both Tolkien and Pope Francis identify the evil done to persons and the evil done to the environment as part of the same philosophy; a philosophy that sees people and the natural world as objects to be used instrumentally rather than as parts of the created world to be stewarded. They also identify evil as coming from a will to dominate and an unwillingness to accept any limits whatsoever. This desire for limitlessness creates both environmental and societal destruction represented by Tolkien in the environmental desolation of Mordor and the moral deformity of its creatures.

Pope Francis, quoting extensively from Romano Guardini, also argues that modern people have a tendency to confuse an increase in power with an increase in "progress" itself and that "goodness and truth flow from technological and economic power" (75–76).[22] He claims, "We have certain superficial mechanisms, but we cannot claim to have a sound ethics, a culture and spirituality genuinely capable of setting limits" (76). Both Tolkien and Pope Francis argue that some of the most moral decisions require limiting our actions.

On a more fundamental level, modern man has what Pope Francis describes as a "subject-object" problem in which man views nature and others as objects to be manipulated in an unlimited way. He acknowledges in *Laudato Si* that

> Men and women have constantly intervened in nature, but for a long time this meant being in tune with and respecting the possibilities offered by the things themselves. It was a matter of receiving what nature itself allowed, as if from its own hand. Now, by contrast, we are the ones to lay our hands on things, attempting to extract everything possible from them while ignoring or forgetting the reality in front of us.[23]

The quote "respecting the possibilities offered by the things themselves" resembles Tolkien's contention that subcreation must have limits and take into account the "givenness" of nature. Note also how Pope Francis subjectifies nature by personifying it; he says that nature has hands and can "allow" things. The result of ignoring these limits and treating nature as an object to be manipulated rather than a subject with which one could cooperate becomes nature's diminishment and destruction.[24] According to Pope Francis, this attempt at total extraction of all value from nature is not only wrong, but fundamentally mistaken since its reductionism fails to see how the reality of the natural is greater than the sum of its useful parts. In our desire to exploit nature fully, we "murder to dissect," as William Wordsworth says.

Tolkien's good and bad societies provide narrative illustrations of what Pope Francis argues. Tolkien's ideal societies "subjectify" and work in harmony with nature to explore its possibilities, while his evil realms objectify and destroy nature to strip it of its value. Tolkien gives different aspects of nature a personhood through the pantheon of the Valar. His just societies build on specific aspects of the "personality" of the nature they inhabit. Therefore, Lothlórien elves integrate their society into the ecology of the woodlands in which they live. In a similar way, Gondolin and Rivendell integrate themselves seamlessly into the mountains that surround them. Finally, the Shire is an agricultural paradise where the hobbits are careful to never take too much from the land and take pride in cultivating its fertility. In each case, Tolkien's benevolent societies arise from the unique qualities of their part of the natural world. On the other hand, Tolkien's evil societies are all about extraction and destruction. The wastelands of Thangorodrim and Mordor are the final product of Morgoth and Sauron's attempt to "extract" all value from them. It is not a coincidence that both these sterile, lifeless lands resemble each other. Evil turns the living into the lifeless, and environmental diversity depends in large part on the diversity of life. Death is the ultimate nullification and absence, just as evil is.

As this review of Catholic thought makes clear, Tolkien's approach to nature has precedent in the Catholic Church's continuous social teaching about the environment, from the Middle Ages, to the nineteenth and twentieth centuries, to the present day. The philosophical connection between the medieval belief in restricting certain intellectual exploration and Pope Francis's advocacy in restricting certain economic development are the same desires to set limits. The need to reject limits is the root of all impious desires. As Tom Shippey noted, the most common fault of our world is the desire to do things because they can be done.[25] Thus, Odysseus's pointless exploration, the desire to maximize worker productivity, and the temptation to exploit the environment's long-term health for short-term gain, all derive from the same desire. This also leads to the same result: to take things that should be treated as "subjects," like human beings or nature, and objectify them so they can be controlled, manipulated, and used up so that all the value is extracted from them. Another Biblical account that describes the consequences of this desire to do things because they can be done no matter the cost is the story of the tree of the knowledge of good and evil from Genesis. The temptation in this story is the same one that seduces Morgoth and Sauron: the desire "to be like gods."

This recognition of the importance of limits and the dangers of unchecked desires is reflected in the utopian hopes and dystopian fears of Tolkien's legendarium. In these ways, Catholic social values appear in Tolkien's stories even without the specifics of Catholic doctrine and worship. As Tolkien wrote in a letter to Robert Murray, referring to *The Lord of the Rings*, he has "not put in, or have cut out, practically all references to 'religion', to cults or practices, in the imaginary world. For the religious element is absorbed into the story and symbolism."[26] Later on, in the same letter, Tolkien argues that this did not mean that he had "consciously planned" to do anything. This letter is very revealing since it implies that Tolkien suggests that the Catholic nature of his legendarium is mostly organic and unplanned. I think a model to understand this idea of how a work can be Christian organically rather than polemically is the art of medieval Christendom. While some medieval people gained their sense of religion through formal teaching, most developed it through the culture that was so inculcated with religious imagery and expression that it was absorbed "naturally."[27] Yet again, this approach seems especially alien to our post-Reformation and Counter-Reformation world, where belief is modulated by oral and written arguments as well as formal instruction rather than art, performance, and music.[28]

Tolkien's ability to demonstrate Catholic doctrine, rather than argue for it, is most obvious in Tolkien's evil societies. Tolkien presents the most fearful ecological trends in our modern society as illustrations rather than arguments. Thangorodrim and Mordor use both people and their environments as objects to exploit rather than subjects to be respected. The end result is the destruction of many people and most of the natural world. This treatment of humans and the wild environment as undifferentiated inputs in a process, rather than living creatures and irreplaceable resources with their inherent worth, is familiar to modern people in the very language that we use. People become abstracted into the word "labor" and paired with true abstractions like "capital." Minerals, plants, animals all become the word "material." This contrasts with older words like craftsman and artisan, or even farmer, which emphasize the subjective nature of the doer rather than their objective use in the process. In a similar way words like the "fruits" of labor seek to make products more like living things, just as our modern language makes living things more like inert matter. Thus language like "raw materials" implies that anything is incomplete until it is made into a consumer product. Whatever value the "materials" have (aesthetic, ecological) as part of their natural environment, the wood or rocks or water becomes discounted by the very terms used to describe them.

While the good societies of Middle-earth do not always live up to the ideal of treating nature and people as subjects, to the extent that they do exhibit this ideal, both their people and environments flourish. These good societies personify both living non-human creatures and inanimate objects. Tolkien does this to re-enchant the world, but this re-enchantment also has environmental implications. For instance, the way Sam personifies his pony Bill means that Sam feels responsible for the animal in ways that he would not if he viewed the pack animal as some sort of transportation abstraction. Bill Ferny (the pony's former owner) treated Bill badly only because of the pony's low use-value. Bill Ferny's ill-treatment of the pony is one of the ways that Tolkien marks Bill Ferny as a villain, but, as often is the case, the pony turns out to be much more useful when he is treated well by Sam and the elves of Rivendell. The short-term demand for efficiency leads to a long-term degradation of performance. We also see examples of environmental stewardship that include the personification of plant life. Tom Bombadil can "sing" to trees like Old Man Willow and thus communicate with them. In a similar way, ents speak to the trees of the Fangorn Forest. Even Legolas, the elf, can sense and in some way communicate with trees. Non-living creatures are also personified in Tolkien's Middle-earth. Goldberry describes Tom Bombadil as the "Master of Wood, Water, and Hill," which suggests that inanimate forces like water and hills have a will that can be "mastered" in some way. Dwarves are given the title "Masters of Stone" in a similar bid to show how even the crafting of stones is more like husbandry than domination.[29] Of course, some may think that these titles of "Masters of" might suggest the totalizing power that Tolkien identifies with his bad societies of Thangorodrim and Mordor based on the categories of "master" and "slave." Tolkien instead is using the title "Master" in the older sense of the word: one who truly understands the thing he has mastered—like "schoolmaster" or "master craftsman" rather than one who has total control over that thing. We can see this especially in Tom Bombadil, who is the opposite of the latter meaning of master; his joking, child-like demeanor suggests a power that comes from understanding rather than dominating nature.

One way Tolkien connects nature to his various creatures is through his deeply symbolic use of trees. This connection encompasses even the most urban part of Middle-earth through the White Trees of Gondor. The trees' genealogy goes all the way back to the tree Galathilion, which was made in the image of Telperion, one of the two trees that provided light for Valinor after the destruction of the enormous lamps that once lit Arda (the Earth that included Middle-earth). The Valar, Yavanna, created Galathilion in Tirion, the city of the Noldor in the Undying Lands. Over the history of Númenór and Gondor, descendants of this tree stayed with the cities that the Númenóreans built. In one way, the trees' connection with the Undying Lands is part of the way that Tolkien re-enchants reality. Still, this re-enchantment takes the form of a tree, an obvious symbol of nature and the natural world. In both, the original tree in Tirion and the descendant trees in Armenolos and Minas Tirith are placed in the middle of cities to symbolically connect nature to city life, which makes sense since the cities themselves were also famous for their gardens and green spaces. Not only do these trees symbolize the harmonious connection between urban life and nature, they also symbolize the moral health of the cities. In morally degraded cities or cities with immoral leadership, the trees weaken, while they flourish during times of good morals and leadership. Thus, the White Trees of Gondor act as a holistic symbol: for man's relationship with the holy, with the natural world, and with the moral absolutes that determine the health of a society.

Trees play a symbolic role in other societies in Middle-earth as well. For instance, the hobbits have their Party Tree, which is the geographic and social center of their community. After Saruman has the tree cut down, Sam replaces it with a mallorn tree, which revives the Shire's social life. The Lothlórien elves' relationship with their mallorn trees is also richly symbolic. They come from Tol Erressëa and are associated with the Undying Lands. At one time both the Númenóreans and elves cultivated them, but they are most famous in Lothlórien, which translated as "Golden Wood," means that the place was named for them. The elves live with and love the trees beyond their usefulness. Interestingly, Tolkien's description of Lothlórien almost always centered on the elusive beauty of the mallorn trees. Tolkien describes the Fellowship of the Ring's first glimpse of the eaves of Lothlórien in this way, "Under the night the trees stood tall before them, arched over the road and stream that run suddenly beneath their spreading boughs. In the dim light of the stars their stems were grey, and their quivering leaves a hint of fallow gold."[30] Later Tolkien describes the ineffable beauty of Lothlórien using mostly negation,

> It seemed to him that he had stepped through a high window that looked on a vanished world. A light was upon it for which his language had no name. All that he saw was shapely, but the shapes seemed at once clear cut, as if they had been conceived and drawn at the uncovering of his eyes, and ancient as if they endured forever... On the land of Lórien there was no stain.[31]

Note how many times Tolkien uses negatives to describe Lothlórien: "vanished," "no name," and "no stain." His image of shapes, both radically new and ancient, simultaneously creates a paradoxical place outside of time. In the end, however, Tolkien is describing a forest. This language of ineffability lends a weighty power to the natural world. It is through imagery like this that Tolkien demonstrates that the value of parts of the world like trees transcends their simple use-value.

It is not a coincidence that trees played such an important part in Tolkien's legendarium; Tolkien famously was obsessed with trees and their significance. In fact, Tolkien's symbolic use of trees is part of his genius for making his utopian and ecological ideas believable and concrete. Trees for Tolkien and many of his readers have become what has been known as a "condensed symbol." Political scientist Doris Graber defines a condensed symbol in her book *Verbal Behavior in Politics* as "a name, word, phrase, or maxim which stirs vivid impressions involving the listener's most basic values and readies the listener for action."[32] For example, political phrases like "family values" or "cultural diversity" imply a whole series of symbolic values that greatly exceed the denotative meaning of the words. Tolkien uses trees as a non-verbal condensed symbol for fundamental environmental, social, and political values. Trees have a three-fold symbolic significance—representing harmony with nature, the connection with the transcendent, and political legitimacy. The connection with nature is obvious since they are the living part of the natural world. The transcendent symbolism comes from the mythology of *The Silmarillion* where the Valar create trees as a central part of Tolkien's world mythology. Further, the residual sacralizing of trees is a fundamental part of many world religions, especially Germanic, pagan religions. Trees' connection with political legitimacy, however, is more subtle. As one of the oldest organisms on earth, trees represent a continuity from past to current generations. Their growth or decline can thus reflect the flourishing or waning of the society. The richness of the symbolism of trees is key to Tolkien anchoring these associations into a condensed symbol. To carelessly cut down trees in Middle-earth signals a person's contempt for nature, God, and the past of his or her political community.

We can see how this condensed symbol works in the decline of the Númenórean civilization. One of the reasons the Númenóreans needed moral barometers like the White Trees was that even societies that started out as good were capable of heading down a path that led to environmental degradation and ruin. As is often the case, it is the race of men, in-between saintly elves and devilish orcs, that Tolkien uses to show how destruction of the environment, and specifically trees, can lead to disaster. In its desire to extract resources, in this case, timber, Númenór starts down its path to destruction as an imperial power in Middle-earth. At first, the Númenóreans come to the people of Middle-earth as benefactors, but quickly descend into colonizers who hunt down and enslave the indigenous peoples of the mainland and wantonly destroy the forests of Middle-earth. The Númenóreans had needed timber in the first place because they had cut down most of the trees on their own island in their pursuit of maritime glory. Later, the Númenóreans' continued imperialism led to their conflict with, capture of, and seduction by Sauron. Still, as we have seen, the first step down the path to evil began with an attack on the environment in order to fulfill purely instrumental desires. Not surprisingly, one of the last steps down this path of error and evil involves destroying Nimloth the Fair, the White Tree of Númenór. This destruction symbolizes the last king of Númenór's, Ar-Pharazôn, rejection of his friendship with the elves, his desire to sacrifice all of nature for power, and his desire to cut himself off from the continuity of the earlier kings of Númenór. Still, this is only the last step in a long progression. The desires of the Kings of Númenór become more and more unlimited, starting with commodities like timber, and ending with a desire for unlimited life itself.

Tolkien also suggests that this instrumental approach to the environment creates blowback for those who try to "extract everything possible" from nature, as Pope Francis says. In *The Silmarillion*, first the Valar and then Eru Ilúvatar remake Middle-earth twice after transgressions by Morgoth and the men of Númenór to end the First and the Second Ages, respectively. In Middle-earth, the Valar do not normally interfere with the lives of men and elves, so free will is allowed. Even so, some transgressions are so great that they cause destruction. Note that these "remakings" involve natural phenomena like earthquakes and tsunamis rather than some obviously supernatural force. Eventually, Morgoth and the Númenóreans' violations of the natural world are paid back by natural forces. At the end of the First Age, both Thangorodrim and large parts of Beleriand are destroyed and sunk beneath the waves. Not coincidentally, the lands that are destroyed, those of Morgoth and the Sons of Fëanor, are the lands of those who had done the most to destroy the Middle-earth of the First Age. Eru Ilúvatar himself remakes the Earth to punish the presumption of the Númenóreans. Not only is the Island of Númenór destroyed, but Eru changes the very shape of the world from flat to round. The Valar's changing of the world in the First Age in their final battle with Morgoth can be interpreted as the result of the blowback that comes from violating nature. The Valar's identity as guardians of the different parts of the natural world: Manwë, the air; Ulmo, the waters; Varda, the heavens, and so on, suggests that their coming to defeat Morgoth meant that the very aspects of nature itself rebelled against Morgoth's triumph in Middle-earth. In the remaking of the world in the Second Age, the change in the world is not so obviously a reaction to the destruction of the natural world as it is in the First Age. After all, the Númenóreans are allowed to ravish large parts of Middle-earth, and Eru only destroys them when they violate the Ban of the Valar and sail to the West and the Undying Lands. Still, the underlying transgression of the Númenóreans is the same when they deforested large parts of Middle-earth and when they attempt to gain eternal life: the desire to have more than what is allotted to them either by nature or God.

This theme of nature striking back carries on into the Third Age as well. The most obvious example is the ents marching on Isengard and destroying Saruman's industrial center, and the Hourns overwhelming the Uruk-hai at the Battle of the Hornburg. We also see an earthquake and the eruption of Mount Doom when Gollum falls into the Cracks of Doom and destroys the Ring of Power. The volcano's eruption destroys the ringwraiths, and the earthquake destroys Sauron's tower, Barad-dûr. Much of the final destruction of the forces of Mordor occurs due to natural phenomena rather than military defeat. The implication is that long-term destruction of nature can have acute, violent, and sudden consequences for those who harm the environment.

Of course, the idea of sudden environmental destruction brought on by humans is a recurring theme in the environmental movement as well, especially in regard to climate change. Many popular science documentaries like *An Inconvenient Truth* and even disaster movies like *The Day After Tomorrow* depend on a theme of a sudden natural disaster caused by human activity. This human activity is often presented morally rather than descriptively. In *The Day After Tomorrow*, for example, the crusading scientist uses language about the evils of greenhouse gases that more resembles the jeremiads of a prophet than the often clinical language employed by most climate scientists. This is one case where the modern environmental movement and Tolkien have a similar approach.

Just as he provides a condensed symbol of good societies living in harmony with nature, the Divine, and the community in the tree, Tolkien also provides a condensed symbol of a society alienated from all these goods—that of the treeless wasteland. The natural result of these evil societies, like Thangorodrim and Mordor, is to create these deserts, but the environmental destruction of these wastelands also symbolizes something well beyond the mere fact of this destruction. I argued earlier that one of the characteristics of evils is substituting a greater good for a lesser one. We see this especially in Sauron's choices: he chooses the ability to terrorize over persuading (substituting his beautiful form in the Second Age to an ugly and terrifying one in the Third), power over bodily integrity, and control for psychic division (Sauron starts as a powerful whole and divides his power through his rings and other means to gain control). The most absolute example of this substitution is the fertile land of Middle-earth for the Wastelands of Thangorodrim or Mordor. This is the final choice of death over life after a series of substitutions of the lesser for the greater.

On a larger scale, this substitution of the lesser for the greater has been going on throughout the history of Middle-earth even with the "good" races. In her book *Splintered Light*, Verilyn Fiegler describes this deterioration through the metaphor of light splintering and dividing from its original source in God. Her analysis suggests that not only does this weakening imply a moral deterioration, but an intellectual one as well. She analyzes *The Silmarillion* using Owen Barfield's theories about language. Barfield argues that at one time words included their metaphorical, spiritual, and literal meanings bound together, and only as language developed did abstractions like "hot" get separated from concrete things like "fire." In the same way, myths were also more unified and became separated and degraded into the various versions we have today.[33] All this reflects the "splintering," as things and ideas lose their holistic sense and power, as suggested by Fiegler's title. The resulting words, ideas, and myths still have beauty and power in them but in an attenuated form. In the long history of Middle-earth, we see a similar progression of separations, divisions, and weakening. *The Silmarillion* describes how at first the world is lit by lamps, then by two trees, and finally the sun and moon. All these are devolutions from the original and more beautiful predecessor. Valinor and Middle-earth are connected in Arda, then the world is changed in the First Age, and the island of Númenór was created between Middle-earth and Valinor, finally Númenór was destroyed and Valinor was forever separated from the lands of the mortals. The city of Tirion upon Túna is memorialized as Gondolin in Middle-earth and finally reflects even more weakly in Imladris's (Rivendell) "Last Homely House" and how the tree Telperion's descendant is Nimloth, whose descendants become the White Trees of Gondor. One could go on for much longer tracing this pattern of diminished repetition in Tolkien's work. The further away people move from God and Creation, the more they will degrade Creation *itself*. This truly brings to life Tolkien's contention that he "did not expect 'history' to be anything but a long defeat."[34]

I started this chapter describing the specific differences between Tolkien's view of environmental stewardship and the views of many in the environmental movement. I hope by now that you see that these specific differences come from much broader philosophical differences. Tolkien does not pit man against nature as part of separate, incommensurate realms, unlike many current environmentalists. Instead, he sees the forces that would destroy and diminish nature as part of the same evil that would destroy and diminish persons. Instead of assuming that the very presence of people would degrade nature, Tolkien argues that a truly "civilized" people (like elves) would enhance rather than destroy the natural world. In the twenty-first century as in Middle-earth, we are following a trajectory away from God and Creation and toward destruction and emptiness. In chapter 2, I argued that the world that Tolkien created resembles the biblical world in that it was "progressive" rather than "cyclical" like many earlier pagan models. My argument does not imply that this definition of "progress" is the same one that many contemporary people hold today. This current definition of progress assumes a Whig view of history that sees people heading toward an ever more free and comfortable society. Tolkien's view is, on the whole, rather more tragic.

It is not, however, completely so. I left out the second part of Tolkien's quote, where he says, "Though it [the long defeat] contains (and legend may contain it more clearly and movingly) some samples or glimpses of final victory." The "samples or glimpses," whether they be Lothlórien or Rivendell or the First White Tree of Gondor, are still worth preserving for their own sake. The damage that has been done can be, to a certain extent, healed. The restoration of Ithilien at the end of *The Lord of the Rings* shows how this is possible. The "final victory" Tolkien discusses is the Parousia rather than utopia, but again I think for many people Tolkien's "samples and glimpses" of good societies like Valinor, Lothlórien, and even the humble Shire appear more real than, say, William Morris's complete environmental program in his eco-utopia, *News from Nowhere*. As I argue earlier, the very precariousness of the goodness of these societies makes them seem more tangible. I also think that their existence as echoes and copies of more utopian forebears ironically makes them more believable to Tolkien's readers. Just a walk in an isolated old growth forest seems to bring back primeval memories that suggest a world of forests that are larger and darker than the remnants left in the world today. Tolkien's isolated images of environmental tranquility tap into Edenic memories of a prelapsarian Paradise, but in a way that suggests an even larger canvas exists or existed elsewhere.

Tolkien makes just this point in his short story "Leaf by Niggle." In it, an artist concentrates on creating a painting of a tree with a forest in the distance only to have his work frustrated by the demands of everyday life (especially his needy neighbor). The artist eventually has to go on a trip (a metaphor for death) even though he has not completed his painting and recuperate at an institution (a metaphor for Purgatory). In the end, he finds all of his painting has been destroyed but a single leaf. Eventually, Niggle is released from the institution and allowed to rest (go to Heaven). Here, he finds the whole tree he has been trying to create all these years in all its completeness and perfection, much better than his artistic attempt. Niggle is offered a chance to care for this tree and make it even more beautiful and complete. In the distance is the vast forest of Niggle's imagination that he cannot begin to comprehend. He also learns that he will have the opportunity to make the forest more beautiful as well. Tolkien's metaphors of the tree and the forest encompass the artistic desire for perfection, the impossibility of completing a great work of art, as well as the vast distance between an artistic vision and the finished product.

Beyond the Platonic interpretation, the story suggests an ecological interpretation as well. Niggle's perfectionism causes him to miss how his artistic vision fits into larger picture of the world. This narrowness of vision can extend to how people treat the environment when they focus on only one part of it. In a broader sense, the story is also a metaphor for how ecology is not only interconnected but larger than we can possibly comprehend—that, like Tolkien's vistas, nature is always somehow beyond our grasp. The story also reinforces the importance of subcreation and the attempt to understand what we can of the world. In the story, a small part of Niggle's creation has been preserved in the "real" world. Of all Niggle's work, only a single leaf has been preserved, but because Niggle strove to make each leaf on his tree unique, it still has enough value for the people still living in the world that it has been preserved in a museum. The leaf also represents the utopian fragment in the sense that it is an incomplete vision of a vaster canvas, but one that was done with absolute care. Tolkien's legendarium is one example of his "leaf." Another is Tolkien's attempt to conserve the trees in his "real" neighborhood (he urged neighbors not to cut down trees, even old and overgrown ones). Note how bound up the desire to preserve the environment in "Leaf by Niggle" comes from the assumption that the good man and the artist are allied with the environment, not rivals to it.

Central to Tolkien's utopianism is an environmental vision mediated through his Catholic faith. His approach to the environment appears similar to many past and current environmentalists, but ironically his underlying philosophy is at odds with most in the environmental movement. The most obvious place one can see this difference is Tolkien's approach to humanity's relationship with the environment. While many modern environmentalists have a zero-sum view of the relationship between people and the environment, Tolkien does not treat people as the enemy of nature. On an even more fundamental level, he not only avoids the assumption held by many environmentalists that humans and nature are pitted against each other. Instead, he challenges the assumption that humans are somehow outside of, or beyond, nature. In some ways, Tolkien's foundation myths in *The Silmarillion* (both humans and other "species" like elves and dwarves) make this point even clearer than the Bible by connecting the creation of people seamlessly with the creation of the rest of the natural world. Still, for the most part, Tolkien's narrative's approach to the environment mirrors most Christian theology, especially the theology of the Catholic Church. Once again, the similarities between the Catholic Church's approach to the environment and Tolkien's approach can be seen most easily in their fundamental philosophical assumptions. The Catholic Church's concerns, as far back as the Middle Ages, involved limiting man's desires for power and knowledge. Later, in the industrial nineteenth century, these translated into fears about workers' treatment as mere parts of the industrial process rather than as persons with individual rights and responsibilities. Finally, in the twentieth and twenty-first centuries, papal statements and encyclicals warned of treating nature, as well as people, in this instrumental way. The development of doctrine is clear throughout this progression: the Church's concern is that the desire for power will lead to crossing boundaries that will result in damage to individuals and society. These limits all focus on recognizing that both people and the natural world have value outside of their immediate utility. Tolkien's evil societies use people and nature as products to be consumed to create power (though this power is often illusory). His good societies respect people and cooperate with the natural world to allow creation to develop its inherent beauty. The distinction between Tolkien and many environmentalists is that Tolkien's concern is not with the "environment" (a typical modern word that strips nature of its transcendent meaning) but with "Creation" (a word that assumes a connection between the divine and the material world). Tolkien's connecting of his good societies with this transcendent nature makes them more than just "environmentally conscious" as we would say today; this connection makes them utopian.

NOTES

1. Stephen Jarvis, "Live Long and Die Out," *The Independent*, 23 April 1994.
2. There are several additional strains of the environmental movement that are important now but are not relevant to my analysis in this chapter. For example, the part of the environmental movement that focuses on climate change and limiting greenhouse gases is quite different from the other strains I have discussed. Though it might seem similar to the Carsonian approach to pesticides, it is actually from a different wing of the environmental movement. Many of the people concerned about global warming offer technocratic solutions like carbon-pricing, tax rebates for "green" technology, and so on that are different from the regulatory approach favored by earlier environmentalists. This form of environmentalism shows how environmentalism has moved from the counterculture to the heart of the establishment. Not surprisingly, this approach is not only favored by many environmentalists, but many corporations as well because such policies might create future business opportunities. They also draw much more from the business, academic, economic, and social elites that were often the targets of the environmental movement of the 1960s.
   In addition, a minority of environmentalists would fit quite well with Tolkien's philosophical assumptions. E. F. Schumacher's *Small Is Beautiful* captures some of the spirit of Tolkien's approach to the environment, as do certain strains of the "crunchy

con" traditionalism of thinkers like Wendell Berry, which I briefly quoted in this chapter. I will discuss these thinkers in more detail in relation to Tolkien's localism in chapter 5. Still, except for the anti–global warming movement, I think these are relatively minor strains in the environmental movement compared to the more mainstream environmental groups like the World Wildlife Fund, Greenpeace, and Friends of the Earth.

3. One cannot help but be struck by the similarity between Arnor and Western Europe shortly after the Fall of Rome (fifth to ninth centuries) and Gondor to the Eastern Roman Empire during a similar period. First, obviously the split between the North and South Númenórean kingdoms looks a lot like a similar split between the Western and Eastern Roman Empire. The rapid fall in material standards of living and the depopulation of that period in Northern Gaul and Britain after the fall of the Western Roman Empire (see the excellent *The Fall of Rome and the End of Civilization* by Bryan Ward-Perkins for the material evidence for this decline) match a very similar collapse in population of Arnor. Even the residual nostalgia for "the king" and the fear of traveling a few miles outside one's village have a familiar early Middle Ages feel about them. One of Tolkien's earliest language obsessions was with Gothic, which was exactly from this period, so he did have an understanding of this period and its people.

Gondor also has many similarities with the Byzantine civilization. Besides its Mediterranean climate, Gondor is a civilization that has ebbed and flowed based on challenges from serious rivals from the East. Despite facing similar issues with depopulation, Gondor also has a city in Minas Tirith that is almost impregnable like Constantinople, which survived many times throughout the Middle Ages because of its excellent defensive fortifications and geographic position.

Of course, there are many differences and Tolkien would have no more liked this comparison than he would the popular 1950s assumption that his works were a metaphor for World War II. Númenóreans were less corrupt than the late Roman Empire, there were no "barbarian" invasions in Arnor and Gondor, and the principal city of Gondor was Osgiliath, not Minas Tirith. I certainly do not think that Tolkien constructed these similarities between Arnor/Gondor and the Eastern/Western Roman Empire as a metaphor or worse yet an allegory (a literary form Tolkien particularly loathed), while I think Tolkien used his extensive knowledge of the early Middle Ages to paint a convincing picture of civilizations in decline and crisis.

4. Wendell Berry, "Conservation Is Good Work," *Sex, Economy, Freedom, & Community* (New York: Pantheon Books, 1993), 34.

5. The exception to this rule are the dwarves, who were not created as part of this world, but later fashioned by Aulë, one of the Valar. Even so, Aulë fashioned them out of the elements of the world, so dwarves also have an intrinsic connection with Creation. One could argue that creatures like orcs, trolls, or dragons were also "created" later by Morgoth, but this is not true since Morgoth cannot "create" in the true sense "out of nothing" but only alter already existing creation.

6. My citing of the "Judeo-Christian" tradition in favor of ex nihilo creation is a bit of a simplification. Genesis 1, for example, states that "the earth was formless and darkness was over the surface of the deep." This suggests that there was "something" to be formed and some "surface" and "deep" from which the world was created despite the dogma that the world was created out of nothing. Still, the position of many Jewish authorities and certainly the Catholic Church was that it was "out of nothing." As I will discuss in some length in chapter 4, myths have a tendency to contradict and complicate the dogmatic beliefs of the very religions that the myths were founded upon.

7. One could argue that certain Christian theologians' emphases on original sin can suggest that creation is evil. Even some of the letters of Saint Paul, with his contrasts between the world of the "flesh" and the world of the "spirit," suggest that Creation is inherently evil or corrupting. Still, Christian doctrine, like the resurrection

of the body and the very words of Genesis where God declares creation as "good," suggests otherwise.

8. Does that mean that Tolkien's metaphysics in *The Silmarillion* and *The Lord of the Rings* are somehow not Christian or Judeo-Christian? Tolkien insisted that they were pre-Christian yet compatible with Christianity. He also did not consider himself a theologian and did not want his work judged on that basis, but rather as a work of art. No doubt certain details of Tolkien's mythology, like the inherent evil of Middle-earth and the moral irredeemability of orcs, are difficult to fit within a completely orthodox Christian framework, but the overall shape of his universe is both remarkably original and orthodox.

9. J.R.R. Tolkien, *The Silmarillion*, ed. Christopher Tolkien (London: Ballantine Books, 1999), 77.

10. Eleanor R. Simpson, "The Evolution of J.R.R. Tolkien's Portrayal of Nature: Foreshadowing Anti-Speciesism," *Tolkien Studies* 14 (2017): 74–75.

11. Tolkien, *The Silmarillion*, 37.

12. The trial of Galileo, the Index of Forbidden Books, and the various Inquisitions are all examples of where the Catholic Church's attempts to police intellectual boundaries were wrong and severely damaged its credibility.

13. Tennyson's famous poem *Ulysses* takes the Dante story as its starting point rather than *The Odyssey*. Ironically, the poem is now widely read as a paean to the human spirit of adventure despite the ambivalence Tennyson brings to the poem when read carefully. This reflexive adulation of transgressing boundaries shows how different the spirit of our time is from when Dante wrote *The Inferno*.

14. I want to be careful here and not imply that Enlightenment thinkers themselves advocated freedom to the point of license. On the contrary, Enlightenment thinkers from Hobbes, to Locke, to the American Founding Fathers, were very concerned about balancing freedom with other "goods," whether they be security, or property, or absence of mob rule. Still, the logic inherent in determining these limits by "reason" has led generally to an erosion of this balance.

15. Right now an embryo over two weeks cannot be used in experiments in Great Britain. This is a law, but only an informal rule in most places like the United States. Still, these rules have a tendency to erode over time, especially if direct benefits appear based on the research.

16. There are some exceptions where this strict utilitarian approach does not appear to win out. For example, chemical, biological, and nuclear warfare has been mostly restrained (though the former has been sporadically violated in the Middle East in the recent past). Eugenics (at least of the negative variety) has also been mostly discarded since the early twentieth century. Still, the particularities of these exceptions are illuminating as well. Chemical, biological, and nuclear warfare (especially the latter) because of the MAD (mutually assured destruction) doctrine often does not pass the test of utilitarian benefit. As for eugenics, it took its association with Nazis, one of the most morally reprehensible regimes of the twentieth century, to morally discredit it. The rejection of eugenics was also helped by the fact that current methods were not scientifically effective. It will be interesting to see if these prohibitions remain in place with potentially more effective gene-editing procedures, like CRISPR, that make eugenic interventions more practicable.

17. Predictably, based on the logic of utilitarian calculation, these bans have been progressively softened over the years. Utilitarian thinking tends to ignore all but the most serious harms and tries to find the least disruptive solutions (financially). Therefore, market-based cap-and-trade schemes have become more popular instead of outright bans.

18. Leo XIII, *Rerum Novarum* (Vatican City: Liberia Editrice Vaticana, 1891), 20.

19. Pius XI, *Quadragesimo Anno* (Vatican City: Liberia Editrice Vaticana, 1931), 135.

20. John Paul II, "Address on the XXIII World Day of Peace" (Vatican City, Liberia Editrice Vaticana, 1990), 7.

21. Francis I, *Laudato Si* (Vatican City: Liberia Editrice Vaticana, 2015), 8, 33, 39.

22. Francis I, *Laudato Si*, 75–76.
23. Francis I, *Laudato Si*, 77.
24. Another way to look at this is that Pope Francis is extending Kant's categorical imperative from persons to the natural world, that we should never look at nature as a mere "means to an end" but as ends in itself.
25. Tom Shippey, *J.R.R. Tolkien: Author of the Century* (Wilmington: Mariner Books, 2002), 171.
26. J.R.R. Tolkien to Robert Murray, December 2, 1953, in *The Letters of J. R. R. Tolkien*, ed. Christopher Tolkien (Boston: Houghton Mifflin Harcourt, 2000), 191.
27. One can see how deep and pervasive religion is in the medieval worldview in narratives like *The Canterbury Tales*. Even the worldliest characters in the *Tales*, like the Wife of Bath, describe their world in the language of theology and religion. In her blasphemous Biblical arguments, in her participation in religious festivals and processions, in her references to saints, and even in her casual oaths, this notorious sinner references religion and God with more frequency and sincerity than the most pious church lady is likely to do today.
28. Indeed, since most art and entertainment are secular in the twenty-first century, it is not surprising that this worldview is being absorbed most consistently by current young people.
29. Michelangelo was famous for being able to "see" the statues lying dormant in the stones he selected. The stone he used to create his most famous statue "David" had been rejected by several sculptors for having too many flaws and had lain untouched for twenty-five years until Michelangelo saw its potential.
30. J.R.R. Tolkien, *The Fellowship of the Ring* (London: Ballantine, 1994), 378.
31. Tolkien, *The Fellowship of the Ring*, 393.
32. Doris Graber, *Verbal Behavior in Politics* (Champaign: University of Illinois Press, 1976), 288.
33. Verilyn Fiegler, *Splintered Light: Logos and Language in Tolkien's World* (Kent, OH: Kent State University Press, 2002), 36–41.
34. J.R.R. Tolkien to Amy Ronald, December 15, 1956, in *The Letters of J.R.R. Tolkien*, ed. Christopher Tolkien (Boston: Houghton Mifflin Harcourt, 2000), 273.

FOUR
Tolkien's Utopian and Dystopian Mythology

Throughout this book I have balanced my discussions of Tolkien's utopian visions with his dystopian ones. Based on my contention that Tolkien's legendarium consists of a series of falls and Tolkien's own statement in which he claimed that "I do not expect 'history' to be anything but a long 'defeat,'" one cannot help but suspect that Tolkien's convictions were more dystopian than utopian. This is ironic since many modern critics assume Tolkien is naively optimistic based on a superficial reading of *The Hobbit* and *The Lord of the Rings* (though it is difficult to imagine how one could continue to have this view after reading *The Silmarillion*). Tolkien's legendarium also mirrored this two-sided character. Tolkien's biographer, Humphrey Carpenter, claims that there were two sides to Tolkien: an outgoing, cheerful, and friendly exterior that masked a melancholy, reserved, and isolated interior. One could say that the journeys in Tolkien's tales mirror this two-sided nature as well, since they start off as places of comfort like Valinor and the Shire and move to places of terror like Thangorodrim and Mordor. Many of Tolkien's works are also the reverse of his personality, so that the interior spirit of his characters is where optimism and hope reside and the exterior world is where fear and despair lurk. No doubt, it is out of these two deep emotional currents that Tolkien created his imaginative world—one with the utopian themes from his optimistic exterior and one with dystopian themes from his pessimistic interior. For Tolkien, these deep emotions come out as myths, and as myths, which help him (and us) understand the world. This chapter shows how Tolkien relies on myth to create a series of narratives that can manage to be inviting and terrifying simultaneously. My contention is that Tolkien's good and bad societies are different from most classic utopias and dystopias because of this mythic approach to narrative.

Tolkien's choice to locate his narratives in the world of myth allows him to generalize about these societies while still making them deep and relevant to our own cultural situation. Indeed, his use of myth allows his legendarium to provide both positive and negative examples for his own society to follow as well as to avoid. Tolkien also uses his good societies' approaches to their myths (from earlier events and people of Middle-earth) to show how myths can inspire virtue and fortitude in ways that the programmatic tours featured in most utopian narratives cannot. In doing so, Tolkien also dismantles most people's modern relationships with myth, which because of its focus on validating individual desires, tends at best, to be solipsistic, and at worst, self-serving.

I realize I have used terms like "myth," "mythic," and "mythology" promiscuously throughout this book to describe Tolkien's sources and elements of his work, but I want to be more precise in what I mean by "myth." Myth has both a common definition and a more technical one. In common parlance, myth has been taken to mean anything that is untrue and especially ideas that have once had widespread currency, but now are no longer believed, for example, internet articles that describe "the ten most common myths about exercise." I do not mean it in that sense at all and agree that, in some sense, myths can be more "true" than, say, history. The more scholarly definition of myth preferred by many classicists and anthropologists is a story that helps define a people that involves supernatural events and deities. Often, myths also provide a group with examples of the culture's ideal behaviors in the deeds of a hero or group of heroes.[1]

I also need to define myth in relation to religion since my analysis often uses both religion and myth as similar, almost interchangeable, objects of analysis. Obviously, part of my justification for including religion under the umbrella of myths is that myths, by the definition I am using, involve "the supernatural and deities," which means that religious myths should be viewed as a subset of myths in general. Even though I have definitional justification because of the modern association between myths and fabrications, some might assume that I am denigrating religion when I analyze it alongside myth, but that is not my intention at all. My assumption, and one that Tolkien shared, is that myth sometimes includes elements of actual truth and nearly always possesses elements of metaphorical truth. One of the surprising findings of archeology since Heinrich Schliemann discovered Troy in Asia Minor is that some aspects of traditional oral legends and myths often can be confirmed by archeology. Beyond historicity of events, even individual personalities likely have been immortalized in myths. Tolkien speculates in his essay "On Fairy-Stories" how many idiosyncratic anthropomorphic qualities of the gods likely came from real people rather than mere abstractions or personifications of the natural world. In this way, "real" life can appear in myths, even in descriptions of deities. The most fantastic myths also can contain metaphorical truth even if the real event did not happen. Freudians would argue, for example, that the Oedipus story reflected "true" psychosocial tensions within the family whether or not the man, Oedipus, ever lived. Similarly, Cain and Abel's story contains truths about human violence, the nature of sibling rivalry, and even the relationship between pastoral and agricultural society.

When Tolkien started constructing his legendarium as a young man, he had just this sort of truth-telling national myth in mind. He confessed,

> I was from my early days grieved by the poverty of my own country: it had no stories of its own . . . Do not laugh! But once upon a time (my crest has long since fallen) I had a mind to make a body of more or less connected legend, ranging from the large and cosmogonic, to the level of romantic fairy-story . . . which I could dedicate simply to: to England, to my country.[2]

Tolkien's original ambition was to make a mythology for England to match the other great mythologies of the world. Tolkien was dissatisfied with the myths that did exist about England and the British Isles: he found the Celtic myths somewhat foreign (since they tended to be Welsh, Scottish, and especially Irish so therefore *not* English in his mind) and Arthurian myth too corrupted by French influence. In the end, as Tolkien's deprecatory remarks suggest, he was not successful in creating a mythology for England. The question then becomes: did he, in fact, create a mythology and, if so, how does its mythological character affect the way he presents his good and evil societies in Middle-earth?

My contention is that Tolkien did create a "mythology" that well matches his original ambitions, but it is not a mythology of England. Tolkien, in his earliest writings, like *The Book of Lost Tales*, does attempt to connect England to Middle-earth and even to the early Middle Ages. In one version, an Anglo-Saxon man named Eriol travels from what is now Norway, escapes his floundering ship, and washes up on the island Tol Eressëa. Clearly Tol Eressëa is meant to be England; so in his earliest version of his tales, Tolkien connects his legendarium to England both geographically and temporally. In contrast, in his later work, *The Silmarillion*, he removes any references to a particular time or place in England. Though Middle-earth retains its Northern European orientation, its time is made ever more remote and is ever more geographically vague. This is especially true since the "remakings" of Middle-earth by Eru Ilúvatar in the First and Second Ages make any references to current maps impossible. The Western Isles that were originally conceived as connected with a specific place, the British Isles, become the more mythological Undying Lands: whereas the Western Isles were more like an Elvish Middle-earth in Tolkien's original vision.

Even though Tolkien did not create a mythology for England, I think he did create a mythology in Middle-earth. Not only that, but these myths were not just intellectual abstractions; they act for Tolkien's audience in ways similar to ways other more "national" mythologies act toward their audiences. If you look at what Tolkien set out to do, "to make a body of more or less connected legend, ranging from the large and cosmogonic, to the level of romantic fairy-story that involves the supernatural events and deities," he succeeds. His *Silmarillion* is cosmogonic and *The Hobbit*, while not exactly "a fairy story," seems to fit its smaller scale, and he includes many stories in-between from tragedy (*Children of Húrin*), epic (*Beren and Lúthien*, the story of the silmarils, written both in prose and poetry), and even forms of the medieval chronicle (like the ones in Tolkien's appendices to *The Lord of the Rings*). Many of the stories involve the supernatural, though Tolkien's later works, including *The Hobbit* and *The Lord of the Rings*, contain much less direct reference to God or "gods." I also think that the way Tolkien's readers react to his narratives is much more like the way audiences react to myths rather than to other forms of literature.

One way this difference manifests itself is in the exegesis-like approach that many Tolkien admirers take to his work. Rather than engaging with Tolkien's works as narratives or as works of art, many Tolkien readers spend hours speculating over the minutiae of Middle-earth. I have already mentioned how intimidating it is to write a book about Tolkien knowing that likely quite a few non-academics have read much more than I have of both Tolkien's primary works and his criticism. In addition, many Tolkien societies, wikis, and conferences have been created, often by fans, to discuss all aspects of Tolkien's works. Of course, this extreme interest in the details of a particular work and the creation of vast archives of fan-based material is a common phenomenon among fans of a variety of pop-culture narratives like the *Star Wars* series, Harry Potter books, and the *Game of Thrones* miniseries and books.[3]

In some ways, these pop-culture phenomena are similar to the relationship between Tolkien's legendarium and Tolkien's readers, but some of the key differences suggest ways in which Tolkien's influence on his readers is unique. Just like fans of these pop-culture franchises, some Tolkien enthusiasts have built fanzines, websites, clubs, fanfiction, and fan art. In most cases, all these structures seem larger for Tolkien fans than for many other pop-culture franchises, but that could be as much because of the longer time that Tolkien has existed compared to these other pop-culture phenomena (though one could also argue that the longer period of time would give the enthusiasm for these works more time to dissipate as well). Also, certainly many of the recent manifestations of fan excitement for Tolkien and his works reflect interest in *The Lord of the Ring* and *Hobbit* movies rather than his books. Therefore, many people could argue that the interest in Tolkien's work is not that different in tone or quality than interest or speculation about other aspects of pop culture, like *Game of Thrones* or *Battlestar Galactica*.[4]

I believe that even though many readers' reactions to Tolkien's legendarium resemble generic reactions to popular literature phenomena, I also think that Tolkien's works generate unique responses that are different from the typical reactions to popular art. The difference is the "mythic" response that I described earlier. I have already defined myth as "the origin story of a people or an example of the people's ideal behavior through a hero or group of heroes." Yet how can Tolkien's narratives act as a "myth" in this way when his readers are anything but a clearly defined "people" and are instead a group that differs radically in nationality and ethnicity? The narratives he tells in *The Silmarillion, The Hobbit*, and *The Lord of the Rings* are not the story of a particular group, like the Torah is the story of the Jews, or *The Iliad* or *The Odyssey* is the story of the Greeks. Tolkien's writings also differ from the organic way in which myths are typically created over long periods of time and through uncertain authorship. Myths typically gain their power from their age. They also tend to start as oral narratives passed down from generation to generation. So, since Tolkien's legendarium was not written for a particular group and does not have the provenance of some ancient story, how can I say that it acts as a myth?

Tolkien's stories can be mythical because of how they answer the needs of his readers and how they operate at the level of symbolic belief rather than as a plausible facsimile of reality. Randel Helms, in his book *Tolkien's World*, writes extensively about how Tolkien's work is mythic and how Tolkien's own writings show his understanding of how to create narratives that have mythic qualities.[5] He argues that *The Hobbit* and *The Lord of the Rings* have a similar quest structure that is developed in the latter and perfected in the former. In both books, the central quest is not to find or discover something of value, as in most quest novels, but to renounce something in an act of self-sacrifice.[6] Helms argues that this renunciation is especially necessary in our times when we have the power to indiscriminately destroy nature and ourselves. I have already mentioned in chapters 1 and 2 how Tolkien's goal of resacralizing reality also fulfills a specific need to re-enchant our increasingly materialistic world. Thus, Tolkien's works can act as myths because they provide ways to re-moralize aspects of our society that have since been de-moralized, so to speak. For example, our society has mostly lost the ability to make moral arguments against the desire for the knowledge and power to understand, control, and remake the natural world. In other words, we have lost our moral vocabulary for abnegation. Perhaps even more importantly, which Tolkien's *The Lord of the Rings* and *The Hobbit* try to remedy, is that we have lost the moral imagination to see what abnegation "feels" like as a way of life rather than an intellectual argument. Especially, Tolkien's Ring of Power serves as a potent symbol for the temptations and dangers of unchecked desire and power. One of the most insidious aspects of the Ring of Power is that it gives its wearer what many people secretly want. Not only does the Ring give its victims a form of immortality, it also allows its wearers to escape from the confines of their existence by rendering them invisible and thus able to avoid the consequences of their actions (ironically this invisibility does not work for truly evil creatures like Sauron and his Ringwraiths). The Ring also has a psychological effect of giving its wearers the confidence that their desires can and should be fulfilled. Finally, the Ring allows its wearers to eventually transcend their own physical limitations and become disembodied spirits. Of course, *The Lord of the Rings* makes it clear that these desires are wrong and produce misery, but is it not surprising how many of these desires seem familiar to early twentieth-first-century readers? The desire to transcend the body and be free from its physical and moral limitations is a perennial theme of the increasingly popular transhumanist movement. The disembodied spirits of the Ringwraiths bear more than a passing resemblance to the dreams of transhumanists who imagine themselves transcending the limits of time and space by uploading themselves into computer code. Both the kings of men in Middle-earth, seduced by Sauron's rings, and the modern-day futurists, like Ray Kurzweil, are ready to trade in their embodied humanity for immortality and power.

Not only did Helms write about myth in relation to Tolkien's works, Tolkien himself wrote extensively about myth, though not in relation to his own legendarium. In "On Fairy-Stories," Tolkien explains that much of what is important about fantasy (of which he considered myth a part) cannot be put into words. As he argues, "Faërie cannot be caught in a net of words; for it is one of its qualities to be indescribable, but not imperceptible."[7] Not only is the fairy world indescribable, according to Tolkien, it is unclassifiable. Fairy, in Tolkien's meaning, is indistinguishable from myth; therefore, he resists the division that some critics and folklorists have used to separate the fairy world into myth, fantasy, and folklore. The one word Tolkien *does* use to describe "Faërie" is "perilous," and he goes to great pains to distinguish what he views as the seriousness and dangers of fairyland from the Shakespearean and Victorian tendency to diminish fairies into little child-like creatures.[8] Instead, he argues that fairy tales and myths tap into "primordial human desires" and that part of their appeal comes from their very ancientness. He also argues that these stories are not just for children or for primitive people, but for adults and especially "modern men" because they both satisfy and whet unbearable desires. Tolkien claims that fantasy, if done well, allows its audience entrance into another world, not through Samuel Taylor Coleridge's "suspension of disbelief," but through a willingness to become immersed in a secondary world. Desires that fantasy can satisfy for modern people are the need for recovery, escape, and consolation. Tolkien defines recovery as "regaining a clear view," which comes from people's ability to see the beauty in ordinary things. Fantasy rehabilitates people's understanding of how to see things like a child, not in the sense of being childish, but in the sense of being open to the wonders of the world. He argues, "We should meet the centaur and the dragon, and then perhaps suddenly behold, like the ancient shepherds, sheep, and dogs, and horses—and wolves."[9] Tolkien also talks about fantasy as a means of escape. By "escape," Tolkien does not mean escapism, but an escape from the warped and unjust reality that is often described as "real life." He compares the escape that fantasy often provides to an escape from a prison or a police state, as opposed to the "desertion" from real life. Finally, fantasy offers its audience a consolation in the form of a "eucatastrophe," which is a happy ending brought about by "a sudden joyous turn" that despite its alignment with the desires of the reader is "never to be counted on to recur."[10] Fairy-tales like Cinderella marrying her prince or Jack defeating the giant gain their power from the sudden shift from certain disaster to unexpected triumph. These fairy tales also work because they and other fairy stories, like "The Little Mermaid," acknowledge the tragic possibility of dyscatastrophe, where the sad ending triumphs, as it often does in Tolkien's own works, where tragedies and bittersweet triumphs both exist in abundance.

Because Tolkien argues that the genre of "fairy stories" is a broader category than just children's tales, he includes myths, historical legends, and folk tales in his examples of the appeal of fairy tales. Therefore, he discusses clearly mythical figures like Thor in his analysis, as well as historical figures who have become "mythologized," like Arthur and Hrothgar. More importantly, Tolkien argues that the category these stories are put into, whether myth, fairy, or folk-tale, does not matter as much as their purpose. Tolkien instead argues that the precise atmosphere and details of the story are what make an effective tale, what he describes as "the soup," that is, the story itself, rather than "the bones," that is, the old legends from which the story was created. What Tolkien particularly objects to is treating stories like an archeological site to gain inferences about the people who made the stories. He argues that myth and fantasy are not important because they allow the reader to speculate about the past, and contends instead that modern people need myths more than the people of the past.

Tolkien's approach to mythology differs markedly from the more typical mythical analysis championed by writers like Joseph Campbell in *The Hero with a Thousand Faces*. In it, Campbell connects various mythologies with a variety of broad themes like the "hero's journey" or the "descent into the underworld." Campbell often ignores the specifics of the mythology ("the soup," to use Tolkien's terms) to concentrate on "the bones" of the mythology. He also ignores the parts of the story that most interested Tolkien in fairy tales: the language, the details, and the atmosphere. The difference suggests a different philosophy of interpretation. As Tolkien argues,

> It is indeed easier to unravel a single *thread*—an incident, a name, a motive—than to trace the history of any *picture* defined by many threads. For with the picture in the tapestry a new element has come in: the picture is greater than, and not explained by the sum of the component threads. Therein lies the inherent weakness of the analytic (or "scientific") method; it finds out much about the things that occur in stories, but little or nothing about their effect in any given story.[11]

Finding and comparing single narrative "threads" (to use Tolkien's terminology) across multiple cultures and mythological systems is Campbell's modus operandi. Because of this, the implication is that these individual threads are more important than the picture they create. Campbell's method also tends to reduce mythical narratives to a series of tropes with a simple symbolic value rather than works of art where the different elements of the story work together to create an artistic effect that is greater than its individual parts. Tolkien has often described his distrust of the critical tendency to dismantle the edifice of stories in search of abstracted elements. Tolkien uses a similar metaphor of destructive unraveling in his essay about Beowulf, "The Monsters and the Critics," in which he complains that critics of *Beowulf* are like archeological vandals who destroy a beautiful tower looking for hidden inscriptions or carvings.

Campbell's analytical method, which focuses on individual elements of myth, comes from Carl Jung's theory of archetypes, which has become the most influential way of interpreting mythology and folktales throughout the humanities. According to Jung, archetypes are common mental images that appear in mythology across all cultures. Mythology in Jung's theory is an irruption of people's universal fears and desires from their unconscious minds. Because these images are universal in Jung's theory, they create what he calls a "collective unconscious," which means that all people share these images (in the sense of genetic inheritance or original sin). Jung also argues that interpreting mythology and bringing into consciousness what these images mean can be a way to self-actualization. He calls this "individuation." Jung's three elements, archetypes, their universality, and the therapeutic nature of myth interpretation are central to the way many contemporary people relate to myths and, increasingly, to religion.

Campbell's adherence to Jungian theory of archetypes and his emphasis on the utility of myths differ from Tolkien's approach. Campbell argues in *Pathways to Bliss* that myths have several functions: "to evoke in the individual a sense of grateful, affirmative awe before the monstrous mystery that is existence," to provide an "image of the cosmos" to help produce this awe, to back the morality of the culture that created the mythology, and finally to help the individual psychologically move through the stages of his or her life. Even though Campbell's four functions of myths seem to have some surface resemblance to Tolkien's view of mythology as escape, recovery, and consolation, Campbell's categories miss what Tolkien sees as the most important part of myth. Part of what Campbell misses comes from his emphasis on efficacy of myths in answering psychological and social needs. Like Jung, Campbell primarily views myths as functional—as ways to help individuals and societies cope with the realities of the world. Therefore, these myths are true insofar as they are useful. That is why he argues that since science has replaced myth as a way to make an "image of the cosmos," myth (and, by myth, Campbell mostly means Christianity) has lost much of its resonance. It would be a mistake, however, to assume that Campbell's analysis of myth is descriptive rather than proscriptive. For example, what Campbell defines as useful also looks suspiciously like what allows individuals the most freedom and comfort. One can see this in the way Campbell approaches the various religious myths. Campbell's approach to different religions and their myths is irenic and ad hoc except for one notable exception. Campbell is comfortable evoking Taoist philosophers, Native American legends, and parts of the Bible to create his personal myth of the hero. Still, while he does not challenge the metaphysical assumptions of almost any mythological system or faith tradition, Campbell makes one noteworthy exception: the Roman Catholic Church. In *Pathways to Bliss*, Campbell faults the Catholic Church (and to a lesser extent, other Christian churches) for two things: its failure to change its dogma on contraceptives and its insistence that Christian redemption takes place in historical time rather than in an indeterminate mythical time. Not surprisingly, these objections stem from the way each of these claims in its own way makes the Christian believer subservient to the narrative of Christian salvation rather than the reverse. The contraceptive claim depends on a reading of church tradition that goes back to the earliest pronouncements of the church (such as the Didache) and one that ignores the convenience of modern medical innovations such as the oral contraceptive pill. In a similar way, the historic claims of the church that Jesus was a specific man born in a specific time and place (hence the insistence of Christian churches to name a historic figure, Pontius Pilate, in their Creeds) orient Christ in history. In other words, the Christian churches insist on contextualizing what Campbell wants to decontextualize. This context makes the believer subservient to the narrative in ways that make Campbell uncomfortable. Myths that have concrete details and enduring claims lose much of their flexibility as a way to personal fulfillment because they place demands on the believer rather than provide a narrative for the believer's desires.

    This contrast between myth as primarily a way of finding personal fulfillment or meaning and myth as primarily a paradigm for challenging the individual to fit him or herself into the confines of a greater narrative highlights the contrast between myth as therapeutic psychology and myth as religion. The relationship between myth and religion is a complex one. I mentioned earlier that the layman's definition of myth is "a lie," so there is a tendency in more secular parts of our society to equate the two. This was C. S. Lewis's approach in his debate with Tolkien before Lewis's conversion back to Christianity in which he famously defined myth as "lies breathed through silver" and therefore worthless as propositions of truth. In the same way, many "spiritual, but not religious" people have taken myth and sheared off its religious elements to make the narrative their "own" rather than their culture's myth. Myth and religion often are overlapping, but not the same. The heart of myth is a narrative, which often is part of religion, but religion has aspects like doctrines, dogmas, and liturgies that can be informed by this narrative but are, to a degree, outside it. To Catholics, every mass is a reenactment of the narrative of Jesus's last supper, but there are elements of the liturgy that go beyond that narrative (the communal singing, the affirmation of creeds, etc.). In a similar way, mythical narratives seem to go beyond the confines of the doctrines and dogmas of religion. Hence, for example, the difficulty of logically fitting the vengeful God of the Old Testament who destroys whole cities with the loving God of the New Testament who cares so much that He counts the hairs on the heads of His beloved creatures. One of the orthodox doctrinal beliefs about God is that He is immutable (unchangeable), yet the God of the Old Testament does seem to change from the family God of Abraham to the tribal God of Moses to the universal God of the later Old Testament and New Testament.[12] Myths seem to go beyond the doctrinal limits of the religions, even as both have co-evolved simultaneously. Just as "spiritual, but not religious" believers take the narrative as their malleable property and treat religious doctrines as optional, pharisaical believers focus on the rules and doctrines of their religion, while neglecting the "spirit" of religion that often comes through in its religious myths.

Of course, for the most part, we do not live in pharisaical times. The separating of myth from religion and the eliminating of the mythical altogether is happening in a large part of the Western world. Campbell's and Jung's utilitarian use of myth was part of a movement that has not only led to a reduction in religious practices, but to a certain hollowing out of myths as well. This can be seen in the rise of Moralistic Therapeutic Deism, which has become the leading religious doctrine of many Americans, especially young Americans. "Moralistic Therapeutic Deism" is a term coined by the sociologists Christian Smith and Melinda Lundquist Denton to describe the religious beliefs of most American teenagers based on their extensive surveys and interviews. One of Smith and Denton's key findings is that many teenagers of all faiths believe that God and religion are about making individuals happy rather than a system of metaphysical beliefs or codes of conduct. Moralistic Therapeutic Deism suggests that many teenagers today deemphasize the theological content of religious beliefs (What is the nature of God? What is the proper form of worship? Etc.) and see religion as a way to fulfill their own needs and desires. Therefore, they create a God with a role more like a divine butler. This God whose primary purpose is to serve them has become the dominant image of divinity in the United States among young people who are, at least nominally, members of wildly disparate religious traditions, including Christians, Muslims, and Hindus. One can see how Campbell's approach to myth and metaphysical questions puts him in the vanguard of this movement to make myth (and eventually religion) into the raw material of this solipsistic therapeutic approach. Because he uses decontextualized versions of myths and legends from a variety of different sources in *Pathways to Bliss*, Campbell implies that the social context of these myths is unimportant. What is important for Campbell is how to "use" these myths to create individuals' own "personal" myths to unlock their ability to "follow their bliss."[13] Thus these most important stories, these illustrations of the metaphysics of a whole people, become a handmaiden to personal desire. It makes sense then that the last logical step is to make God a servant to this desire.

This lack of interest in the details contrasts with the typical "fan behavior" I discussed earlier and with serious religious believers. Fans are often less interested in the broad themes of popular culture works, but obsess over the details. As Tolkien predicted, the details that make the story sui generis (the soup rather than the bones) are what engages the serious fan. These details also generate much of the effect that Tolkien talks about: the details make myths and fairy stories attractive and perilous. Why are the details so important to fans? Because the details are pathways to the Secondary World that Tolkien describes (and not just the suspension of disbelief assumed by Coleridge). The details are more than the stage-setting that makes Tolkien's fantasy world believable, they are the essence of the story. If the details are done well and are intellectually consistent, they also have the ability to create not just alternative worlds but alternative worldviews.[14] If properly constructed, the fantasy worldview can be so compelling compared to the reader's own worldview that the reader experiences what Tolkien describes as "unbearable desire." The plausibility of the alternate world depends on understanding the implications of the "rules" of this new world so that readers forget that this is a secondary world at all. As Tolkien says, "But if they really like it [the fairy-story], for itself, they would not have to suspend disbelief: they would believe."[15]

This last step is what makes fairyland so perilous. The danger of fairyland is that it is so enchanting that people's attempt to travel there either causes them to leave the current world or pine endlessly for the fairyland world that they have visited but to which they can never return. This metaphor has a long pedigree in folktales where adventurers make trips to fairyland either to never return or, even more tragically, return home but fruitlessly attempt to find their lost fairyland. Not only does this journey create an unquenchable desire for fairyland's exiles, but their brief sojourns in the magical realm make them exiles in the real world as well. Tolkien wrote about the melancholy desire for fairyland in the poem "The Sea Bell," where the speaker travels by sea to a distant island, which is obviously a type of fairyland. On this island, he hears the music and dimly discerns the dancing of the elves, but they flee when he approaches. Eventually, the speaker gives up chasing after the elves. He then makes a crown of flowers and a mace of reeds and declares himself king of the enchanted island. When night falls, the poem takes a dark turn as the speaker grows prematurely old and gray in a prolonged night. He eventually returns home an old, damaged man alienated from the real world and ignored by his former companions. This type of poetry has a long history in Irish Celtic literature as *immram* poetry, which involves a hero's journey by sea to the "Otherworld," often islands to the west of Ireland. The poem is also reminiscent of Keats's "La Belle Sans Merci," where a knight is enchanted by a fairy woman and pines away in sickness and hunger waiting for his fairy love to return. In Tolkien's and Keats's poems, the exposure to fairyland leads to the ennui of longing for a desire that can never be quenched. The artistic metaphor for fantasy narratives is obvious: these narratives offer the ability to inhabit a different world, since Tolkien argues that the best of these narratives do not merely evoke a "sentimental state of mind" but instead, unsuspended belief. With this belief comes the danger that this new world will be so enchanting that it will cause permanent estrangement from the "real" world. Tolkien the artist understood that this desire to live in the world of the artist's own creation could lead to discontent and unrequited longing as well as to wonder and enchantment.

This feeling of estrangement and desire mirrors the feeling of desire that many people have for utopian societies. I listed many of the dangers of utopian societies in my first chapter, not least of which is that many utopian projects in the "real" world have ended as dystopian nightmares. Even so, the perils that Tolkien describes from these mythical utopias are of a different kind than the failed political utopias of the nineteenth and twentieth centuries. Tolkien's fairyland is not a materialist utopia where everyone's physical needs are fulfilled and all political oppression is eliminated, but a spiritual utopia where the voyager to fairyland has an aesthetic and mystical experience with the supernatural that answers to his or her aesthetic desires. Even more surprising, these encounters hardly lead to material comfort but quite the opposite. Indeed, the myths of fairyland are characterized as much by hardship as by ease. Nowhere is this clearer than in Tolkien's self-described childhood "dragon-desire" (which continued into his adulthood). The desire to see dragons is quite different from the utopian desire of perfect peace and comfort. To seek out dragons is to seek out wonders, no matter how dangerous they may be, and this represents a different vision than utopia and one more mediated by wonder than by comfort.

The physical perils of utopian fairyland pale, however, compared to the metaphysical demands of fairyland, the demands of enchantment. What Tolkien writes about in "The Sea Bell" and what Keats describes in "La Belle Sans Merci" involve a loss of not only comfort and peace, but of the autonomy for the enchanted one. This loss of autonomy comes from the realization that the enchanted person becomes a part of, and not outside of, the narrative. I earlier defined myth as the story of a people that represented their ideals. One of the most important parts of a myth is that the myth owns the people more than the people own the myth. To live up to the myth puts demands on the listener, even if it is just by example. This is why Tolkien describes myths as "perilous."

Tolkien acknowledges the power of myth to both challenge and comfort when his characters, Frodo and Sam, have an extended discussion about the nature of tales and the choices of the stories' protagonists in "The Stairs of Cirith Ungol" chapter of *The Two Towers*. In comparing their dilemma to the ancient tales of Middle-earth, Sam points out to Frodo that the heroes of those tales are forced into circumstances where heroic acts are required and yet have a chance to renounce their heroism. Sam observes,

> But that's not the way of it with the tales that really mattered, or the ones that stay in the mind. Folks seem to have been just landed in them, usually—their paths were laid that way, as you put it. But I expect they had lots of chances, like us, of turning back, only they didn't. And if they had, we shouldn't know, because they'd have been forgotten. We hear about those that just went on—and not all to a good end, mind you; at least not to what folk inside a story and not outside it call a good end. You know, coming home, and finding things all right, though not quite the same—like old Mr. Bilbo. But those aren't the best tales to hear, though they may be the best tales to get landed in![16]

Sam notes that the heroes of his tales do not choose their circumstances but do *choose* their heroism, even at great cost. Frodo, in the same conversation, reminds Sam that the heroes of the tales do not know if their stories will be ones that have happy endings or not. Sam agrees and brings up the tale of Beren and Lúthien as the prime example of a hero acting well, despite uncertainty. Sam argues that not only did Beren not know if he would be able to pry the silmaril from Morgoth's crown, but that Beren likely, like Frodo and Sam, thought his quest was impossible and that his story would not have a happy ending. Then Sam has the realization that part of the silmaril's light exists in the star-glass that Galadriel gave to Frodo. He exclaims, "Why to think of it, we're in the same tale still. It's going on. Don't the great tales never end?"[17] Nowhere can one find a better example of the power of myth to shape the expectations and actions of its audience than in this dialogue. In this case, the audience for the myth is not just the readers of *The Lord of the Rings* but the characters Sam and Frodo in the story itself. The dialogue starts with Sam and Frodo explicitly modeling their behaviors on heroes of old tales. It is not a coincidence that Sam picks the Beren and Lúthien tale as his example. Thingol gave Beren the task of wrestling a silmaril from the crown of Morgoth because it was the quintessential impossible quest. As a mythical example, the quest for the silmaril matches Sam and Frodo's seemingly hopeless quest to destroy the Ring in the fires of Mount Doom. Sam's choice of this story shows how myth can become more than a dead story, but the measure by which Sam and Frodo conduct themselves. Beren and Lúthien's courage in the face of impossible odds and their decision to continue to the heart of evil even when all seems lost gives hope to the hobbits and courage to continue on their path. Even so, Tolkien's conception of myth goes beyond using myth just as the ideal for heroic conduct. Frodo and Sam finally recognize that their quest is a continuation of Beren and Lúthien's tale. Not only that, but they identify so strongly with the myth that their own quest becomes subordinate to it. These are the dangers of myth that I spoke about earlier: Sam and Frodo not only decide to emulate the heroes of old, but they agree to surrender their very autonomy to the demands of the myth.

The subordination of an individual to a larger narrative should sound familiar to serious Christians. From the idea of life as a pilgrimage to the admonition for Christians to "take up their cross and fellow me," Christian imagery merges the life of the believer with the life of its founder, Jesus Christ. Sometimes, this merging can be quite literal, as in Thomas à Kempis's *Imitation of Christ* or subsuming as in *Soli Deo Gloria*, one of the Five Solas of the Protestant Reformation. Of course, one may object that religious belief is different from myth, but Tolkien did not consider them so far apart. In his famous disputation with C. S. Lewis before the latter's conversion, Tolkien described Christ's story as a "true myth." To be a Christian means to accept not the just the truths spoken by Jesus, but to accept the narrative of redemption and resurrection. In this way, the believer not only believes in the "myth" of Jesus's life and mission, but that in some way, he or she participates in the re-creation of that narrative. Just as Christ is born without original sin, the Christian is reborn again in baptism without sin. Just as Christ dies and then experiences a bodily resurrection, so too will the Christian believer die and his or her glorified body be resurrected on the last day. Thus, the Christian myth becomes not just the story of some distant ancestor or hero, but a story that continues with and to the individual believer.

This relationship of dominance that myths hold over Frodo and Sam is the opposite of the approach that Campbell and the people who subscribe to Moral Therapeutic Deism take toward myth as a path to self-fulfillment (or even self-gratification). First, the holistic content of the myth is unimportant to Campbell and the believers in Moral Therapeutic Deism. Because Campbell has an essentially functional view of myth, he can pull apart different aspects and themes of radically different mythological traditions and "use" them to construct his own personal myth. Therefore, the individual elements and the internal consistency of different myths are relatively unimportant to him. Instead, broad themes stripped of their context are all that matter to him. The heroes of *Gilgamesh*, *The Iliad*, or *The Bhagavad Gita* are all just the representations of Campbell's hero with a thousand faces, no matter what individual adventures they have or what settings they inhabit. In a similar way, believers in Moral Therapeutic Deism (MTD) are uninterested in the theological particulars of the religion that MTD has colonized. By definition, the practitioners of MTD do not understand concepts like irresistible grace or the Immaculate Conception or they would realize that elements of MTD are inconsistent with the orthodox beliefs of their religions. In that sense, believers in MTD are even less wedded to the mythological foundations of their religions than Campbell is to his myths. At least Campbell must examine the particulars of the myths he intends to reassemble to create his personal mythology and "follow his bliss." The deracinated, ersatz Christianity, Buddhism, or Islam of MTD takes even less effort since it replaces the particulars of the religion it colonizes with the latest societal pabulum. MTD retains the outer husk of the original religion without any of the particularities that make that religion unique.

MTD also belies the underlying assumption of Jungian psychology: that this collective unconscious belief of people manifests itself in a common set of images across multiple cultures. MTD has not only hollowed out the theological complexity of many of its host religions, it has also laid waste to the mythical imaginary that once cut across classes, races, and other divisions in Western society. Over the years I have been teaching, the loss of common religious touchstones such as Noah's Ark, the Garden of Eden, Abraham's covenant, and even the resurrection of Jesus has become apparent for nominally Christian and Jewish students. Not only that, but there has also been a corresponding loss in the passing on of secular myth as well. It is likely that many students do not have knowledge of, say, the mythology surrounding the founding fathers. Similarly, many students from the New Worlds of America and Australia have lost the organic connection with the cultures of their ancestors. How can one have a collective unconscious if specific images like Arthur pulling the sword from the stone or George Washington cutting down the cherry tree have started to fade from popular consciousness? Other myth systems (*Star Wars*, *Harry Potter*, *Star Trek*) from popular culture do not seem to be replacing these touchstones as widespread societal myths because these popular-culture replacements for the Jungian unconscious are so fragmented that they only influence specific subcultures rather than the whole society.[18] The one exception to this extirpation of common religious imagery and theology is MTD itself, where the more robust symbols and theology are replaced by MTD's simpler, less demanding ones. The sort of Butler-God of MTD (a God who takes care of the believer's problems, does not demand much from the believer but makes sure that the worshiper will go to heaven if they are "nice") does not resemble the Christian God the Father, the Hindu supreme spirit Brahma, or the Allah of Islam, and like many aspects of contemporary society, takes the complex and various forms of religious identity and makes them less complex and more general. Campbell's ecumenical approach takes the individual elements of the various mythologies and harmonizes them as best it can, while the MTD believer just replaces the complex and demanding religion with the simpler and easier version. These are both examples of the cultural "thinning" of a thicker culture that characterizes the Modernism and Postmodernism I discuss in chapter 2.

This utilitarian view of myth and religion helps explain why both Campbell's approach to myth and many MTD approaches to Christianity are especially inimical to the particular historical claims and traditions of orthodox Christianity. Religions that have historical claims anchor the religious tradition in a specific time and place and perhaps even to a specific people. Myths that exist in a real time and place, rather than in an indeterminate "once upon a time," cannot be taken out of that temporal historical context to be used as a piece of Campbell's private mythology. Myths that are historically grounded also tend to be part of a holistic mythical structure that not only presents a coherent view of the past, but also attempts to influence and/or predict the future. All these aspects of myth are especially true of traditional religion: its connection with specific cultures, its relationship with a particular time, and its predictions about a future. These elements limit religion's relative flexibility and make it more difficult for believers to contextualize away the more demanding aspects of the faith. This context is also found not only in the general principles of the religion, but in the details of how the religion is lived: in its orthopraxy even more so than its orthodoxy. This point about how specifics and particularity define religious beliefs and mythological systems mirrors Tolkien's distinction between the soup and the bones of myth-making that he makes in "On Fairy-Stories." Remember that Tolkien argues that the atmosphere and particularities of the story (the soup) are more important than the general themes (the bones). This is because Tolkien focused on myths not merely as receptacles of the Jungian unconscious images, but as works of art whose aesthetic qualities, what Tolkien calls "the atmosphere," depend on these details. Not only that, but Tolkien recognized that in the oral tradition of many of these myths, individual storytellers would keep the central themes of the stories but vary the details to create quite different aesthetic effects. Indeed, throughout much of his life, Tolkien did just that by writing and rewriting various versions of his stories with different details and genres in order to achieve different aesthetic effects. These aesthetic effects create emotions that place demands on us that are particular to the myth and to the culture that created it. Alexander the Great supposedly carried a box with *The Iliad* in it throughout his conquests, and his approach to the world was inextricably linked to his conception of the hero, whether it be Achilles or Odysseus. Myths both explain cultures and shape them. The details and peculiarities of the myths remind us of their ongoing influence, and much to the irritation of Campbell, how that influence is not always subordinate to the desires of the individual.

I have discussed how myth influenced characters like Frodo and Sam in *The Lord of the Rings*, how both traditional and religious myths influence and have influenced people in the "real" world, and how many readers of Tolkien's legendarium treat it as a modern-day myth: my final task is to connect all these threads together and argue that Tolkien's works are a modern-day myth with a specifically utopian purpose. I have spent a good deal of time discussing the mythological approaches of Jung, Campbell, and the purveyors of Moralistic Therapeutic Deism in order to show how Tolkien's mythological approach, both in his legendarium and his criticism, does not fit these models. More modern approaches to myth assume that the most important parts of myths are their general themes, which derive their power from some collective unconscious, while Tolkien's approach focuses on the specifics of the works and how the details create an atmosphere that, in turn, creates an emotional response. Therefore, Tolkien's understanding of myth is aesthetic rather than scientific or analytical. He also assumes that different cultures create different myths that have different aesthetics. Tolkien admitted that he had a particular affinity for Northern European myths, but he made it clear that his affinity was a matter of aesthetic preference rather than because he thought the myths were, in some sense, better or more moral. A fundamental difference between Tolkien and these advocates of a more comparative approach to myths is that while Jungians and Campbellians saw myths as functional tools for self-discovery, Tolkien saw myths as aspirational goals that the audience strove to emulate rather than analyze.

The mythical features of Tolkien's legendarium, though presented as part of the mythical past, point his readers toward the possibility of both a utopian and a dystopian future. I hope I have made the case that myth is as much about the present and the future as the past, whether the myths provide a template for emulation or suggest a world renewed by prophecy. That is why it was so important to Tolkien that his legendarium have an internal consistency that made it believable in its own terms. Tolkien's myths derive their power from their effectiveness as parts of a holistic, complex narrative that feels as believable as our own world. That is why Tolkien argued that a myth is more than the sum of its parts. The fan behavior associated with Tolkien's legendarium suggests that they, too, understand how the details that make up the broth of the myth are not some incidental part of it but central to the myth's power as guide to the future. The power of Tolkien's myth is that it points to something believably utopian (to use a somewhat oxymoronic turn of phrase). Thus, the debates fans have about the more obscure lore from Middle-earth, such as whether orcs have souls or what happened to the blue wizards, are important because they affect the moral import of the works in important ways. If orcs are irredeemable, then can other persons, like humans, become so alienated from the world and themselves that they, too, lose all possibility of redemption? Did the blue wizards succumb to the temptations of Middle-earth and establish cults to enhance their own power or did they remain faithful to their mission of thwarting Sauron in the East? While arguments like this seem like pointless quibbles over minutiae, they have important metaphysical implications in the complex world of Tolkien's legendarium. If orcs are irredeemable and the blue wizards failed in the East, Tolkien's story takes on a much darker cast and suggests a negative view of a person's ability to resist evil. The reverse suggests a much more optimistic worldview. Therefore, when fans argue about Middle-earth, they are often indirectly arguing about the moral nature of our world and the possibilities for its future.

We can see a possible future in Tolkien's loving description of the practices and foibles of the Shire's hobbits. In the Shire, he uses myth to create a believable utopian alternative (but not a utopia) to our current world. In Tolkien's early hobbit chapters in both *The Hobbit* and *The Lord of the Rings*, he connects hobbits to present reality by suggesting that the creatures are still among us. For instance he, as the conspiratorial narrator of *The Hobbit*, says of hobbits that "there is little or no magic about them, except the ordinary sort which helps them to disappear quietly and quickly when large stupid folk like you and me come blundering along,"[19] implying to the children reading the story that the hobbits might be hiding in the more rural parts of their neighborhood. In this way, Tolkien puts hobbits clearly in the mythical folklore category, like fairies, brownies, or leprechauns, but also tantalizingly suggests that hobbits are not completely outside of the reality of our world.

While Tolkien hints that hobbits might still inhabit our world, his Shire appears to be located completely in a mythological past. Even so, it appears to be a place that *could* be recognizably part of our world. I argued that myths often have a unifying purpose in that they tell the stories of a people and its heroes: how Achilles defines Greek *arête* and Beowulf demonstrates Northern courage in the face of impossible odds. The beauty of the Shire is that it also tells the story of a "people" and their virtues, but it is the story of rural people everywhere. It represents the good parts of the rural world in a generic but believable fashion, so people from England, Germany, and Japan can see the beauty of the simple life and people, as if Tolkien is telling the story of *their* country place and country people. As I argued, I think Tolkien created a mythology, not just for England but a mythology for the world. This is why Tolkien used the word "shire," it is the most English, yet the most generic word possible for the homeland of his hobbits; Tolkien's naming of the home of the hobbits "The Shire" is like naming it "The County" or "The Parish." He takes this generic rural place and shows its utopian possibilities. Not surprisingly for Tolkien, this utopia has ecological and anarchic characteristics. The Shire depends on the hobbits seeing themselves as stewards of the natural world they inhabit. Thus, their homes are literally integrated into the landscape, and trees are their most treasured landmarks. The hobbits' social structure, with its relatively flat social class, lack of violence, and limited government, also points to a utopian ideal. Another way to look at the Shire is as a backwater. Like places around the world that have been neglected by official government, the rural people have had to make it on their own, which means they had to become integrated with each other and the land. The hobbits show what this integration would look like if conducted by people morally better than ourselves. Perhaps this is why the Shire can appeal to people as far away as Kyrgyzstan.

In a similar way, Bilbo, Frodo, and Sam are recognizable as rural folk heroes around the world: simple people who succeed where more sophisticated and educated people fail. Of course, now I seem to be arguing from a more Campbellian point of view by assuming that readers admire the Shire's inhabitants for generic features and themes rather than idiosyncrasies: the bones more than the soup. Tolkien certainly gave his hobbits the conventional habits of rural people the world, over including a love of genealogy, distrust of strangers, and a fondness for good gossip, but he also provides enough idiosyncratic details to make hobbits sui generis, including hobbit holes, birthday presents for everyone but the hobbit having the birthday, an inordinate love of mushrooms, and six meals a day. All these details make the Shire and its inhabitants believably unique. As Philip Irving notes in his article "Conceptions of the Pastoral," characters like Sam "have a great power in belonging to a place and being shaped by it."[20] In this way, hobbits become both familiar yet strangely exotic. They are part-brownie or leprechaun, part Victorian gentleman with tea times and pocket-handkerchiefs. In other ways, however, hobbits are heroic in ways that seem to cut against their rural everyman identity. Once again, their heroism suggests the utopian possibilities beyond their prosaic selves.

Tolkien's other good civilizations, while not as well developed as the Shire, also point toward utopian possibilities. Part of the way Tolkien does this is by consciously drawing some of the societies from *The Silmarillion* in mythic terms. Tolkien takes on a deliberately mythical or even scriptural style in his descriptions of Valinor and Túna so that they resemble the Garden of Eden in Genesis more than they do the conventions of the novel. Lothlórien also seems like a mythical fairyland, but a lesser one that is in danger and surrounded by anxieties. Gondolin and Gondor are similarly Edenic oases amid ever-widening wastelands of evil and violence. Like the Shire, these civilizations all have some similar characteristics: a love of beauty, a society built in cooperation with the natural world, and government that depends on legitimate (if aristocratic) authority.

These societies' utopian characteristics are transmitted effectively through Tolkien's use of mythology as a vehicle. Remember, I defined myth as the origin story of a people and/or a story of a people's most representative heroes. Obviously, hobbits or elves are not of the same "people" (in the sense of an ethnic or national group) as the readers from around the world who have read the different parts of Tolkien's legendarium. Still, as I have noted, Middle-earth's combination of alterity and familiarity allows people from vastly different backgrounds to identify with the legendarium and its characters, so much so that it has become an alternative legendary history for them. I also noted how in the world of Middle-earth, Frodo and Sam call upon the former heroes of the First Age, Beren and Lúthein, as exemplars of how to behave in difficult circumstances. Similarly, the various heroes in Tolkien's legendarium have become models for their readers to emulate in ways that are similar to how Greek children might have emulated Achilles or American children might imitate Davy Crockett.

The question becomes then how are Bilbo, Frodo, Túrin, and Lúthien mythological figures in ways that characters like Robinson Crusoe or Anna Karenina are not? I think a large part of the difference is the distance that Tolkien creates through his atmosphere of remote ancientness; an ancientness that exists not only in relation to the readers of his tales, but in his characters who in the Second and Third Ages view their world as ancient. Tolkien's Middle-earth is both old and vast; its very size is suggested by the sheer volume, and maybe even the disorderliness, of Tolkien's legendarium. While novels can be large, their scope is generally limited to one time period or to the current generation of its characters. Since they are almost always contemporary or from the relatively recent past, most novels do not have the patina of ancientness that Tolkien tries to convey in his legendarium.

Another way that Tolkien's legendarium differs from the average novel is in its atmosphere, "atmosphere" meaning the non-plot elements of the story that establish not only what happens in the story but how the story feels. Once again, we are talking about the "soup" that Tolkien describes in "On Fairy-Stories" rather than the "bones," and it is this soup that makes Tolkien's legendarium an effective myth for its readers. The soup is an atmosphere that separates the reader from his or her prosaic time and place. Myth and fairy stories can speak to atavistic desires because they live in that "once upon a time" place that seems familiar, non-descript, and strangely detailed. Tolkien famously referred to this as "the secondary world." The purpose of the setting for the hero of a realistic novel is quite the opposite: to immerse the reader in a place that feels like it can exist plausibly in a recognizable time and place. The secondary world in a fantasy or romance can only "work" if the artist can create a world so real that his readers forget the existence of the primary world and lose themselves in the author's secondary world. This is what myths do as well. The myths of "Merrie Old England" are the myths of the England inhabited by King Arthur, not Edward II, and therefore outside any identifiable historical period.

Because myths exist outside the confines of a particular culture, they are an especially excellent vehicle to convey values to diverse audiences. That is why they are so often provided to children in the form of fairy stories. This is also why it is not a coincidence that *The Hobbit*, and to a lesser extent *The Lord of the Rings*, are some of the most popular books to be read aloud to children. So how, exactly, does myth become such an effective vehicle for these values? I argue that it is not the broad themes of the stories (the aspects of myths that interested Campbell and Jung), but in the atmosphere. We all know from the elements of genre literature how atmosphere can be created by details in the setting that have little to do with the plot of the narrative. In suspense stories, for example, simple elements like storms, darkness, or strange noises create feelings that activate our most primitive fears. Other forms of "genre literature," like romance novels and science fiction stories, have similar conventions that help set the mood for the story. Tolkien, as the progenitor of his own genre of fantasy literature, has determined what a fantasy atmosphere should entail. He generates his atmosphere from melding the different sources I discussed in chapter 2: medieval literature, Victorian medievalism, Modernism, his experience in World War I. In that chapter, I spoke mostly about how these sources influence Tolkien's plots, but in this chapter I focus on how they helped create this "mythic" atmosphere. Part of what makes something feel mythic rather than historical is the very mixing of time periods and attitudes. When I think of fairy tales like "Jack and the Beanstalk" or "Cinderella," I envision, like many other readers, scenes with a series of historically inaccurate anachronisms that include elements from the High-Middle-Ages-like castles mixed promiscuously with clothes that belong in the sixteenth or even seventeenth century in a political setting that might be more reminiscent of the Dark Ages of the fifth and sixth centuries. Part of my mental images comes no doubt from illustrations I saw as a child (or in books that I have read to my children), which only shows how much this type of chronological incongruity has become a convention. Of course, just like these fairy tales, Tolkien's stories include a similar mixture of anachronistic features, like waistcoats, dragons, and medieval keeps. Fairy tales and Tolkien's tales, both types of myths, generate their atmosphere by not having to follow rules like sticking to a single chronology or zoology. Myths allow readers to inhabit parallel worlds and accept realities that they would not ordinarily accept. Of course, this mixing of elements from different time periods without making these anachronisms irritating takes some skill so as to not break the "spell" that Tolkien weaves around his readers. Anyone who has read bad fantasy fiction has experienced the phenomenon of characters who seem much more at home in the contemporary world unconvincingly inhabiting some medieval landscape and costumed in medieval clothing. To be truly transported to the realm of fantasy or fairy tale, a successful writer must pay the most judicious attention to atmosphere to make it seem at once familiar and foreign, at a place removed from our time yet somehow a place for all time.

The best way to see how this plausible mixing of anachronism creates this mythic atmosphere is to look at some specific examples from Tolkien's works. In Tolkien's Prologue to *The Lord of the Rings*, for example, he discusses the anachronistic pipe-weed, which the reader immediately recognizes as tobacco. Obviously, it does not make sense to include tobacco in Middle-earth since tobacco did not come to Europe from North America until the sixteenth century and most every other part of the trilogy suggests a European location in some distant past. That is not the only American import since Sam also cooks potatoes with his rabbits in Ithilien even though potatoes also came from South America to Europe in the sixteenth century. Both tobacco and potatoes do little to affect the broad themes of *The Lord of the Rings*, but do much to improve the cozy atmosphere of the tales (especially for the middle-aged author who would no doubt find the pub life he so enjoyed less congenial without his pipe and chips). These anachronisms also make it clear that *The Lord of the Rings* is not a work of historical fiction but in the same category as myth and fairy tale, and most of his readers happily accept these anachronisms.

Of course, another aspect of the mythological quality of Tolkien's novel, besides its anachronisms, comes from its unabashed supernaturalism. I mentioned that one of the characteristics of myths is that they involve deities. Certainly, parts of *The Silmarillion* are literally mythological in the sense that Tolkien includes God in the form of Eru Ilúvatar and "gods" in the form of the various members of the Valar. In the world of *The Lord of the Rings*, however, both Eru and the Valar are now, at best, remote presences. Still, supernatural activity occurs regularly throughout Middle-earth. The Ring of Power is the most potent and obvious example of this supernatural power. It controls the will of those who wear it and changes them physically; like Gollum, who through the Ring's influence has his life extended and his body made monstrous. The even more extreme example of the Ring's power extends to the Ringwraiths, who become liminal half-spirit, half material specters due to the influence of the Ring. Beyond the Ring, the supernatural is everywhere: in Middle-earth in its Barrow-wights, palentirs, magical untying ropes, password-opened doors, and light-generating vials. Tolkien also populates his legendarium with the monsters that operate in the mythology of fairy tale and myth, including dragons, werewolves, giant spiders, trolls, goblins, enormous bats, and other creatures.

We "accept" these elements of the supernatural because we know we are entering into the world of myths, which has its own rules, just as in the world of dreams, the dreamer accepts all manner of implausible events like the ability to fly, or talk to animals, or to open a door to a closet and find the outdoors.[21] More so than in dreams, however, Tolkien's myths are disciplined by the characteristics of the genre. One of those characteristics I mentioned earlier is that mythology often involves the "story of a people," whether it is Israelites in the Bible or the Romans in *The Aeneid*. *The Silmarillion* is certainly a story of a people, and eventually, peoples. It is many other things, including a creation story, various tragedies, and a series of chronicles. The various elves' migration to Middle-earth bears a negative resemblance to the biblical Israelites' migration to the Promised Land. In this case, however, the elves exile themselves from the Promised Land rather than letting God lead them to the land of milk and honey. Even so, just as the Jews struggled with following God's laws and with worshiping other gods, the elves also allow themselves to become degraded in their disobedient pursuit of the silmarils and their desire to revenge themselves on Morgoth. In addition to elves, certain tribes of men, like the ones who would eventually become the Númenóreans, also take up this mantle as the "chosen people" especially favored by the Valar or Eru.

Some critics have interpreted Tolkien's use of a "chosen people" mythology as a disreputable form of racialism or even racism. Certainly the milieu of late nineteenth- and early twentieth-century Europe was a high point of racist-influenced historical theories. Despite this, I think that the focus on individual peoples as the vehicle for God's plan is a much more likely explanation for Tolkien's focus on the "races" of Middle-earth, rather than the assumption that Tolkien re-inscribed his society's racist assumptions into his legendarium.[22] For one, there is little evidence to suggest that Tolkien harbored racially problematic attitudes except for one incident. Dimitra Fimi describes a racially insensitive remark that was attributed to nineteen-year-old Tolkien during a debate about whether Shakespeare's works were really written by Francis Bacon (a popular theory at the time). Tolkien had supposedly compared the idea of the brilliant Shakespeare's birth in "filthy" Stratford-upon-Avon to "the belief that a fair-haired European infant could have a woolly-haired prognathous Papuan parent" in order to suggest that Shakespeare was not the author of his plays.[23] This apparently racist remark is a bit more ambiguous after careful examination. One could argue that Tolkien assumes that being a Papuan is "filthy" and thus denigrates Stratford by the comparison. But then again, that makes an English village and Papuans comparable. A more charitable and straightforward reading of Tolkien's statement is that his use of "woolly-haired" and "prognathous" is simply describing phenotypes of Papuan parents that would not likely suddenly change to make a fair-haired child.[24]

In contrast to this remark, Tolkien wrote hundreds of letters to a variety of people, and it is striking that so little of the ubiquitous racist sentiment of the early twentieth century ended up in his letters. On the contrary, in his famous letter to the German publisher Rütten & Loening, Tolkien unequivocally rejects the anti-Semitism that was unfortunately commonplace at that time. Also, even though Tolkien appears to present a racial hierarchy with distinctive higher and lower races (in both a physical and moral sense) from High Elves to orcs, he does much to complicate this simple hierarchy. Part of this involves allowing "lesser races" central roles in many of the key events, starting with the men in *The Silmarillion*. Despite the greater strength and wisdom of elves, men are chosen (by the Valar and indirectly, Eru) to do the greatest deeds. It is Beren, the man, who pries the silmaril from Morgoth's crown, and it is Tuor who is chosen by Ulmo to warn Gondolin and it is he who rescues the surviving remnants of the city after its fall. This pattern continues in *The Hobbit* and *The Lord of the Rings*, where lowly hobbits are the key to defeating or saving much mightier and wiser races. Even the primitive Drúedain play a key role in the defeat of Sauron's armies at Gondor. Finally, the ultimate irony is that the "highest" and "lowest" races of Middle-earth are intimately related to each other since orcs are a corruption of elves.

Once again, Christians will be familiar with the motif of the unlikely hero from the Bible. The Bible is replete with unlikely and disfavored sons who go on to great things: for every first-born Isaac, there are many latter-born Jacobs, Josephs, and Davids. Once again, Jesus serves as the model of the most unlikely of heroes: a carpenter's son from the most backwater part of Galilee ("Can anything good come out of Nazareth" [John 1:46]) from the most backwater part of the Roman Empire.

Tolkien's focus on the metaphysical and chosen people aspects of mythology lends itself to a more utopian approach, especially considering the part of traditional mythology that he leaves out. I already mentioned the elements of traditional mythology that Tolkien includes: creation myths, stories about the creation of "a people," and tales about ideal heroes. Tolkien leaves out a strand of myth that especially fascinated Freud and many of his disciples including Jung and Otto Rank, the so-called family romance myths. These are stories that focused on conflicts between family members in royal households, mostly between fathers and sons (or father figures), including Laius and Oedipus, Abraham and his sons Ishmael and Isaac, Acrisius and Perseus, and others. In these stories, fathers actively try to kill their sons through exposure or sacrifice. Many Freudian interpreters argued that these murderous fathers were a projection of the son's desire to get rid of the father because of the son's subconscious sexual desire for the mother. Tolkien's mythology has little of these interfamily struggles between fathers and sons (except perhaps Morgoth's rejection of his creator-father, Eru). Instead, Tolkien has numerous father figures in his works who are almost always portrayed positively. The most obvious of these figures is Gandalf, who acts as a sort of surrogate parent for Frodo and especially Bilbo. But other father figures appear throughout Tolkien's legendarium. The closest to the family romance story is the Beren and Lúthien saga where Beren, like many Greek heroes, is given an impossible task by a father figure, Thingol, the father of Lúthien. Still, the classic pattern is disrupted because even though Beren cannot complete the mission, Thingol accepts Beren as his son-in-law. Instead of fathers as dangers to their sons, Tolkien's foster fathers adopt orphan children who are hungry for a father figure. Frodo, Túrin, and Aragorn all either lost their fathers or were raised without their fathers and found father substitutes. For both men, their foster fathers were elves and for Frodo, his father figures were both his Uncle Bilbo and Gandalf.

Knowing Tolkien's biography, one can understand his longing for a father and wanting the acceptance of an alien foster father. Tolkien's own father died in Africa when Tolkien was a small child. Later, after his mother died, Tolkien was raised by the Catholic priest Father Francis Morgan (an adoption in his own mostly Protestant society almost as strange and unprecedented as a human getting adopted by an elf king in Middle-earth). Perhaps because of this unusual upbringing, Tolkien's views about fatherhood in particular, and families in general, are very different from the standard Freudian approach to the family as a place of unconscious sexual conflict. Instead of fathers and sons fearing and wishing to replace each other, Tolkien presents characters who miss and deeply desire to have paternal relationships. Of course, mythology and sacred texts often present examples of substitute or foster fathers who provide paternal care; Saint Joseph, known as the foster father of Jesus, is the obvious example. This is another way in which Tolkien might connect with many present-day readers since so many more young people now grow up with absent fathers and have a father-longing as opposed to those who are raised by an overbearing paterfamilias and wish to escape his influence, as so often portrayed by Freud, Jung, and Rank.[25] In this case, the myth of a replacement father would seem more desirable and real than the myth of the overbearing father. Instead of viewing family relationships as a source of threat, Tolkien nearly always presents them as a way of character rehabilitation and fulfillment.

Despite his generally positive approach to myths, Tolkien also shows how enduring myths can reinforce negative behaviors. The "Oath of Fëanor" in which the sons and grandsons pursue their pointless war against Morgoth and all other races in hopeless quest for the silmarils becomes a negative myth that doomed the Noldor into a downward spiral of ever more pointless struggles. Another example of the negative effect of myths is the enmity between elves and dwarves caused in part by ancient grudges based on legendary slights from thousands of years ago. In these cases, mythic narratives model chauvinistic behavior and establish irrational prejudices and create boundaries between people.

Tolkien also exploits fears of the dystopia in mythic terms as well. Thangorodrim and Mordor play upon mythic fears of an underworld. In many myths, characters go through journeys to the underworld, like Odysseus's trip to Hades or Beowulf's journey to the cave of Grendel's mother. Tolkien's narratives have similar journeys into a type of underworld, such as when Beren and Lúthein travel to Thangorodrim and Sam and Frodo travel through the Dead Marshes and into Mordor. Unlike many of the Greek myths, however, the underworlds of Mordor and Thangorodrim threaten to leave their boundaries and overtake the whole world. This more apocalyptic scenario resembles the mythology of both Christianity and Northern Paganism. For example, in the world of *Beowulf's* Heorot, monsters threaten to overtake the world of men in a way that resembles the precarious First Age of *The Silmarillion* where the kingdoms of man are often marginalized and threatened by the creatures of Morgoth. In *The Lord of the Rings*, Sauron's battle to control Middle-earth has more than a passing resemblance to the antichrist's triumph in Revelation. In both cases, the evil Lords seem to be true "Lords of the World."

Like Christian and Norse mythology, Tolkien's legendarium assumes that "history is one long defeat" but that there are still moral choices to be made in this world. In this way, he rejects the assumed metaphysics of much of the modern and postmodern world: a metaphysics that assumes either a progressive "Whig view of history" or the increasingly popular nihilistic view that our moral choices make no difference at all. In Tolkien's evil societies there are echoes of the antichrist as well as the monstrous serpents and wolves who destroy Asgard. The future is determined to be bleak, but it is still a world of choices that are not Nietzschean and so still within the realm of the morality of good and evil.

In this chapter, I hope I have made a convincing case that Tolkien consciously built his legendarium with mythic qualities. In it, he answers the questions that myths seek to answer: where do we come from, what is our relationship with the world, who are we as a people, who are our heroes? For Tolkien, the complete answers to these questions can never be found on the thin reed of fact, but only in the rich symbolism of myth. Though he started his legendarium as a myth for England, Tolkien's myth grew to be a myth for the whole world. He also illustrated his own theory of what myth is and what makes it an effective conveyor of values by the way he constructed his legendarium.

In doing so, Tolkien also contradicted the most popular interpretations about the meaning of myth of his time and our own. He rejected the scientific study of comparative mythology, which sought to dissect and decontextualize the idiosyncratic elements of myths. Tolkien also ignored the psychoanalytic approach to myth as a repository of an individual and society's forbidden sexual and antisocial desires. His myths also are constructed in such a way so that they undermine the therapeutic approach to both myth and religion favored by Joseph Campbell and the purveyors of Moralistic Therapeutic Deism. Tolkien showed that myths are not lies told to people who are too ignorant to understand facts or vehicles for personal validation. Instead, his myths point to higher truths that cannot be expressed in any other form than story and are not the property of individuals but of "peoples." Tolkien showed how myths can place demands on the people who profess them and take them seriously. He argued that the important part of myths are not their broad themes that can be compared across cultures, but instead their idiosyncratic atmosphere that is created by specific details. Tolkien showed how myths socialize a people and demonstrated how myths ripple through generations and influence people in both good and bad ways. He rejected the idea that myths are about personal validation or "following one's bliss." Instead, his myths, in their communal nature, function as exemplars of ideal behavior, and finally their status as works of art makes them more than objects of study or self-gratification. In this way, they are utopian in demanding not just a new way of living, but a new way of imagining the world.

NOTES

1. E. J. Michael Witzel in his book *The Origin of the World Mythologies* provides an especially comprehensive definition of myth. He describes it "as a narrative

- that is told or recited at certain special occasions
- that is standardized (to some extent)
- that is collectively owned and managed (often by specialists)
- that is considered by its owners to be of great and enduring significance
- that (whether or not these owners are consciously aware of this point) contains and brings out such images of the world (a cosmology) of past and present society (a history and sociology), and of the human condition (an anthropology) as are eminently constitutive of the life society in which the narrative circulates, or at least where it circulated originally
- that, if this constitutive aspect is consciously realized by the owners, may be evoked (etiologically) to explain and justify present-day conditions
- and that is therefore a powerful device to create collectively underpinned meaning and collectively recognized truth (regardless of whether such truth would be recognized outside the community whose myth it is)."

2. J.R.R. Tolkien to Milton Waldman (undated), in *The Letters of J. R. R. Tolkien*, ed. Humphrey Carpenter (Boston: Houghton Mifflin Harcourt, 2000), 144.

3. From the other direction, we can also see a similar shift in academic interest from works of "high" literature or art to works of popular culture.

4. Though in terms of staying power, world-building complexity, and even invented languages, the *Star Trek* universe seems closest to the epic-like nature of Tolkien's

legendarium. I don't think that it is a coincidence that it is also one of the more utopian products of popular culture. Once again, I think part of its staying power comes from its role as an exemplar.

5. One part of Helms's theory about Tolkien's mythic development is clearly inaccurate in hindsight (Helms wrote his book in 1974). Helms argues that Tolkien's *The Hobbit* was a sort of dry run for creating a mythic story that Tolkien later perfected in *The Lord of the Rings*. Helms therefore tends to approach *The Hobbit* as Tolkien's "first" narrative. Unfortunately, Helms did not have access to *The Silmarillion* or *The Lost Tales* or a real understanding that Tolkien had been working and reworking elements of his legendarium for decades before he started *The Hobbit*. Helms also assumes that *The Lord of the Rings* was the only successful mythic narrative that Tolkien created. A more complete understanding of Tolkien's work suggests that he was constantly experimenting with a variety of genres (poetry, prose, chronicle, folktale, children's literature, epic, romance novel, etc.) to create his legendarium and often reworked the same narratives (like his Beren and Lúthien tale) in a variety of versions and genres over the decades.

6. Randel Helms, *Tolkien's World* (Boston: Houghton Mifflin, 1974), 40.

7. J.R.R. Tolkien, "On Fairy-Stories," *Tolkien on Fairy-Stories Expanded Edition, with Commentary and Notes*, eds. Verilyn Fliegler and Douglas A. Anderson (London: HarperCollins, 2008), 32.

8. The diminishment of fairies and elves from supernatural creatures that were held in awe to cutesy decorative creatures seems very similar to the way angels that were once viewed as terrifying messengers of God's power are now often portrayed as beautiful women or fat toddlers in artistic representations and the popular imagination. After all, one of the most common greetings from Biblical angels is "be not afraid," suggesting angelic apparitions are neither sexy nor cherubic. One wonders if the same principles worked for the artistic diminishment of both types of creatures.

9. Tolkien, "On Fairy-Stories," 67.

10. Tolkien, "On Fairy-Stories," 75.

11. J.R.R. Tolkien, "On Fairy-Stories," footnote 1, 40.

12. Not that theologians cannot reconcile the two. Perhaps God spoke to his people in ways that they understood and only revealed Himself later. Perhaps the fallible writers of the Bible interpreted God's actions and motivations incorrectly. In any case, the need to explain or qualify the myth shows how they tend to go beyond the limits of doctrine.

13. This Jungian-based analysis has also been specifically applied to Tolkien's legendarium in Timothy R. O'Neill's *The Individuated Hobbit: Jung, Tolkien, and the Archetypes of Middle-earth*.

14. This consistency of worldview separates Tolkien's view of fantasy from other narratives that might have fantastic elements. For example, though I have not seen direct evidence of this I suspect that Tolkien would not have approved of "magical realism" where the fantastical intrudes upon the prosaic reality of everyday life. This literary school violates Tolkienian principles in two ways: first, the fantastical elements are not made consistent within the narrative and second, the fantastical and realistic parts of the narrative are not only combined, but the contrast is emphasized.

15. Tolkien, "On Fairy-Stories," 53.

16. J.R.R. Tolkien, *The Return of the King* (New York: Ballantine Books, 1994), 362.

17. Tolkien, *The Return of the King*, 363.

18. I have no way of knowing this, but I suspect that these religious and civic myths have been replaced by other complex myths. For example, a surprising number of my students seem fascinated by conspiracy theories, like the supposed occult power of the Illuminati in controlling powerful individuals and world events. In the past, views like this might be part of a web of other beliefs, but the relative lack of other strong belief systems makes these beliefs more intense and all-encompassing. It also appears to me that people's political (and sometimes racial) beliefs are forming a much more salient part of people's identities as their familial, civic, and religious identities have receded.

19. J.R.R. Tolkien, *The Hobbit* (London: Ballantine Books, 2014), 2.

20. Philip Irving Mitchell, "Conceptions of the Pastoral," in *Approaches to Teaching Tolkien's* Lord of the Rings *and Other Works*, ed. Leslie A. Donovan (New York: Modern Language Association, 2015), 111.

21. One of the universal assumptions of mythology that started with Freud is that dreams and mythology are intimately connected. This belief reached its high point with Jung and his belief in the "collective unconscious" that I discussed earlier in the chapter.

22. Assuming that Middle-earth creatures like orcs and elves are somehow equivalent to races is problematic for several reasons, as I mentioned in chapter 1.

23. Dimitra Fimi, *Tolkien, Race and Cultural History* (London: Palgrave Macmillan, 2009), 134.

24. What makes the statement seem especially racist to modern ears is the language used, especially "woolly-haired." Still, I suspect part of that effect is its association with racist ideas rather than its actual meaning in the early twentieth century. For example, words like "colored" and "negro" have a racist connotation in the early twenty-first century though they were considered the non-racist nomenclature in the 1920s and 1950s, respectively.

25. Probably the closest Tolkien comes to creating a "family romance" story with a disturbing sexual subtext is in his epic of Túrin. With the ill-fated Kullervo from the *Kalevala* as the model, the narrative has the most disturbing family dynamics of any of Tolkien's works. Húrin, Túrin's father, while not directly malevolent, instigates his son's suffering by taunting Morgoth and causing Morgoth to curse his family. The curse leads Túrin to mistakenly marry his sister Nienor and leads to both characters' suicides. In a way, Morgoth, as Lord of Middle-earth, acts as an even more sinister father figure than other filicidal fathers like Laius and Acrisius.

FIVE
Tolkien's Utopian and Dystopian Politics

In a tangential way, I have already discussed the relationship between Tolkien's works and utopian and dystopian politics. I have noted that Tolkien's good societies, like the Shire, Rivendell, Gondolin, and Lothlórien, are small and isolated, while his evil ones, like Thangorodrim and Mordor, are large and centralized. It would be a mistake, however, to assume some simple formula where small is good and large is bad. As we shall see, Tolkien's approach to scale depends on context. Even so, his instincts are to be suspicious of large and controlling institutions. This suspicion reflects Tolkien's unique political perspective. However, I hesitate to use the world "political" when discussing Tolkien's views, since Tolkien's approach to these questions tends to be broad and philosophical, whereas many people's approach to politics (especially today) is narrow, technical, and tribal. In general, Tolkien's anarchistic views depend on granting individuals the maximum freedom to live their lives. This position makes him mostly at odds with his contemporaries on the left and the right for different reasons, as well as at odds with most people today. Despite this hostility toward interference in people's daily lives, Tolkien, in many ways, is more accepting of the concept of legitimate authority than many contemporary people. Reconciling this contradiction will help explain how Tolkien's utopian vision depends on different assumptions about the relationship between leaders and followers than most current political theorists. Tolkien's anarchy does not require an absence of hierarchy and leadership. On the contrary, he believes that lack of freedom comes from a lack of authority. It is not a coincidence that Tolkien's malevolent societies feature both a breakdown of legitimate authority and its replacement with power that seeks to control rather than to lead. These paradoxical beliefs resonate with many of his readers, who are discontent with societies that strangely seem at once leaderless and controlling. Once again, the believability of Tolkien's political utopianism comes from his tapping into what his readers found and find lacking in their political world.

Tolkien addresses two deficits in our current politics: the first comes from a current political environment that ignores the dangers of efficiency and control, and the second comes from a lack of courageous leaders who will take the right action, even if that action might lead to bad consequences. By filling these deficits, Tolkien creates ideal societies that allow freedom and encourage virtue. As always, Tolkien also provides bad societies that exaggerate modern vices, especially this penchant for efficiency and control, as a contrast. In order to examine this contrast, the first part of this chapter explores Tolkien's overall political framework in relation to his utopian and dystopian themes and their relationship with the politics of his and our time. The second part examines political leaders in his good and bad societies and how they compare to current and recent theories about political leadership.

TOLKIEN'S POLITICAL FRAMEWORK

Not surprisingly, Tolkien's political vision, like much of his other views, is idiosyncratic. His views not only are out of the mainstream in our time, but did not fit in with the most popular political views of his own time. The contentious period that Tolkien lived most of his life, the early to mid-twentieth century, was filled with economic and political upheaval, including a worldwide depression and two world wars. During that time, Britain maintained a mostly capitalist society that incorporated some aspects of socialism. In politics, the final aristocratic bastions of power were dismantled and replaced with mass democracy, after weakening throughout most of the nineteenth century. It is safe to say that before World War I, many Britons had an optimistic view of the future (it was the heyday of utopian literature), whereas after the war many people had a deeply pessimistic view.[1] Not many people were thinking in terms of anarchistic solutions to their problems and, in general, statist solutions became increasingly more popular during Tolkien's lifetime. In terms of politics, Tolkien was not very interested in the mainstream political currents of his time. Not surprisingly, none of Tolkien's good societies resembled the Britain in which he lived, though some aspects of his bad ones did.

The one group of his contemporaries whose political and economic beliefs did resemble Tolkien's preference for small-scale politics were distributionists. Distributionists believed in a political and economic philosophy called distributionism, based on Catholic social teaching principles that are outlined in the papal encyclicals *Rerum Novarum* and *Quad-*

ragesimo Anno. The basic principles of distributionism depend on two concepts from Catholic social teaching: subsidiarity and solidarity. Subsidiary means that decisions should be made whenever possible by the smallest, closest authority to the community. Therefore if a political decision needs to be made, it should be done at the local level unless there is some reason for it not to be, such as national defense. Solidarity, on the other hand, refers to the ideal of Christian brotherhood where different groups identify and share their goods and hardships together. This means both within groups, such as workers having solidarity with each other, or even more importantly, between groups, such as workers and capitalistic owners who are also supposed to be in solidarity with each other. As often the case in Catholic social teaching, these two approaches are in tension with each other.[2] Subsidiarity suggests that personal and intimate relationships should be valued above others and that outside interference should be avoided. In contrast, solidarity emphasizes the bond that people have both inside and outside the group and the principles that transcend the merely local and parochial. Because of its attempt to balance these conflicting mandates, distributionism does not fit neatly into most of the political ideology of the past two centuries, which tends to value either collective or individual approaches to the relationship between the government and the governed.[3]

In England, the biggest proponents of distributionism were Hilaire Belloc and G. K. Chesterton. Their particularly British form of distributionism emphasized the dispersal of property to as many people as possible in order to break up concentrations of market or economic power and "distribute" the responsibility and dignity that come from owning one's property. Distributionism differs from free-market capitalism in that it discourages concentrations of wealth and property, whether or not they came about through the workings of the market's "invisible hand." It differed from socialism in that distributionists did not view property as a problem, but instead wanted property to be spread as widely as possible rather than to be controlled by the state or eliminated altogether. Distributionist thinkers also argued that the most important unit of society is the family, rather than the Enlightenment assumption that the individual is the basic building block of society. This assumption of the centrality of the family goes against the individuality that is central to the logic of both capitalism and socialism. Other tenets of distributionist ideology are an interest in the revival of crafts and medieval guilds, a nostalgia for agricultural society, and suspicion of large banks and financial institutions. According to distributionist ideology, both the government and business should be limited in power and as small as possible.

The Shire has many of the attributes of an ideal distributionist society. The population seems to consist of mostly small freeholders, so it fits the requirement of a society that has an agricultural base and widespread ownership of property. The society is mostly organized in family and clan units, rather than as individual citizens. For example, the Tooks all live together as a communal extended family in Took Hall. There are few concentrations of wealth or power in the Shire, though there are definitely some hobbits who are more well off than others (the Bagginses versus the Gamgees, for example). Even so, the Shire offers opportunities for social and economic movement so that someone like Sam Gamgee can start off in the servant class and end up as the mayor. Rather than large-scale production of goods, most products are artisanal and made at home rather than in factories. Almost no government exists, and much of it is more ceremonial than executive. Thus the Shirriffs, the coercive arm of the state in the Shire, are used more to police animals than people, and the mayor's most important function is to host banquets and parties.

While distributionist ideas were somewhat influential in continental Europe in the mid-twentieth century through various Christian democratic parties (like the Christian Democratic Union of Germany), they made little headway in Great Britain. No doubt part of the reason was their association with Catholicism and Catholic social teaching. As I said, the leading proponents of distributionism in Great Britain, Belloc and Chesterton, were also probably the most famous Catholic apologists of early twentieth-century England. Anti-Catholicism in England made any political or social movement associated with the Catholic Church suspect for many British people. Another likely reason for its unpopularity was the communal nature of distributionism, which was not a good fit for the commercial and individualistic nature of twentieth-century Britain. The theoretical way the leaders of distributionism presented it was also a barrier for it to become a prominent political party or movement in Great Britain. Chesterton promoted distributionism through essays written in his highly allusive fashion that focused more on convincing people of the evils of the current system than the correctness of distributionism. Like Marx, Chesterton was much better at describing the ills of the systems he sought to dismantle than providing a workable program for what should replace them. Unlike Marx, Chesterton did not organize a political program, promote specific policies, or create a party. For example, in his explanation of distributionism titled *Outline of Sanity*, Chesterton spends much of his essay describing, often with his famous paradoxical word play, what he sees as the insanity of overreaching government, big businesses, monopolies, and trusts, while providing little space for outlining his program to create a distributionist society. Here is an example of the maddening degree of non-specificity typical of Chesterton's political program:

> But I mean my utopia would contain different things of different types holding on different tenures; that as in medieval states there would be some things nationalized, some machines owned corporately, some

guilds sharing common profits, and so on, as well as many absolute individual owners, where some individual owners are most possible.[4]

Note that Chesterton provides very little guidance about what things should be collectivized and what things should be held as individual property and how this is to be decided. As a political action plan, *The Outline of Sanity* could not be more vague. The most specific proposal he suggests is to create a peasantry, though how twentieth-century Britain is going to make that happen is not made particularly clear.

Even though many aspects of Tolkien's utopian societies seem to be based on distributionist principles, most of the resemblance to distributionism comes more from a common genealogy than from Tolkien consciously illustrating distributionism in his legendarium. Certainly, Tolkien read Chesterton, but Tolkien was never much interested in political philosophy, so I think it is unlikely that Tolkien studied Chesterton's political program in detail. What seems more likely to me is that Tolkien, Chesterton, and the nineteenth-century Church all drew from similar sources: medieval social organization and papal encyclicals. I explained earlier how Tolkien was influenced by both medieval and Victorian medieval sources. Chesterton also had an appreciation for the medieval period that reflected the type of Victorian medievalism so admired by conservatives in Chesterton's childhood and youth. Therefore, both Chesterton and Tolkien viewed a desirable society through their Victorian medieval ideology. The Catholic Church, while not quite as influenced by the peculiarities of British Victorian medievalism, looked back to some of the economic structures of the late Middle Ages in *Rerum Novarum* and *Quadragesimo Anno*. Medieval guilds, for example, certainly seem to be the type of organizations that serve as a model for the twin principles of subsidiarity and solidarity. Since Tolkien, the distributionist, and the Catholic Church drew from the same sources, they, not surprisingly, appear to have a family resemblance.

Instead of calling himself a distributionist, Tolkien used a more fraught term to classify his politics: anarchist. How exactly to define what Tolkien meant by this term takes some unpacking because defining clearly what is meant by the word "anarchy" is difficult for a variety of reasons. The simplest dictionary definition is an absence of government. More extreme versions of anarchy reject all forms of authority, coercion, and hierarchy. Of course, this is all the denotative definition of anarchy; the connotations of the word "anarchy" are different and mostly more negative. For most people, anarchy is associated with lawlessness, crime, lack of order, and other social ills, such that dysfunctional governments like Somalia or Syria are described as being in a state of anarchy. Anarchy also had an association with violence, especially around the turn of the twentieth century when assassinations and terrorist acts were often committed by anarchists.[5] This connotation was more prevalent in the twentieth than the twenty-first centuries, which is why when Tolkien admitted his anarchist sympathies, he was quick to separate himself from "whiskered men with bombs."[6] Anarchism is also strange because it is an ideology that exists in both left- and right-wing forms. As Giorel Curran notes, anarchism's seemingly schizophrenic ideology comes from how it "draws from two main, seemingly oppositional traditions: liberalism and Marxism."[7] Even so, she argues the left/right dichotomy is not the most meaningful way to categorize anarchistic thought. Instead of viewing anarchists as "right anarchists" versus "left anarchists" or through the huge variety of anarchist "schools," she makes the case that

> A much simpler distinction can be drawn between "individual" anarchism and "social" anarchism since this encapsulates the key elements of anarchist thought and of the different schools within it. Generally speaking, individual anarchists privilege the individual within the community and favour autonomous solutions to social problems. Social anarchists instead favour communal responses to social problems. While viewing the individual as key, social anarchists believe that individual flourishing can only occur in a communal society. But both promote, if in different ways, maximum freedom for individual expression in a community that sponsors harmonious relationships with fellow human beings.[8]

Based on these two categories, Tolkien's anarchism ironically seems to favor the communal rather than individual approach to anarchism. This is ironic since communal anarchism has often been associated with left anarchist figures, like Mikhail Bakunin, and Tolkien was not remotely a man of the left. On the other hand, Tolkien would likely find the individual anarchism that is often associated with the libertarian right (especially in the United States) particularly repulsive. Once again, trying to place Tolkien within the conventional political categories for anarchy (or any political affiliation) is difficult both in his time and our own. So in what sense is Tolkien an anarchist and what does that mean for him?

The first distinction that must be made between most anarchists and Tolkien is that, for Tolkien, the freedom that anarchism offers is a freedom that is for *a people*, rather than for *individuals*. Just like in chapter 4 when I discuss how, for Tolkien, myths are property of peoples rather than individuals, the freedom that Tolkien is interested in creating in his anarchistic societies is the freedom to act as a community rather than the radical freedom to act as an individual. In this, Tolkien continues to reject the Enlightenment assumption that humans should be viewed primarily as individual agents rather than parts of a social group (especially the family).[9] Still, while this type of freedom can be classified as communal freedom, it is not the same type of "communal" that thinkers like Bakunin express. The "communities" that Bakunin refers to are workers' collectives joined together by class rather than by ethnic groups or families.

Bakunin envisioned the leadership of these communal organizations chosen democratically and rotating after short terms in office to discourage the acquisition of power. The ultimate goal of these communal anarchists is the eventual abolishment of all hierarchy and authority.

For Tolkien, unlike these classic anarchists, anarchy does not mean the rejection of all authority. Tolkien not only did not reject hierarchy, but in many ways was more comfortable with it than most people in his and our own time. One can see this clearly in the way Tolkien promoted the class-based groupings in almost all his societies. As I have mentioned, hobbits have a servant class and a sort of squireocracy, though these classes are not permanent and people can rise to a higher class and fall to a lower one. Most of the societies of men in Middle-earth also are based on a semirigid class system that is passed on from father to son (and perhaps mother to daughter). Not only do we have an inherited position of Steward to the King, but even positions like Guards of the Citadel appear to be hereditary. Similarly, elven societies also seem to be run as monarchies with an entrenched aristocratic class. We do not see many indications of democratic norms or institutions except for the ents' informal assembly called the Entmoot.

Still, despite Middle-earth's mostly medieval social structure, we do not see many trappings that we would expect of a medieval monarchy. There are no palaces to be seen, for example. Instead, we see a lot of communal architecture, various meeting and gathering places including the storytelling halls in Rivendell, the giant dwarf-hall in Moria, the Golden Hall at Meduseld, and others. These serve as communal places that have multiple functions: places of council, room for debate, and even areas for artistic expression. We, in general, also do not see the ceremony that one expects to see in a monarchy. Just as Tolkien's Middle-earth is mostly stripped of the liturgical pomp of the Middle Ages, it does not include much of the spectacle of the monarchy that we see in the high Middle Ages. Because of Middle-earth's lack of liturgical religion, we also do not see the way in which religious authority either confirmed or challenged monarchial authority; this is another perennial theme of medieval politics absent from Middle-earth (unless one considers wizards, like Gandalf, a sort of clergy). In short, we have a hierarchical structure, but one that seems stripped of many of the privileges and markers of class power.

Not only does Tolkien reject the outward privileges of class power, he also rejects a form of power that is most legitimate in today's world: electoral power. Rather than rejecting the idea of authority itself, Tolkien's anarchistic beliefs reject the more modern form of legitimacy that comes from elected legislatures or parliaments. It appears that though Tolkien was comfortable with some forms of hierarchy, he was much less comfortable with democracy.[10] In the same statement where Tolkien claimed to be an anarchist, he also said the only form of government he would support was an "unconstitutional Monarchy." Yannick Imbert, in his essay "Tolkien's Shire," argues that this reference to "unconstitutional" monarchy means that Tolkien is not only rejecting constitutions, but also legislative bodies and parliaments.[11] Tolkien did not approve of constitutional government because he did not like the Enlightenment way of constructing societies based on "reason" and instead preferred a government that was created organically through the traditions of people. In a similar way, Imbert posits that Tolkien's rejection of legislatures comes from Chesterton and Belloc's rejection of party politics. Imbert also notes that Tolkien's descriptions of the evils of the modern world bear a resemblance to historian Christopher Dawson's fear of what he calls "radical Parliamentalism."[12] The problem with this democratic institution (according to Chesterton and Belloc) is that they tended to increase factionalism and party loyalty rather than trying to create the common good.[13] This helps explain an unusual aspect of the Shire—there is no governing body of any sort to make decisions: no parliament, legislature, not even the "council of elders" that one often sees in primitive societies. While occasionally the reader sees ad hoc assemblies to make decisions in Middle-earth, such as when Elrond gathers the free people to Rivendell to decide what to do with the Ring or when Treebeard convenes the Entmoot to decide what to do about Saruman, these assemblies are never permanent or institutionalized.[14]

Imbert argues that the sum total of these different positions makes the term "Tory anarchism" the best description of Tolkien's political views. Tory anarchism is a term coined by George Orwell to describe his own and Jonathan Swift's seemingly contradictory political beliefs. On the one hand, Swift believed deeply in preserving the aristocratic way of life while at the same time mercilessly satirizing the follies and excesses of that very class. In a similar way, the leftist Orwell attacked many of the modern aspects of his society, like the mass media and a moral decline, as well as admiring aspects of the past, especially a past that was less dominated by money and capitalism. According to Imbert, various twentieth-century thinkers fell into this Tory anarchist category, including Tolkien, Evelyn Waugh, and sometimes Chesterton.

Peter Wilkin in his book, *The Strange Case of Tory Anarchism*, explains the phenomenon of Tory anarchism in twentieth-century Britain. He argues that figures as politically disparate as George Orwell and Evelyn Waugh can be described using the same term because they have these characteristics:

> To be a Tory anarchist is to share a conservative moral and cultural critique of the modern world rather than a right-wing political ideology, and it is in this sense that Waugh and Orwell share common ground. Thus they and other Tory anarchists are concerned with such themes and issues as the nation's traditional cultural practices, its apparent moral decline and the need to defend the individual from au-

thoritarian institutions such as the state and the mass media. In order to do this they often deploy humour as a weapon with which to take on their adversaries.[15]

Anyone who has read Tolkien's letters can see almost all these themes throughout his correspondence. Still, one must draw a distinction between Tolkien's letters and his fiction. While Tolkien often seems to promote traditional values in his legendarium, the way he advocates for these values differs substantially in both form and goals from most of the thinkers who have been characterized as Tory anarchists. Wilkin describes dependence on satire as the most distinguishing feature of most Tory anarchists' works. This dependence on satire is most obvious in Orwell's naming Swift as the prototypical Tory anarchist. Not surprisingly, the satirists Orwell and Waugh also become Wilkin's most important case studies into the phenomenon of the twentieth-century Tory anarchist. Thus, one obvious distinction between Tolkien and Swift or Waugh is that satire is a register that Tolkien rarely employed or was much interested in pursuing. This is especially true in Tolkien's writing before *The Hobbit* and *The Lord of the Rings*. Almost all of the stories that became *The Silmarillion* are serious, and practically the only satire that is employed in them are litotes meant to express the hardy courage of its heroes. Tolkien provides some gentle satire in both *The Hobbit* and *The Lord of the Rings* but it is mostly the good-humored kind in which the targets would appreciate being in on or part of the joke. His ironic barbs in tales like *Farmer Giles of Ham* are gentle enough for children. Nothing could be further from Waugh's bitter satire in *Decline and Fall* and *Vile Bodies* or Swift's often scatological humor in *Gulliver's Travels* or *Battle of the Books* than Tolkien's legendarium. Instead, Tolkien spends almost all his time attempting to rehabilitate old values rather than mock new ones. Even his evil societies, which are modeled on the worst aspects of the contemporary world, portray cultures so evil that irony cannot exist. The cliché that "hypocrisy is a tribute vice pays to virtue" makes no sense in Morgoth's Thangorodrim or Sauron's Mordor. The type of duplicity we see in Lady Beste-Chetwynde, who pretends to be a respectable socialite while she is actually a brothel owner in Britain, is unnecessary in the evil realms of Middle-earth, where evil characters have no need for hypocrisy to mask their evil. Perhaps because of this lack of satirical bite, Wilkin does not mention Tolkien as one of the twentieth-century Tory anarchists he discusses in his book.

This distinction, between Tory anarchists and Tolkien, highlights once again the difficulties in describing Tolkien in political terms like "conservative" or "reactionary." Part of the issue becomes what exactly are Tolkien and the Tory anarchists trying to conserve or revive. One can imagine Waugh's ideal time period several centuries before his own when the aristocracy thrived and the aesthetic values he admired were in full bloom. Perhaps Waugh would feel most comfortable in the Georgian or Regency period, except for the fact that they were Protestant (to be Waugh's ideal they would have to be part of an alternate history where these were Catholic rather than Protestant dynasties). At one time, Waugh suggested that he would prefer to live in the twelfth century, but for the sybaritic artist this hardly seems like a good fit. The English literature of the seventeenth and eighteenth centuries, with its master satirists like John Dryden, Alexander Pope, and Jonathan Swift, also fits Waugh's literary style much better than any earlier period. Tolkien's ideal time, however, seems to be in a much more distant past. For example, Tolkien lamented the Norman Conquest, and as a schoolboy, argued it was one of the greatest catastrophes in English history and language. The past that Tolkien yearned for was the Anglo-Saxon England of his favorite poetry like "Dream of the Rood" and *Beowulf*. Stylistically, most of Tolkien's legendarium reflects the heroic and powerful tone of these Old English works. What Tolkien wants to conserve or revive is quite different from say, the typical American conservative whose ideal period might be the mid-1950s rather than the mid-ninth century.

There are those who argue, despite what Tolkien said about his political beliefs, that much of his work espoused more conventionally conservative values (in the twenty-first-century sense).[16] Jay Richards and Jonathan Witt, in their book *The Hobbit Party*, argue that the political views espoused in *The Hobbit* and *The Lord of the Rings* reflect a belief in the traditional conservative values of small government and economic liberty. For instance, they note that in *The Hobbit*, Bilbo joins the party of dwarves only after a legal document (a sort of contract) is drawn up delineating the duties and compensation that Bilbo would receive for his "burgling" services (discreetly described by Thorin as "professional assistance").[17] According to Richards and Witt, this contract serves as a model of free exchange of goods and labor. They describe how the fastidious manners of the hobbits help create the trust necessary to conduct business according to established rules and conventions (derived from Christendom).[18] In addition to the contract, they note the various trading relationships that the elves of Mirkwood and the men of Laketown have developed over the years to suggest that Tolkien was commenting favorably on trade and the principle of comparative advantage and the dangers of crony capitalism interfering with that trade. Finally, they describe how in Middle-earth, tyranny often goes hand-in-hand with the stealing and hoarding of goods by centralizing tyrants, whether they be the dragon Smaug or the wizard Saruman. What they glean from these books is that government should not interfere with the free exchange between people and that the greatest danger to freedom comes from outside forces confiscating people's property. It appears that they see Tolkien's ideas as arguments that help them in the conventional struggle between the left and right poles in American politics and argue that these arguments firmly come down on the right side (as opposed to the left side) of free enterprise and small government. They argue that Tolkien is not arguing for completely uncontrolled economic freedom. Tolkien constrains his version of free enterprise with Christian moral principles and a belief in the common good, rather than an unchecked, amoral libertarian economy subject only to market forces.

Richards and Witt make a compelling case that Tolkien did not have much use for socialist governments and authorities interfering in the free exchange of goods between people. Tolkien's disdain for government interference is clear from his "Scouring of the Shire" chapter in *The Lord of the Rings*. Saruman creates a society where goods are "gathered" and "shared" by his henchmen. As it turns out, these henchmen were much better at the gathering than the sharing and kept most of what they had stolen. Beyond the economic theft, the society that Saruman creates also focuses a lot on rules that do not necessarily have much to do with economics. Indeed, rules like forbidding hobbits to drink beer would do more to dampen economic activity than promote it. The lists of petty rules that Saruman forced hobbits to conform to bear more than a passing resemblance to the "petty and counterproductive regulations" of interfering government agencies that modern American conservatives claim stifle innovation.

I agree that Tolkien had no problem with free exchange and commerce. Therefore, the "Scouring of the Shire" chapter and parts of *The Hobbit* can be read as condemnations of the evils of socialism and centralized planning. Even so, these observations do not mean that Tolkien was an advocate for American-style economic conservatism. Take, for example, the "contract" that Bilbo accepts to begin his burgling career. I think it is a bit of a stretch to describe it as a contract at all. It is a small note that Thorin leaves on Bilbo's mantel. There is no negotiation between the parties to an agreed-upon set of actions and compensation; instead, Thorin unilaterally sets the conditions of Bilbo's employment, so it is hardly an argument for the beauty of capitalist contract law. Even if the reader takes the contract as binding, one of the clear themes of the novel is Bilbo's transformation from a low-level hired hand to a full-fledged leader of the group. Therefore, Bilbo's relationship with the dwarves becomes less commercial as the plot of *The Hobbit* unfolds, and the contract's relative unimportance becomes clearer. Indeed, the central turning point of the novel comes when Bilbo deliberately *breaks* his contract with the dwarves and offers the Arkenstone to Bard of Lake-town and Thranduil of the Mirkwood elves. As a professional burglar, he should have turned over the Arkenstone to the dwarves immediately instead of giving it to the dwarves considered "enemies." As a contractor, he had no right to make that decision, but as the de facto moral leader of the dwarf party, he could. Instead of the contract defining his association with the dwarves, it is Bilbo's taking on increasing responsibilities throughout his journey to the Lonely Mountain that ends up defining his relationship with them. Another indication that Bilbo's approach to the dwarves is not commercial comes at the end of the novel. After the Battle of the Five Armies, the dwarves offer to repay their bargain strictly and give Bilbo an equal share of the treasure that he has earned by the agreement, but he accepts only a small portion of the enormous treasure that is due him.[19] He leaves with just one chest each of silver and gold. However the reader interprets the novel, Bilbo is hardly the best businessman, and he did not do nearly enough to maximize his profits; in the final analysis, Bilbo did not make the best capitalist and his stockholders would have been unhappy with him (if he had any).

In a similar way, Richards and Witt's celebration of the commercial ties between Lake-town and the elves comes with the important caveat that commercial activity and wealth are not necessarily good in themselves, but only in context with how they are used. Tolkien makes this contrast by comparing the Master of Lake-town with the newly created King of Lake-town, Bard. Bard generously gives the money he receives after the Battle of the Five Armies to help rebuild Lake-town and make for a more prosperous relationship between the dwarves, elves, and men. He also gives money to the Master of Lake-town, who rather than make a similarly good use of it, flees with the gold to the wastes and ends up starving amid all his treasure. Tolkien clearly has no problem with people owning property, but the implications of these two characters' relationship with wealth suggest that wealth comes with responsibilities. One of the primary responsibilities is to distribute it (note, not invest it), which is exactly what Bard did. This contrast between Bard's generosity and the Master of Lake-town's hoarding of his gold shows the lesson that Tolkien clearly meant to send to his young readers: with great wealth comes great responsibility, or to put in terms of Catholic social justice, with an obligation to act with solidarity. Not coincidentally, Bard also acts using the principle of subsidiarity as well; the wealth he uses is spent as close to home as possible and with his closest neighbors. Richards and Witt argue that the Master of Lake-town's greed is not a reflection of capitalist desire because he is an administrative official—more of a bureaucrat than a businessman. Therefore, Tolkien's lesson is more about the dangers of government officials and their promotion of crony capitalism than about the dangers of capitalism itself. This ignores the fact that Bard, as the eventual King of Dale, is even less a businessman than the Master of Lake-town, yet seems capable of acting in the interests of his community. The focus of this incident suggests that there is a danger in the greed of capitalism just as there is in the oppression of socialism.

Tolkien's inclusion of dwarves as one party to the transaction also hints that his story was not meant to be a simple paean to free-market capitalism. In the larger mythological world that Tolkien created, dwarves have a specific attitude toward the material world that sheds light on their function in *The Hobbit*. From the very beginning, dwarves have virtues and vices that lead them to certain patterns of behavior. I mentioned in chapter 1 how elves had a particular weakness—that of wanting to keep the world the same. This vice was coupled with the virtue of appreciating and preserving the beauty of the natural world. In a similar way, the dwarves have a particular vice, greed that is also associated with a particular virtue, toughness. This combination of vices and virtues makes dwarves difficult to control by the forces of evil, but also suspicious and close-fisted in their dealings with the forces of good. The dwarves were greedy for minerals of the earth specifically and often behaved irrationally in order to protect or obtain beautiful stones or medals. Throughout the history of Middle-earth, the dwarves' avarice for these goods leads them to disaster. In the First Age, the dwarves forged the necklace Nauglamír using jewels taken from Valinor. Thingol later commissioned the dwarves to attach the silmaril that Beren had recovered from Morgoth to the existing necklace. The dwarves who remade the necklace became so enamored with it that they demanded Thingol give them the whole necklace as payment for their craftsmanship. This demand leads to the slaughter of the dwarves by the elves of Doriath. In retaliation, the dwarves of Nogrod attack Doriath and kill Thingol. As a result of this attack, the enmity between dwarves and elves lasts into the Third Age, many thousands of years later. In *The Hobbit*, Thorin's refusal to share his wealth with the men of Lake-town and the elves of Mirkwood nearly leads to a pointless battle between potential allies on the eve of the Battle of the Five Armies. Also in the Third Age, the dwarves of Khazad-Dûm (Moria), in their greed from mithril, mine too deeply into the earth and awaken the Balrog. It is clear from this repeated history of avarice that the besetting sin of the dwarves is greed. This is the context of the dwarves' "contract" with Bilbo. With this understanding of the character of the dwarves and their penchant for hard bargaining, we see that it is unlikely that Tolkien included this document in *The Hobbit* as a way to justify free-market economics to children (though he was not opposed to the free exchange of goods).

Because of the close-fisted nature of the dwarves, the biggest change in attitude toward material goods happens to the dwarves in *The Hobbit*. Bilbo never seems particularly interested in personal gain as a motive for his journey, but is tempted by promptings of his Tookish inclination for adventure to join the dwarf party. On the other hand, the dwarves, and Thorin in particular, are hyper-focused on material gain. So, along with Bilbo's growth as a heroic character and leader throughout the novel, the dwarves also undergo a transformation, though this transformation does not happen until the end of *The Hobbit*. The stubbornness of the dwarves, and Thorin in particular, when they refuse to share Smaug's treasures almost leads to a fraternal war between the various "good" races that are located around the Lonely Mountain. When forced to negotiate with Bard and Thranduil, Thorin still schemed to keep all of his treasure and regain the Arkenstone, even after he promised to give Bilbo's fourteenth share of the treasure to Bard and the Elvenking.

It is only after the Battle of the Five Armies that Thorin and the dwarves learn to value personal relationships more than treasure. After the battle, the dwarves agree to keep their bargain and Thorin dies reconciled to Bilbo. They also insist on sharing their wealth with Bilbo even though he had technically broken his agreement with them. When Dain becomes the new King under the Mountain, he becomes a great king "because he dealt his treasure well";[20] in other words, Dain was a good gift giver. We can see here the final resolution of one of the central conflicts of the novel: the dwarves move from a commercial contract-oriented approach to material goods to the gift-giving approach. As I mentioned in chapter 1, Tolkien took his model of the correct approach to wealth from the poem he knew best, *Beowulf*. In *Beowulf*, the definition of a good king is a ring-giver, a lord who rewards his thanes. This reward does not have a commercial intent, like the wages given by a boss to an employee, but instead signifies a relationship rather than a payment. By the end of *The Hobbit*, the dwarves realize that they cannot truly "pay" Bilbo for his services in money. The relationship between the dwarves and the hobbit transcends the commercial. This change in the relationship between Bilbo and the dwarves shows that Tolkien's concern was not to justify capitalism and the creation of commercial contracts, but to show how personal relationships are much more important than financial gain.

That Tolkien was not primarily concerned with advocating for free-market capitalism is even more apparent in *The Lord of the Rings*. In addition to attacking the "socialist" policies of Saruman with his "gatherers and sharers," Tolkien also attacks the industrialization of the Shire (which was a prominent feature of twentieth-century capitalism as well as of socialism). Some of the most negative imagery that Tolkien uses to describe the Saruman-transformed Shire is reserved for the newly created mill. Even though this description comes from Farmer Cotton, one cannot help but feel that it represents Tolkien's view of industrial development:

> Take Sandyman's mill now. Pimple [Lotho Sackville-Baggins] knocked it down almost as soon as he came to Bag End. Then he brought in a lot o' dirty looking Men to build a bigger one and fill it full of wheels and outlandish contraptions. Only that fool Ted was pleased by that, and now he works there cleaning the wheels for the Men, where his dad was the Miller and his own master. Pimple's idea was to grind more and faster or so he said. He's got other mills like it. But you got to have grist before you can grind; and there was no more for the new mill to do than the old. But since Sharkey came they don't grind no more corn at all. They're always a-hammering and a-letting out smoke and a stench, and there is no peace even at night in Hobbiton. And they pour

out filth on purpose; they've fouled all the lower Water, and it is getting down into Brandywine.[21]

I have quoted this passage at length because Farmer Cotton's speech combines many of Tolkien's complaints and suspicions about industrial development into one passage. First, the original mill is destroyed for no good reason except as an example of creative destruction. The new mill is sold as a means to grind more grain and is promised to be a means of greater efficiency. The centralization of production makes people who were once owners, like Ted Sandyman, into employees, and worse than that, slaves to the machines, rather than masters of their trade. In the end, however, the hobbits do not even get the "efficiency" they were promised and the mill is used for other, apparently more nefarious, purposes. Finally, instead of milling more grain, the mill creates air, water, and noise pollution. In this example, Farmer Cotton (speaking for Tolkien) combines his suspicion of the necessity, purpose, and results of industrial development all in one succinct passage. Few arguments in classical free-market theory can be marshaled to suggest why building the mill was wrong,[22] but one can see why this project would not pass muster based on distributionist or anarchist principles. Rather than prioritizing efficiency and profit like market capitalism, distributionism focuses on building solidarity and serving the needs of the immediate community.

Tolkien's suspicion of machines and mechanical devices is also apparent in *The Hobbit*. He makes goblins the most mechanical of the Middle-earth races. The narrator in *The Hobbit* describes goblins' skills in this way,

> They make no beautiful things, but they make many clever ones. They can tunnel and mine as well as any but the most skilled dwarves, when they take the trouble, though they are usually untidy and dirty.... It is not unlikely that they invented some of the machines that have since troubled the world, especially ingenious devices for killing large numbers of people at once, for wheels and engines and explosions always delighted them.[23]

This fascination with machines comes in direct contrast with hobbits who "do not and did not understand or like machines more complicated than a forge-bellows, a water-mill, or hand-loom, though they were skillful with tools."[24] Tolkien has two complaints about industrial machines. The first is that they are utilitarian without being beautiful. Therefore, Tolkien first condemns the goblins because "they make no beautiful things." More surprising, Tolkien's complaints about machinery also focus on what they do well and what many would consider the benefit of machinery: that they produce lots of something with relatively little effort. Of course, in the case of the orcs, it is efficiently doing something evil, killing large numbers of people, but Tolkien also implies that doing anything efficiently might not be worth the bargain. Tolkien, in a letter to his son,

Christopher Tolkien, argues even more directly that "labour-saving machinery only creates endless and worse labour."[25] I think part of what Tolkien objects to is that this machinery separates the producer from the product in unhealthy ways. Some of this recalls the Marxist idea of "alienation of labor," where the worker starts to feel more like a cog in a machine rather than the creator of his or her own products. At the most degraded end of this spectrum is Ted Sandyman, who traded in his heritage as the master of the mill later to become a slave to men and their machines.

Tolkien's negative response to industry was not just a feature of his fiction. Throughout his correspondence, Tolkien complains about the effects of machines and technology. Sometimes, his disgust came about in conversation, like when he pointed out a motorcyclist to Clyde Kilby and casually observed, "That is an Orc." He also wrote of his disgust of industry and technology in his letters and essays. In a letter to his son, he goes as far as to exclaim, "How I wish the 'infernal combustion' engine had never been invented."[26] In "On Fairy-Stories," he describes his reaction to an academic who claimed that he enjoyed living near an automobile factory because it helped him experience "real life." In response, Tolkien caustically observed, "The notion that motor-cars are more 'alive' than say centaurs or dragons is curious; that they are more 'real' than horses is pathetically absurd."[27] Finally, in another letter to Christopher, he argues, "It is the aeroplane of war that is the real villain," and says of the British air war that "my sentiments are more or less those of Frodo if he had discovered some hobbits learning to ride Nazgûl-birds 'for the liberation of the Shire.'"[28]

His animus toward machines, like most of his beliefs, does not just reflect his personal tastes, but shows a deeper philosophical objection to what the machines represent about people's desire for power, their relationship with other people, and their approach to the material world. I have already touched on this issue in chapter 1 when I discussed the desire for evil to replace the greater with the lesser and also in chapter 3 with people's inability to accept limits. For Tolkien, these sins all come from a root evil: our desire for control and speed. In his letter to Milton Waldman, Tolkien describes the temptation to do evil by accelerating and controlling the material world:

> This desire [for creativity of art] is at once wedded to a passionate love of the real primary world, and hence filled with the sense of mortality, and yet unsatisfied by it. It has various opportunities of "Fall." It may become possessive, clinging to the things made as "its own," the sub-creator wishes to be the Lord and God of his private creation. He will rebel against the laws of the Creator—especially against mortality. Both of these (alone or together) will lead to the desire for Power, for making the will more quickly effective—and so to the Machine (or Magic). By the last I intend all use of external plans or devices (apparatus) instead

of development of the inherent inner powers or talents—or even the use of these talents with the corrupted motive of dominating: bulldozing the real world, or coercing other wills. The Machine is our more obvious modern form though more closely related to Magic than is usually recognised.[29]

In this complex passage, Tolkien links several things together that help explain his antipathy to the "Machine" in general and "machines" in particular. On a basic level, the creative impulse that makes machines is a desire for control, which he traces all the way back to the desire to control mortality. Because the physical world is mortal, this control will always become frustratingly temporary. This leads to the desire to have permanent power over Creation and to create without God rather than recognizing that power ultimately belongs to the Creator: in other words, to make his Creation, our creation. At the heart of this desire for control is a rebellion against limits, in general, and mortality, in particular. Power over Creation depends on speed and effectiveness because this mortality can only seem to be thwarted ("seem to be" because this control is illusory) by taking control over time, that is, "making the will more quickly effective." This leads to "bulldozing the real world, or coercing other wills."[30] Note that the chain of causes that leads to the machine starts with a desire to create, which is not evil at all. It is only when this desire goes outside the bounds of morality and attempts to defeat mortality that it becomes evil. One can also see the link between mortality and speed. The desire for speed is often a desire to control time, by placing reality under our schedule, as if we can slow down time by doing tasks more quickly and efficiently.

I think most contemporary people can follow Tolkien's reasoning until they get to the most fascinating part of the quote: when Tolkien associates machines with magic. To most twenty-first-century people, machines and magic are two completely different phenomena, with machines being real and practical, while magic is false and impossible. Yet Tolkien classes them together because both machines and magic imply unacceptable shortcuts. For the average person, this goes beyond the obvious insight that some of the most sophisticated machines appear almost to be operated by magic. For example, Kirk Honeycutt describes breakthroughs like the 3-D animation technology for the movie *Avatar* using a familiar cliché that "movie magic is back."[31] Certainly, many of the movie's viewers unconsciously think of the immersive, easy nature of the experience as magical. Tolkien sees the very effectiveness, ease, and speed that both magic and machines promise as the danger.

Another draft of a letter he wrote, Letter 155 to Naomi Mitchison, helps to explain what Tolkien means by the word "magic." In that letter, Tolkien makes a distinction between what he calls *magia* and *goeteia*, with *magia* meaning magic that affects the real physical world and *goeteia* meaning magic in the sense of enchantment, creating an illusion that does not really exist.[32] According to Tolkien, both types of magic can be used for good or for ill. The danger of using *magia* is that its power can be used "to bulldoze both people and things" (note how Tolkien uses the same verb "bulldoze" in both letters). The danger of *goeteia* is that the illusion can be used as a lie, to fool people. When Tolkien compares machines to magic, he most certainly is speaking of *magia*. According to Tolkien, the temptations of *magia* are caused by its "immediacy: speed, reduction of labor, and reduction also to a minimum (or vanishing point) the gap between the idea or desire and the result or effect."[33] It is pretty clear that Tolkien's description of the purpose of *magia* bears a striking resemblance to most contemporary people's view of the ideal purpose of machinery and technology: to reduce the result desired to a "vanishing point." Consider, for example, people's desire for instantaneous entertainment (not willing to wait even a few seconds for a video to load) or the desire to have goods shipped to them immediately (sometimes with the goods manufactured to their personal specifications). Tolkien connects magic and machines through their similar promise of immediacy of desire.

We can see now how Tolkien's description of Saruman's mill in the Shire speaks as much to Tolkien's politics as to his aesthetics. Everything about the mill represents the aspects of the Machine[34] that Tolkien hated. The original mill, which worked well enough, was torn down in haste to make room for this quickly built mill. The unnecessary speed shows Saruman's impatience for power and dominance. Its great size suggests that the mill was built for efficiency rather than to supply a real need. Finally, the fact that the mill stopped filling the need that the old mill fulfilled suggests that it was built on false pretenses. This suggests that the hobbits both individually and collectively lost control over the use of the mill. As a community, they no longer could rely on the mill to grind their grain, and individually they ceded control of the mill to men. All of this suggests that the mill had a political significance; Tolkien saw the new mill as a symbol of how people choose to organize themselves rather than just an example of impersonal economic forces, which is the language most twentieth- and twenty-first-century people use for these types of economic decisions. His attack on machines, and indirectly the division of labor, goes to the heart of the free-market system since Adam Smith. The assumption is that the most efficient solution is best and the only decision is to find out what solution is the most efficient. This is how people come to view political decisions as the inevitable result of market forces rather than policy decisions by those in power. Think about how trade agreements or technology are introduced in our society. Almost no one argues about whether the agreements or technology are good for people, but whether they will create jobs or economic return. If the new product or service has a net economic benefit, no one bothers to ask whether it contributes to human flourishing. Tolkien's attack on the very idea of economic efficiency is in some ways a more basic challenge than socialist economics, which after all often comes down to how to control and distribute this efficiency rather than suggesting it should be eliminated altogether.

In the end, as is often the case, using Tolkien as an ally in contemporary political struggles only works if one takes him selectively and out of context. I agree with Richards and Witt that there is no direct evidence that Tolkien was a distributionist, despite his disdain for a purely free-market approach. Based on his dislike for coercion in all its forms, I find it unlikely that Tolkien would have approved of the coercive measures necessary to distribute property advocated by thinkers like Hilaire Belloc. Still, proving that Tolkien did not believe in the modern political philosophy of distributionism or socialism, for that matter, does not imply that he was an advocate for the current market economy and its effects. Certainly, the societies that Tolkien created and had the most affection for do not resemble our free-market, industrial, and post-industrial society. Richards and Witt counter that Tolkien's affection for the Shire was primarily an aesthetic one and that he included many other types of societies, like Gondor, that were "good" yet created on a much larger political and economic scale than is favored by distributionist theory.[35] It is true that Tolkien did not have a simple political philosophy where good equals small and bad equals large. Still, it is mistake to separate Tolkien's aesthetics from his politics since they are both based on his overarching philosophical principles. The one area that Tolkien did seem to be dogmatic about was his distaste for industrialization in general and machines in particular. In none of Tolkien's "good" societies do labor-saving machines play a role and in all his bad societies they do, so it is hard to imagine that Tolkien is not criticizing our industrialized world.

What was writ small in the mill in the Shire was writ large in the evil realms of Thangorodrim and Mordor. The three social imperatives that dominate these societies are increased control, speed, and scale. These societies are built for control, even to the point of diminishing the power of their leaders. Morgoth and Sauron are willing to give up their power, and even parts of themselves, in return for gaining control over their subordinates (despite these sacrifices, their control was incomplete and fleeting). These societies are willing to destroy their environments and use up their subjects in order to increase the speed of their production of weapons and armies. Finally, everything is done on the largest scale possible, with huge armies, arms, and resources that always exceed those of the free peoples they attempt to conquer and dominate. Like the Shire and Rivendell, the implications of these tendencies in Thangorodrim and Mordor suggest a political philosophy. In order to create this speed and scale, these evil states depend on sacrificing today for the promise of tomorrow.

DYSTOPIAN AND UTOPIAN LEADERSHIP IN TOLKIEN'S LEGENDARIUM

To see how this philosophy played out, it makes sense to look at it at the micro as well as the macro level by seeing it through the eyes of those living in Tolkien's evil realms. Looking closely at individuals' roles in these societies will also allow us to see how Tolkien's approach to leadership is intimately connected with his approach to politics. We never see the inside of Thangorodrim, but we get a glimpse into Mordor's governance in the way orcs behave toward each other. In *The Lord of the Rings*, the reader sees how Mordor is organized when Sam overhears the conversation between two orc officers, Shagrat and Gorbag, at the entrance of Mordor. The crux of their discussion involves power, who wields it, and whether the leaders of Mordor are making the right decisions. Unsurprisingly, when Tolkien first introduces Shagrat and Gorbag, they are engaged in an orc-like power struggle:

> "Hola, Gorbag! What are you doing up here? Had enough of war, already?"
>
> "Orders, you lubber. And what are you doing, Shagrat? Tired of lurking up there? Thinking of coming down to fight?"
>
> "Orders to you. I'm in command of the pass. So speak civil. What's your report?"
>
> "Nothing."[36]

Note that the first instinct of both orcs is to rely on their military authority to establish their pecking order. The discussion of "orders" and who is in command is an obvious power play in which each of the orcs tries to gain the advantage over the other using the command structure of their organization. The discerning reader will also note how this dialogue sounds much more like the modern military than interactions between the troops and their leaders among the good societies of Middle-earth, like Gondor and Rohan, whose soldiers speak in much more medieval language. This connection with the twentieth century suggests that Tolkien was commenting on his society and its relationship with power, especially the power dynamics within modern militaries.

The dialogue is interrupted as the orcs search for the "elf-warrior" (actually Sam) who has wounded Shelob. When it continues, the orcs debate about their future and whether their superiors have got control over the situation. Shagrat argues that the "big bosses" have "let things slip" and Gorbag agrees that "ay, even the Biggest [referring to Sauron] can make mistakes." All of this is said as quietly as possible because Shagrat warns that "they have got eyes and ears everywhere; some among my lot, like as not."[37] This debate highlights the doubts even mid-level orcs have about their leadership and the paranoia that is created to enforce discipline. Even so, the orcs chafe at the control and long for an opportunity to escape the discipline of "the big bosses." Shagrat goes as far as to suggest that they escape with a "few trusty lads" and set up their own personal fiefdom "where there's good loot nice and handy, and no big bosses." They also make it clear that orcs feel the same kind of personal antipathy that humans do for the Nazgûl, and Gorbag admits that these wraith leaders give him the "creeps."

This brief dialogue gives us a lot of insight into the way Mordor is run. First, the jockeying of the orcs about their relative authority focuses exclusively on their rank or the rank of their superiors. This is ironic since their later conversation suggests that they actually had some doubts about how the war was being conducted by those in power over them (doubts that turned out to be justified). What is clear is that power comes through both formal channels and informal relationships. Indeed, elements like informers among the orcs' own troops suggest that the leadership of Mordor wants to poison both these professional and personal relationships in order to maintain control. This leads to the other remarkable aspect of the conversation: how vertically integrated the command structure is. These orcs, though they are only midlevel officers, feel that they are being surveilled and controlled by leaders at the very top of Mordor's leadership, so much so that they wish to escape the domination. Even though these orcs want to evade this control, they feel ambivalent about defying their masters. In the same dialogue, Gorbag warns Shagrat, "But don't forget: the enemies don't love us any more than they love Him [Sauron], and if they get topsides of Him, we're done too."[38] So on the one hand, they desperately desire to escape Sauron and, on the other, they depend on his triumph to survive. At the same time, they doubt the competence of their leaders. All these conflicting priorities lead to fractiousness, especially since the orcs are only concerned with their personal well-being. Besides using rank to jockey for power, these leaders also use more informal types of power against their rivals within the military structure. Thus, the orcs place great emphasis on which soldiers are "my lot" or "my lads." We saw this in the orc party that kidnapped Merry and Pippin as well. Some of the rivalry was based on loyalty to either Mordor or Isengard, but much of it was personalized as a rivalry between Uglúk and Grishnákh. All this points to the central obsession of both Mordor's leaders and subordinates: control.

We see an even more violent skirmish for control between two orcs tracking Sam and Frodo within Mordor itself. It highlights the fragility of the political structure of Mordor and the pattern of irrational conflict and dysfunctional politics repeats itself. As Sam and Frodo struggle toward Mount Doom, they spy two orcs: a larger Uruk warrior and a smaller scout/tracker orc, arguing over whether they should continue their search for "spies." The smaller orc wants to give up the search and the bigger one wants to continue. They also debate over who is to blame for losing the trail of the fugitives. The small orc was supposed to track his prey by smell, like a bloodhound, but he had lost the scent. The bigger orc also bungled killing or capturing Gollum, who might have given them some useful intelligence. Despite their recriminations, they do not limit their blame to each other; the only subject they both agree about is the incompetence of their leadership. The soldier orc complains that the "Higher Up" did not give them a specific-enough description: "First they say it's a great Elf in bright armor, then it's a sort of small dwarf-man, then it must be a pack of rebel Uruk-hai; or maybe the lot together."[39] The tracker agrees, "They've [the bosses] lost their heads, that's what it is." Despite this initial agreement, the tracker orc makes the argument personal by blaming warrior orcs (as a group) for their recent reversals: "Tower raided and all, and hundreds of your lads done in, and prisoners got away. If that's the way your fighters go on, small wonder there is bad news for the battles [referring to the defeat at Pelennor Fields]." The allusion to the defeat is too much for the soldier orc. He threatens the tracker with the warning: "That's cursed rebel-talk, and I'll stick you if you don't shut it down." Despite this warning, the scout orc has had enough and abandons the search, and starts to head home. In response, the Uruk orc threatens to give the trackers' "name and number" to the Nazgûl. Alarmed, the tracker exclaims, "Go to your filthy Shriekers [Nazgûl], and may they freeze the flesh off you. If the enemy does not get to them first. They've done in Number One [the Witch-King, the head of the Nazgûl], I've heard, and I hope it's true."[40] After this, the orcs attack each other: finally, the tracker shoots an arrow into the eye of the warrior orc, kills him, and runs away.

Like the discussion between Shagrat and Gorbag, this dialogue between the orcs is essentially a political one, in that these low-level soldiers debate about those in power and their relationship (as foot soldiers) with leaders of Mordor. As in the earlier debate, part of what the orcs argue about is whether to obey or resist their leaders. That they can even debate this question suggests that the orcs have free will and that free will leads to the possibility of conflict. Even before the debate begins, however, there are already various sources of division. Tolkien mentions that the different orcs come from different orc tribes, which is why they speak in Common Tongue rather than Orcish. Part of the hostility that the orcs feel for one another is tribal, or maybe in some sense "racial" differences. Perhaps an even better word for their physical and temperamental variation would be differences in "breed" since they seem to have been created for specific purposes, like different breeds of working dogs. Another source of the hostility is their respective military units, since the warrior orc comes from Minas Morgul (he bears the token of the Eye), whereas the tracker orc appears to come from some other unit. Still, the most interesting source of the conflict is their debate over Mordor's leadership. I already mentioned in the first chapter how Tolkienian evil societies differ from many classical dystopian societies in the degree of insubordination and chaos that seem to be inherent in their very structure, as opposed to the discipline and control that seem to be the most prominent feature of classic dystopias like *Brave New World, We,* and *1984*. This particular dialogue takes this insubordination to an extreme. The orcs not only question the competence and wisdom of their leaders, but the tracker orc expresses satisfaction at the possible death of the "Number One" (the Witch-King). One possible reason for this animus is the way that control is exercised in Mordor. Once again, we see how even individual orcs, equivalent to mere foot soldiers in a vast army, fear retribution from the Nazgûl, the very top of the leadership of Mordor. The scout's willingness to kill the warrior orc over the promise that his "name and number" will be turned in to the Nazgûl suggests that the turning in of individual soldiers to the wraiths was no idle threat. This extraordinary level of scrutiny that the leadership gives to individual orcs suggests a chain of command in total disarray. With no expectation that subordinate leaders will act with any sort of initiative, the leaders of Mordor must engage in inefficient levels of coercion because they cannot rely on their officers to provide guidance or discipline. The most extraordinary aspect of this incident is that it occurs close to the summit of Mordor's objective power. At this very moment, Sauron was supremely confident that he had the forces necessary to crush the remaining resistance from Gondor. This event happens as Sauron is gathering his forces for what he assumes is his final victory at the Battle of the Black Gate. Therefore, this should be the point when the forces of Mordor experience their highest morale. Instead, his soldiers doubt their leadership at the apex of Mordor's military strength. In this way, Tolkien ably conveys how the political structure of Mordor with all its military power and efficiency is actually brittle to its core.

This fragility goes beyond Mordor's weak political structure and suggests a weakness inherent in the shaped personalities of the creatures. Morgoth created orcs to be "evil." One of the effects of the orcs' malice is their inability to trust each other, so this disability is inherent in their very natures.[41] Even so, this inability to trust is exacerbated by their environment as well. The narrowing of personality that surveillance causes has a personal as well as a social dimension. Because Tolkien saw evil as the choosing of the lesser over the greater, choosing evil means loss. We can see this in the diminishment of both Morgoth and Sauron as they trade their essence for greater and greater control. This diminishment also occurs at the level of foot soldiers. Just as the leaders of Thangorodrim and Mordor diminish themselves to gain control, this control weakens the effectiveness of their minions, ironically even their military effectiveness. This desire for total control bypasses local leaders and makes those subordinates afraid to make decisions. The threat of constant punishment means that orcs spend as much time casting or avoiding blame as they do completing their missions. Their mania for control also weakens the intermediate leaders in the chain of command since, as I have already demonstrated, the leaders micromanage discipline so that the top leaders in Mordor routinely punish individual soldiers. In the end, soldiers and their leaders do not feel responsible for their decisions but live in constant fear that they will be punished or scapegoated for others' actions. Part of the dysfunction of Mordor comes from this desire for speed as well as control that Tolkien described as "The Machine." The hasty and incoherent orders that the leaders of Mordor provide for their foot soldiers and the distrust the orc foot soldiers have in their leadership are symptoms of this frantic desire to take action quickly.

This desire for speed and efficiency has led Mordor to narrow the natures of its minions as well as their responsibilities. As I mentioned, these orcs appear as "breeds" with different physical and temperamental qualities, like the big, fighting Uruk or the smaller olfactory tracking orc. Just as dogs have been created to do certain tasks, these orcs have been specialized to make them more "efficient." This specialization is not limited to orcs: "the Mouth of Sauron," who was once a man, has become a specialized spokesman for Sauron and the Ringwraiths who were once kings but are now couriers and enforcers of his will. This narrowness means that the servants of Sauron must operate in teams, yet the real differences in their natures make them struggle to cooperate, as happens any time large groups of orcs have to work together.

In this limitation and specialization, the politics and reality of Mordor mirror Tolkien's concerns about machines. In order to make his society run more efficiently, Sauron, and Morgoth before him, narrows his subjects into parts of a giant mechanism. Indeed, the language that Tolkien often uses to describe Thangorodrim and Mordor as being great factories or workshops reflects this separation of labor. Specialization means that these military societies can produce larger armies more quickly and effectively than the "free" peoples like Gondor and Rohan. The one constant in Tolkien's legendarium from the First Age in *The Silmarillion* to the Third Age in *The Hobbit* and *The Lord of the Rings* is that the armies of Thangorodrim and Mordor always vastly outnumber their opponents. Another way to look at these evil realms is that they practice total war and that their people and economies are entirely organized to create and sustain military conflict. Despite how efficient and effective Thangorodrim and Mordor are at conducting warfare, this very specialization is a weakness, and this weakness derives from the same principles that Tolkien sees in machines. The narrowing of personality is intended to reduce the time and effort it takes to construct an army. The surveillance, punitive discipline, and personal control that the leaders of the armies of Thangorodrim and Mordor exercise over their forces all make them effective. Remember that, in discussing machines, Tolkien argues that effectiveness can actually be an evil because all these measures of control and speed come at the cost of damaging the environments of Thangorodrim and Mordor. But maybe even more importantly, this effectiveness breaks down the relationship between people who see each other as means to an end rather than ends in themselves (to use the language of Immanuel Kant).[42]

Still, the advantages of control and speed that characterize magic and machines are difficult to resist. The advantage of magic is its speed in answering the desires of its conjurers. This is not always evil; after all, Gandalf wields magic for good. Still, based on Gandalf's example, there are reasons to believe that magic should be used sparingly. He never uses magic to coerce or overpower other people. For one thing, magic's strength can lead to damage because of its bluntness and power. We can see this damage in Denethor's use of the palantír to spy on Sauron and Mordor. The potency of the magic overwhelmed him and led to his downfall. Again, the verb that Tolkien repeatedly uses when describing the effects of both magic and machines is "bulldoze." When one thinks about bulldozing and bulldozers, images of wholesale and indiscriminate destruction come to mind. I think this image would be especially powerful and painful to Tolkien, who was particularly in touch with plant life, since one of the primary purposes of bulldozing is to raze any plants and leave the ground barren before the beginning of a construction project. This bulldozing form of magic is best characterized by Saruman's destruction of land and forests around Isengard. In Saruman, the mechanical and the magical come together to show the destructive effects of trying to build a military force without any regard to the environment.

Yet not all forms of magic in Middle-earth involve this "bulldozing." The elves' purpose for magic is quite the opposite; they use magic to preserve rather than to destroy. In places like Lothlórien and Rivendell, the elves' magic helps maintain the beauty of their surroundings. However, there is a danger even in this. Tolkien uses the word "embalming" to describe the elves' attempt to preserve the world unchanged throughout the ages. Though not as damaging as more destructive forms of magic, this preservation is unhealthy in the long run for the elves themselves (though not for the nature that they preserve) because the elves end up unable to shape the future because of their obsessions with the past.

While magic often leads to the narrowing of possibilities that comes with too much power wedded to too much haste, the narrowing of personality fits especially well in terms of serving what Tolkien calls "the Machine." Like the finely honed wheels and gears of a mechanical object, the leaders of Thangorodrim and Mordor want to make their servants specialized so that they operate as efficiently as possible. Additional complexity to a personality, like nonessential parts to a machine, interferes with the machine's overall efficiency. The leaders have simplified their own beings to increase their efficiency. Morgoth, the spirit, embodies himself in Arda so that he can operate there more effectively. Sauron, a Maiar, also becomes corporeal, and then effectively more one-dimensional as the ages pass. In the First Age, Sauron is most notable as a shapeshifter, able to embody many forms at will, from a werewolf to a vampire. Later, in the Second Age, he is capable of seeming beautiful in order to seduce the Númenóreans. Even later, in The Third Age, he becomes terrible in appearance, but still in an embodied form that resembles the basic form of men, elves, trolls, and orcs. This type of incompleteness was not only a characteristic of Sauron; Treebeard describes a similar but mental, rather than physical, devolution in Saruman. He laments that "he [Saruman] has a mind of metal and wheels."[43] This self-limiting the leaders of Thangorodrim and Mordor practice ends up being their undoing: in various ways they make themselves more vulnerable through incarnating themselves as creatures and through dividing themselves to gain control, as Sauron does when he creates the Ring of Power. But perhaps the greatest weakness comes from their inability to understand benevolence and therefore predict how good creatures would behave. In other words, their greatest weakness is, as Auden describes it, their "lack of imagination."

While the evil leaders voluntarily limit themselves, they also naturally want servants who are limited in order to maintain their machine-like efficiency. Still, the limited nature of the creatures of Mordor and Thangorodrim makes them brittle and unreliable instruments. Organizations need a minimum level of trust and goodwill to operate effectively. Orcs not only have trouble trusting each other, they can barely restrain themselves from killing each other. Trolls, made in the mockery of ents, are associated with inanimate objects, like stones or caves, just as ents are associated with living trees. Not surprisingly then, trolls, while they are similar to ents in strength, are stupid, while ents are the wisest of creatures. Because of their one-dimensionality, these evil creatures must play their specific roles, which lack the flexibility that comes with having more capabilities.

In contrast to this dystopian one-dimensionality is the complexity exhibited by the leaders in Tolkien's utopian societies. Aragorn is the case in point as the veritable Renaissance man of Middle-earth. When the hobbits first meet the man they call Strider, he is introduced as a woodsman and tracker. Later, Aragorn saves Frodo's life as a healer at the Ford of Bruinen. His healing is not just an emergency measure; as King of Gondor, he spends as much time as a healer as he does warrior. Aragorn is also a scholar of languages and lore, and can speak the elven languages of Sindarin and Quenya. Before he met the hobbits, he served as a mercenary for both Thengel of Rohan and Echthelion, the Steward of Gondor. *The Lord of the Rings* also gives examples of Aragorn's poetry and lyrics. Aragorn shows his political acumen when he refuses to enter the city of Gondor after the Battle of Pelennor Fields and when he challenges Sauron and causes him to release his armies prematurely. Eventually, as

King Elessar, he becomes responsible for maintaining his realms in peace as an administrator, rather than a war leader.

Aragorn's many and varied abilities are characteristic of other leaders of the free peoples of Middle-earth as well. Gandalf plays many parts as a wizard in Middle-earth. He is involved in the politics of almost all the known peoples of Middle-earth, from Gondor, to Rohan, to the dwarf and elf kingdoms. Most significant is his interest in the Shire, which appears to be motivated more by curiosity than by any political need. As often is the case, Gandalf's seemingly "inefficient" concern for the Shire pays much greater dividends than any of his more conventionally prudent interests in more powerful states like Rohan and Gondor. More than just a political advisor, Gandalf acts as a diplomat, leader, and even warrior. Similarly, Faramir is known for his interest in lore and music. This is why he ended up being a better and nobler leader in Gondor than either his brother or his father. Even the hobbits, who appear to be one-dimensional at first, have many interests: gardening, tale-telling, song-making, brewing, pipe-smoking, and most surprisingly, adventuring.

As if to provide counterexamples to these successful leaders with varied interests, Tolkien provides examples of monomaniacal and obsessive leaders who lead themselves and their people to ruin, despite their often noble intentions. These leaders are otherwise "good" elves and men whose focus on one thing leads them to make enormous errors in judgment. The prototypical example of this compulsive, unbalanced personality from the First Age of Middle-earth is the most personally gifted and powerful of the elves, Fëanor. His obsessive desire to create and possess beautiful objects leads him and his sons into a fruitless conflict with Morgoth throughout the First Age. I have already mentioned how the dwarves' single-minded desire for jewels and metals leads them to many disastrous and unnecessary conflicts, especially with the elves. Denethor and his son, Boromir's, unhealthy fixation on the security of Gondor leads them ironically to betray their country with rash acts of despair: Boromir, in his attempt to seize the Ring of Power to defend Gondor, and Denethor in his use of the palantír to try to see the plans of Sauron. In both Denethor and Boromir, we see the dangers of one-dimensionality, especially a focus on professional militarism.

The epic *The Children of Húrin* even more clearly illustrates Tolkien's suspicion of military aggressiveness and glory-seeking one-dimensionality. In the story, Túrin's belligerence and desire to make a name for himself end up destroying him and all that he loves. First, Túrin's rash punishment leads to the death of the elf Sauros, and Túrin's banishment from Doriath. Similarly, Túrin kills his best friend, Beleg, when Túrin strikes him after mistaking Beleg for an orc. Most significantly, however, is how the policy of offensive attack that he formulates for the forces of Nargothrond leads to the destruction of that city, which had held off Morgoth's forces for centuries. Before Túrin arrives, the elves of Nargothrond had wisely relied on stealth and secrecy to hide themselves from the forces of Thangorodrim. Túrin convinces them to abandon stealth and openly attack Morgoth's forces. Even more fatally, Túrin convinces the King of Nargothrond, Orodreth, to build a great bridge before the gates of the city so that the forces of Nargothrond could be quickly mustered against Morgoth's forces. Túrin's military activity leads Morgoth to discover the location of Nargothrond and the bridge Túrin constructs allows the city to be quickly taken and sacked by the forces of Thangorodrim. Finally, Túrin returns to his home in search of his mother and sister. When he fails to find them, he rashly kills the Easterling lord, Brodda, which causes his aunt to take her own life and guarantees that his own kin will be even more oppressed by the Easterlings. The pattern here is clear: rash violence leads to suffering even if the violence is, in some sense, justified. Certainly, the message is different than many of the tales of chivalry with which Tolkien would have been familiar that emphasize speedy and reckless courage. Tolkien's message in *The Children of Húrin* differs even from *The Lord of the Rings* where the emphasis is on rousing cautious or despairing allies into action rather than illustrating the folly of rash deeds. Instead, *The Children of Húrin*'s tragic and fatalistic outcome is more in line with earlier examples of Northern sagas like *Beowulf* and *The Story of Sigurd the Volsung*.

The complex and flexible leadership provided by the more utopian societies in Middle-earth contrasts with the simplistic and rigid militarism of Mordor and Thangorodrim, even with these cautionary examples of good men and elves who cannot resist fateful errors because they voluntarily limit themselves through singular desires. One scene in particular in *The Lord of the Rings*, the conflict over the Pyre of Denethor and Faramir, shows a complex interplay between military discipline, legitimate authority, and personal loyalty that would be impossible to imagine among the more limited and narrowed personalities of Mordor. In the scene, Denethor, driven mad by despair, attempts to immolate himself and his son, Faramir, with the aid of his servants. Pippin, after he has been released of his oath of service to Denethor, tries to warn his friend, Beregond, of the Tower Guard, about the threat to Faramir's life. Pippin also warns Gandalf, who is busy directing the defense of Gondor. Gandalf abandons his unofficial role as leader of the city's defenses and rushes to save Faramir. When Pippin and Gandalf arrive, they find Beregond fighting with the servants of Denethor to protect Faramir. They prevent Faramir's death, but Denethor still manages to burn himself alive.

Like the scenes with the orcs, the drama in the citadel tells us a lot about the relationship between leaders and followers in Gondor. On some levels, there are some similarities between the dilemmas faced by Shagrat and Gorbag and the ones faced by Pippin and Beregond. What should a subordinate do if his leader is behaving incorrectly or even erratically? The orcs and the members of the Tower Guard (Beregond and Pippin) respond very differently to the challenge. Whereas the orcs complain and do nothing, Pippin and Beregond take action: Pippin by going to get Gandalf and Beregond by trying to defend Faramir. Pippin uses his own initiative to tell both Beregond and Gandalf of Denethor's behavior. Denethor had released Pippin of his oath to him, so he had no military or feudal obligation to the House of the Stewards and was within his rights as a newly released subject to wash his hands of the whole affair. Pippin's decision to get Gandalf in the midst of a violent siege is a high-risk one, though not as high-risk as Beregond's. By deserting his post and drawing blood in the Houses of the Dead, he violates his oath and commits a capital crime. He also ignores the direct orders of Denethor, his legitimate leader. In this straightforward conflict between personal loyalty and military discipline, Beregond, despite his position as an officer of the guard, chooses personal loyalty.

The orcs' approach to loyalty and rule violation as opposed to Pippin and Beregond's reaction to similar dilemmas is an instructive contrast because Tolkien provides just enough similarity to make the comparison interesting. Part of the reason is that, as I have mentioned many times before, orcs are not automatons; they can and do make decisions. One of the decisions they have to make is between loyalty to their peers and obedience to their superiors. Shagrat and Gorbag imply that they want to choose loyalty to each other over their more powerful leaders, but at the same time fear the repercussions of acting independently. There is a similar conflict between the two orcs who hunt Frodo and Sam. In this case, the Uruk orc chooses loyalty to the leadership, which causes his death. Still, whether orcs obey or disobey, or whether they are loyal or disloyal depends only on their judgments of their own self-interest. Not surprisingly, this translates into a low-risk approach for the individual orcs. Surprisingly, what is a low-risk approach to decision making for individual orcs translates into a high-risk situation for the orcs in general. This is because, for most orcs, the lowest-risk decision often involves killing other orcs before they are killed first. The exception to this rule is when all the orcs are united against some common enemy. This means that though orcs can make decisions, their range of moral decision-making is narrow, violent, and often counterproductive.

On the other hand, good characters, like Pippin and Beregond, are not constrained by the narrow moral confines of self-interest, so they have the ability to make a greater range of decisions. So, even though the moral questions are similar between the orcs and characters like Frodo or Aragorn, the possible range of reasons for their actions is much greater. In this case, Pippin chooses the life of Faramir over his personal safety and over his former loyalty to Denethor. Beregond's decision is even more fraught: he chooses to disobey his oath and desert his post because of his love for his leader, even at the possible cost of Beregond's own life.

In a sense, he is betraying two levels of loyalty, the military one that demands he remain at his post unless given other orders and the feudal one that requires him to be a loyal thane to his leader. I have already mentioned that the forces of Mordor rely much more on the modern model of military organization and discipline, whereas the free forces of Middle-earth depend on the more medieval model. Because the duties of a soldier in the modern military are formalized and there is an explicit emphasis on obeying orders, one might assume that Beregond's violation of military discipline was a more serious crime than his lack of medieval fealty to his "king" (in the sense that the Steward of Gondor is acting for the king). Nothing can be further from the truth. The relationship between the thane and his king is a much thicker relationship than between a soldier and his commanding officer. The relationship is more like the bonds between family members, like the one between fathers and sons, rather than the contractual relationship between the soldier and the state. What the relationship lacks in formal duties, it more than makes up in unstated, but understood, obligations. Therefore, disobeying a medieval king more closely resembles the betrayal of a father than disobedience to a superior. The religious dimension adds to the seriousness of such a betrayal that is missing from most contemporary military organizations. According to medieval Christian doctrine, legitimate kings were not just political figures, but God's representatives on Earth, and it is the subjects' Christian duty to obey them.[44] This sense of familial and even religious betrayal that comes from defying authority is why Dante put betrayers of patrons in the lowest circle of Hell. Therefore, Beregond's decision, based on conflicting loyalties and duties, is much more laden with moral possibilities than any decision an orc could make.

Though Beregond's decision is the most personally risky, in some ways Gandalf's decision to abandon the defense of the city to rescue Faramir is even more surprising. What is especially interesting about Gandalf's decision-making is how non-utilitarian it is. Why rescue a single man, when the fate of an entire city hangs in the balance? Gandalf himself speaks to this dilemma, when he answers Pippin's question, "Can't you save Faramir?" Gandalf responds, "Maybe I can . . . but if I do than others will die, I fear. Well, I must come, since no other help can reach him. But evil and sorrow will come of this. Even in the heart of our stronghold the enemy has power to strike us; for his will it is that is at work."[45] The inclination of many contemporary ethicists would be to do some sort of hedonic calculation and conclude that since Gandalf would preserve many more lives by defending the city, he would be obligated to do so. Perhaps the exception could be made that Gandalf had more of a personal relationship with Faramir than with more anonymous others who might die fighting in the battle. As it turns out, Théoden, another man Gandalf knew well and loved, dies at the hands of the Witch-king likely due to Gandalf's decision to abandon the battlefield. Even more interesting is that Gandalf goes to rescue Faramir even though he recognizes that in some way he is doing the will of the enemy and that he is playing right into Sauron's hand. In no way does Gandalf's decision make sense based on the outcome, so the question remains: why does he choose to save Faramir?

The answer comes from Gandalf's own words: he must save him because "no other help can reach him." Thus, Gandalf judges his responsibility to Faramir based on the fact that he is the only one who could potentially save him. This suggests that Gandalf assumes that Faramir's individual fate is as important as the fate of everyone in the city, even if that "everyone" is a larger group of individuals. To be more precise, Gandalf assumes that the decision to save a particular person or group of people cannot be evaluated in terms of numbers because everyone's (not just Faramir's) fate is infinitely valuable.[46] It is this assumption, which contrasts with the utilitarian calculus, that is likely the bedrock ethical assumption of most of the readers of *The Lord of the Rings* past and present.[47] If Faramir as an individual has infinite value along with everyone else, no hedonic calculation can happen, since infinite value exists on both sides of the equation.[48]

Gandalf's approach to seeing individuals as having infinite value also exists independently of their personal qualities or virtues. We can see this in the way he talks about and behaves toward two particularly loathsome characters in *The Lord of the Rings*: Gollum and Saruman. When he describes Gollum's story to Frodo, Gandalf expresses understanding and sympathy for the creature despite Gollum's manifest wickedness. Gandalf's first instinct is to try to understand him, so he concludes that "even Gollum was not totally ruined [by the Ring of Power]" and "that he was altogether wretched."[49] His pity for Gollum is shared by many of the good characters of the novel, from Bilbo, to the elves of Mirkwood, to Aragorn, to Sam, and to Frodo himself (despite his original protestation that "what a pity that Bilbo did not stab that vile creature, when he had the chance!").[50] In a similar way, Saruman is treated with pity despite his betrayal of the good people of Middle-earth. When Gandalf confronts Saruman at the Orthanc, he offers Saruman the opportunity to leave Orthanc and be free; this is an unconditional freedom: "free from bond, of chain, or command: to go where you will, even to Mordor."[51] This is an extraordinarily generous offer, considering that Saruman had already imprisoned Gandalf, made an alliance with Mordor, and waged a genocidal war with Rohan. Even in Saruman's weakened state, he likely could still do much evil. Later, after the final defeat of Sauron, the victorious party approaches a beggarly Saruman on the road and again Gandalf, as well as Galadriel, offers to help the disgraced wizard. Once again, Saruman rebuffs their offers.

The consequences of extending mercy to Gollum and to Saruman are quite different. Gollum's attack on Frodo and the creature's inadvertent destruction of the ring (and himself) are the pivotal events in *The Lord of the Rings*, and they lead to Sauron's defeat and the victory of the free peoples of Middle-earth. Gollum is also the only possible guide who could lead Frodo and Sam through the Dead Marshes and into Mordor. Therefore, the many people who spare his life were instrumental to the events leading to the defeat of Sauron. In this sense, their mercy was providential.

Tolkien provides no equivalent providential purpose for Saruman. Saruman continues his evil acts despite the mercy shown to him and despite the fact that no inadvertent good comes from them. Not only that, his malicious actions hurt the most innocent victims possible: the hobbits of the Shire. In showing how mercy to Saruman results in evil, Tolkien shows that good intentions can have bad consequences.[52] Despite this final betrayal, Frodo again forgives the defeated Saruman in the Shire and allows him to escape. While Saruman gets what he deserves, the justice comes from his corrupt, persecuted servant, Wormtongue, rather than through the hobbits Saruman had wronged. Just like in the "real" world, in Tolkien's legendarium, choices have consequences. The differing results of mercy shown to Gollum and to Saruman demonstrate that Tolkien ignores utility in determining what is good and what is not. For Tolkien, the goodness and badness of the decision is not dependent on outcome, but principle.

By dwelling on examples of leadership, or lack of it, from Tolkien's good and bad societies, we can see a pattern emerge. In Tolkien's dystopian Mordor, leaders are controlling, narrow, paranoid, and effective at carrying out their will, but thwarted by the incompetence of their limited subordinates. In a similar way, their followers are paranoid, specialized, unreliable, and primarily interested in their own survival. In contrast, the leaders of Tolkien's more utopian societies are more laissez-faire, multi-talented, sometimes actively betrayed by those they mistake as being on their own side, inefficient, yet more flexible since they are willing to take risks and responsibility. And this willingness to take chances allows these leaders to engage in high-risk strategies that belie the image of "good" people and societies as cautious and safe. Not surprisingly, the nature of these malevolent and benevolent societies both mirrors and helps create the leadership in a sort of feedback loop. Sauron is paranoid because his subordinates cannot be trusted, while his paranoia makes his subordinates more untrustworthy. He must necessarily divide himself and his attention to gain control over his subordinates, and yet his subordinates do irrational things to avoid being controlled. In contrast, Aragorn's willingness to allow others to make choices, such as when he defers to Frodo's decision to enter the Mines of Moria and Théoden's decision to retreat to Helm's Deep, creates trust when Aragorn asks others to trust his leadership. Therefore, Gandalf and Aragorn can ask their followers to gamble (and likely lose their very lives) at the Battle of the Black Gate without having to doubt their commitment or attempting to control their actions. The operative word here is "ask" since their leaders give the soldiers of Gondor and Rohan the opportunity to leave the host before it heads for the Black Gate.

Aragorn's leadership style illustrates how Tolkien's vision of a legitimate authority can be married to his anarchist views (even if that legitimate authority appears to be authoritarian in our current context). After all, Tolkien argues that people should not be told what to do, yet he presents a king and a wizard as the ideal leaders. How can both these concepts be true? Don't monarchs command people to do what they want (or it is "off with their heads")? Don't wizards have the power to make people do their will through magic? To the modern reader the idea that these traditionally authoritarian rulers are the ones who will guarantee anarchy certainly should appear absurd on its face. Still, many readers of *The Lord of the Rings* accept the idea of non-constitutional leadership not leading to tyranny, but to greater freedom. The only way this works is through legitimate leadership (i.e., Aragorn and Gandalf) exercising their authority almost entirely through persuasion. This is exactly what the reader sees. Over and over again those in authority ask rather than command. From the Council of Rivendell, to the Battle at Helm's Deep, to the Battle at Pelennor Fields, to the Battle of the Black Gate, and even to Frodo's asking Gollum to guide them, those in power are willing to trust their subordinates to make their own decisions, even when faced with the possibility of defeat.

The one exception to this practice of granting authority through individual requests is the authority granted by a binding oath, which is seen throughout the good societies of Middle-earth. Oaths are exclusive to Tolkien's good societies and central to their functioning. The most obvious reason for centrality is that they are the only form of long-lasting commitment we see in the societies of Middle-earth, and the only way these societies coerce behavior, even if this coercion is mild by our contemporary standards. Thus we see oaths everywhere, for good and for ill: the Oath of Fëanor, the Oath of Eorl, the Oath of the King of the Mountains to the King of Gondor, the Oath of Merry to Théoden, and the Oath of Pippin to Denethor. Breaking of oaths even for "good" reasons is always a serious matter in Middle-earth. This helps explain why Aragorn exiles Beregond from Gondor for his defense of Faramir. Based on the ethical assumptions of most modern people, Beregond deserves no punishment for protecting his leader from a literal madman, but that is not the approach Aragorn takes. First, he cites Beregond's "crimes" and says, "For these things, of old, death was the penalty. Now therefore I must pronounce your doom"[53] Aragorn's monarchial language conveys the seriousness with which he viewed the oath-breaking. Despite this ominous language, Aragorn shows mercy to Beregond and exiles him to the realm of his beloved leader. Still, this is a real consequence in that Beregond is forever exiled from the city he loves.

Despite the power that Aragorn exercises in this unique situation in regard to oath-breaking, what distinguishes him is both his reluctance to use his monarchical power and the possibility that he does not have much power anyway. In the end, the ironic reason Tolkien found "unconstitutional monarchy" so appealing was not that it was an *effective* government, but precisely that it was *not*. The monarch rarely could coerce anybody to do anything and that is just the way Tolkien liked it. We see this at the end of *The Lord of the Rings* where the Shire has a king who demands little and does not even bother to visit the hobbits. Tolkien sees anarchy and monarchy more closely related to each other than most people, whose idea of a monarch is more like a dictator rather than the often politically weak and circumscribed medieval monarchs Tolkien the medievalist knew well. These medieval monarchs usually had very little direct impact on the lives of their ordinary subjects except in periods of war or emergency (though they often had a big effect on the aristocratic class).

The final irony is that Tolkien the localist, the lover of independence, and the anarchist also was a member of the largest organization in the world, the Catholic Church, which had and has quite a lot of very specific rules about how one should live his or her life. I think the reason why this seems like a contradiction to many people, but not to Tolkien, comes from the way he viewed the Catholic Church, as a medieval, rather than a twentieth-century, institution. The Church in this medieval configuration allowed a lot of independence and respect for local tradition because of its syncretic nature and the difficulty of exerting central control because of the limited communications that existed during the Middle Ages. Even today, the Catholic Church's glacial pace of change comes in part out of this respect for local institutions, since any change comes slowly with lots of feedback from interested parties. Similarly, for logistical reasons the Church could not operate as a centralized bureaucracy for much of the Middle Ages and relied on local bishops to help do its will (ironically, many of these bishops were appointed by political leaders who were rivals to the institutional church). Finally, the Catholic Church is not supposed to coerce people based on its own doctrine. For example, forced conversions to Christianity violate Catholic and Christian doctrine.[54] Of course, in many places and times, the Catholic Church failed in this policy of non-coercion, but when it lived up to its own principles they could be accepted even by an anarchist. Again, rather like a medieval monarchy, Tolkien liked the medieval church not because it was effective and efficient in coercing people, but because it was not. Certainly compared to the ever more effective surveillance and carceral state that has been growing in the twentieth and twenty-first centuries throughout much of the world, the medieval church's ability to police conformity looks very primitive indeed.

This chapter's survey of Tolkien's approach to "politics" and leadership in his legendarium again shows how, as a thinker, Tolkien was sui generis. While most current approaches to politics take a consciously, or unconsciously, utilitarian and material approach to the best forms of government (i.e., the society that produces the most "stuff" for the most people ends up best or "happiest"), Tolkien sees the ability to create lots of stuff easily as more of a danger than an aspiration. Thus, his suspicion of machines and magic. Similarly, the consensus position of many of the elites that coercion is a legitimate technocratic tool to nudge society into a more "just" configuration was anathema for Tolkien. Instead, he envisions an anarchical society. Still, despite his anarchist sympathies, he departs from most anarchists in configuring his societies so that they are completely, or mostly, unequal. Instead, his societies have clearly defined classes and hierarchies (though they are permeable). While most political thinkers in the twentieth and twenty-first centuries think in terms of people as independent, individual actors, Tolkien conceives of them as parts of groups starting with families and ending with "peoples."

In the end, however, it would be a mistake to read Tolkien's novels as some sort of political or social blueprint as the typical utopian and dystopian narrative. He conceived them first and foremost as tales and works of art. Still, even if his societies are not blueprints, they do offer an aspirational glimpse of how humans could organize themselves. Finally, the success of his societies mostly comes from the virtues of the societies' citizens rather than their political organization (or lack of it compared to modern models). In this sense, Tolkien is utopian not because he believes in the wisdom of unconstitutional monarchy per se, but because he believes in the leadership of characters like Gandalf, Aragorn, Galadriel, Legolas, Gimli, and Frodo.[55] It is out of the virtues of these characters, more than the structure of his societies, that Tolkien creates his utopian political vision.

NOTES

1. Though as often is the case with social and political trends, one must be careful of generalizing. The period before World War I was also the high point of fin de siècle literature, which was anything but confident about the future. As I mention in chapter 2, this period was also the beginning of the Modernist movement, which signaled a discontent with the very idea of tradition and suggested revolutionary changes. Still, I think the distinction I made in chapter 2 between avant garde cultural pessimism versus the more mainstream optimism of the masses holds true in this case as well.

2. This is rather similar to the Catholic Church's teaching about salvation's relationship to faith and works. A careful reading of Church doctrine suggests a both/and approach to salvation rather than an either/or belief in faith and works as a means of redemption.

3. One could argue that the debate between these two approaches is not so much between two distinct groups that are either individualists and collectivists in totality, but two groups that are debating *what* should be left to individual decisions and *what* should be regulated collectively by the state. People who are described as "conservative" today often are more comfortable with collective approaches to sexual morality and individualist approaches to economics, for example, while people who are described as "liberals" are often more comfortable with collective approaches to economic regulations and individualist approaches to sexual behavior (though with the leftist Me Too movement and the rightist economic nationalism, these traditional distinctions are in flux). Both groups are quick to cast the other as either oppressive or reckless depending on what was to be controlled or tolerated.

4. G. K. Chesterton, *Outline of Sanity* (Norfolk: IHS Press, 2002), 98.

5. For example, an anarchist assassinated President William McKinley, and another injured himself trying to set a bomb at the Greenwich Observatory.

6. J.R.R. Tolkien to Christopher Tolkien, November 29, 1943, in *The Letters of J. R. R. Tolkien*, ed. Humphrey Carpenter (Boston: Houghton Mifflin Harcourt, 2000), 63.

7. Giorel Curran, *21st Century Dissent: Anarchism, Ant-Globalization, and Environmentalism* (London: Palgrave Macmillan, 2006), 21.

8. Curran, *21st Century Dissent*, 23.

9. This distinction between the Enlightenment assumption that people are individual agents versus Tolkien's assumption that they were part of collectives echoes a central argument in the book *The Virtue of Nationalism* by Yoram Hazony. In it, Hazony argues that people naturally associate parts of their identity with groups, whether they be family, clans, or nations and that the individualistic, rationalistic assumptions of Enlightenment thinkers like John Locke and David Hume do not accurately describe most people's political behavior.

10. He says this directly. In the draft of a letter to Joanna de Bortadano, Tolkien argues, "I am not a 'democrat' only because 'humility' and equality are spiritual principles corrupted by the attempt to mechanize and formalize them, with the result that we get not universal smallness and humility, but universal greatness and pride, till some Orc gets hold of a ring of power—and then we get and are getting slavery."

11. Yannick Imbert, "Tolkien's Shire: The Ideal of a Conservative-Anarchist Distributist Governance," *Journal of Inkling Studies* 3, no. 1 (2013): 38.

12. Imbert, "Tolkien's Shire," 39–40.

13. Advocates of democratic societies also have recognized this danger. Both James Madison and John Stewart Mill expressed their fears of the tyranny of a democratic majority in *The Federalist Papers* and "On Liberty," respectively.

14. In this sense, this is another way that makes Tolkien's literary world less "medieval" than it appears at first since various permanent legislative assemblies started as far back as the Middle Ages, with the British Parliament established by the Magna Carta, various King's Councils, and so on. Even before that, there was also the Anglo-Saxon *Witanagemot*, a kind of council of elders.

15. Peter Wilkin, *The Strange Case of Tory Anarchism* (Faringdon: Libri, 2010), 12.

16. Just like the word "anarchy," what it means to be a "conservative" is highly contingent based on time and place. After all, in some sense Tolkien's anarchistic beliefs are "conservative" if one views "conserving" or reviving older medieval social forms, like guilds. In this case, I mean conservative in the American sense of the word that is generally pro-business and libertarian. This would likely be called "liberalism" or "neo-liberalism" in the European context.

17. Jay Richards and Jonathan Witt, *The Hobbit Party: The Vision of Freedom That Tolkien Got and the West Forgot* (San Francisco: Ignatius Press, 2014), 33.

18. Richards and Witt, *The Hobbit Party*, 34.

19. The fact that the dwarves agree to pay Bilbo reflects their moral development as well. At one point, Bilbo agrees to give his share of the gold to the people of Laketown. If the dwarves had stuck with their hard-bargaining ways, they would have an excuse not to give Bilbo *any* share of the dragon treasure.

20. J.R.R. Tolkien, *The Hobbit* (London: Ballantine Books, 2014), 293.
21. J.R.R. Tolkien, *The Return of the King* (New York: Ballantine Books, 1994), 318.
22. Perhaps the only relevant criterion is in order for a market to be free there must be equal knowledge among all the market participants. In this case, clearly there was information that was withheld, so one could argue that the market was not truly "free." Of course, it is not unusual for information to be withheld or given only to a select few market participants in the real world as well.
23. Tolkien, *The Hobbit*, 62.
24. J.R.R. Tolkien, *The Fellowship of the Ring* (New York: Ballantine Books, 1994), 1.
25. Tolkien, *The Letters of J. R. R. Tolkien*, 88.
26. Tolkien, *The Letters of J. R. R. Tolkien*, 77.
27. Tolkien, "On Fairy-Stories" *Tolkien on Fairy-Stories Expanded Edition, with Commentary and Notes*, eds. Verilyn Fliegler and Douglas A. Anderson (London: HarperCollins, 2008), 71.
28. Tolkien, *The Letters of J.R.R. Tolkien*, 115.
29. Tolkien, *The Letters of J.R.R. Tolkien*, 145–46.
30. As I mentioned in chapter 3, Tolkien always contends that damage done to nature and damage done to people are connected by the same moral error.
31. Kirk Honeycutt, "*Avatar* Film Review," *Hollywood Reporter*, December 10, 2009. Accessed December 19, 2018, https://www.hollywoodreporter.com/review/avatar-film-review-93803.
32. The use of the words *goeteia* and *magia* by Tolkien is not necessarily the traditional distinction between them. At least since the Renaissance the word *goeteia* or *goetia* refers to the summoning of demons and is therefore associated with black magic, while the word *magia* is just the Latin word for "magic," which has mostly benign associations with entertainment.
33. Tolkien, *The Letters of J.R.R. Tolkien*, 199–200.
34. Tolkien capitalizes "Machine" to indicate he is discussing the machine as an abstract concept rather than the individual characteristics of machines as manufactured items.
35. Richards and Witt, *The Hobbit Party*, 156–57.
36. Tolkien, *The Two Towers*, 389.
37. Tolkien, *The Two Towers*, 392.
38. Tolkien, *The Two Towers*, 393.
39. Tolkien, *The Return of the King*, 214–15.
40. Tolkien, *The Return of the King*, 215.
41. I put "evil" in quotes because it is my contention that even orcs cannot be "pure" evil. I discuss this issue in chapter 1.
42. It is hard to imagine a more countercultural thought in today's economic and political environment.
43. Tolkien, *The Two Towers*, 76.
44. Even pagan authorities, according to 1 Peter 2:13–17: "Be subject for the Lord's sake to every human institution, whether it to the emperors as supreme, or to governors as sent by him to punish those who do wrong and praise those who do right. For it is God's will that by doing right you should put to silence the ignorance of foolish men. Live as free men, yet without using your freedom as a pretext for evil; but live as servants of God. Honor all men. Love the Brotherhood. Fear God. Honor the Emperor."
45. Tolkien, *The Return of the King*, 127.
46. This means that Gandalf would not be pushing obese people in front of trolley cars, as one of the more common utilitarian ethical dilemmas posits as an option.
47. As a college teacher who has taught essays that involve ethical dilemmas for many years, I am often amazed at how universally and consistently college students view ethical matters through the lens of utility. There is virtually no difference between liberal and conservative, high and low income, or religious and non-religious students when it comes to discussing whether a decision is ethical or not. Almost all of

them instinctively think in terms of adding up benefits and harms and subtracting one from the other; the debate revolves around the relative size of the various benefits and harms rather than any other overarching ethical principle. Therefore, these students almost always think in terms of the ends justifying the means (though I am sure many would not state it that way). Occasionally students will use a form of Divine Command ethics or, even more commonly, argue from some sort of scientific authority, but those types of arguments usually appear for positions that they do not feel that they have good arguments for so they fall back to argument-by-authority. Often, I can tell that their hearts are not in it.

48. In this sense, Gandalf's ethics seem closest to the twentieth- and twenty-first-century ethical philosophy of personalism.

49. Tolkien, *The Fellowship of the Ring*, 60.

50. Tolkien, *The Fellowship of the Ring*, 65.

51. Tolkien, *The Two Towers*, 207.

52. In a similar way, Tolkien's chapter "The Scouring of the Shire" shows that the defeat of Sauron did not mean that the evil was defeated once and for all.

53. Tolkien, *The Return of the King*, 267.

54. See, for example, the encyclical *Mystici Corporis Christi*, which specifically forbids forced conversions.

55. You will note that I do not include any characters from Tolkien's other works like *The Silmarillion* or *The Book of Lost Tales* as the foundations of Tolkien's utopian political ideas. Only in *The Hobbit* and *The Lord of the Rings* do we see any form of *political* utopianism in Tolkien. That was why this chapter has focused so much on *The Hobbit* and *The Lord of the Rings*.

Epilogue

The Struggle for Tolkien's Utopian and Dystopian Legacy

What follows is a discussion of some of the adaptations and reimaginings of Tolkien's works that have occurred since the publication of *The Hobbit, The Lord of the Rings*, and *The Silmarillion*. My survey will certainly not be extensive and only starts in the twenty-first century with the release of Peter Jackson's *The Lord of the Rings* movies and does not discuss the earlier adaptations of Tolkien's works in the twentieth century. I am not including adaptations of Tolkien's own works that are being published posthumously (and edited by his son, Christopher Tolkien) in the twenty-first century, such as *The Children of Húrin* and *Beren and Lúthien*. Since Tolkien's works are proven moneymakers, even his relatively obscure and incomplete works are being published today, like *The Fall of Arthur*.[1] I also avoid fanfiction, YouTube videos, and other ephemera that influence a relatively small number of fans. Instead, my focus is only on adaptations that are for the mass market, which means a sampling of the most important and popular films and video games. I chose these adaptations in particular because these are popular enough that one could argue that many young people's ideas about Tolkien's works and Middle-earth in general come more from these movies and video games rather than from the books themselves. This is in contrast to earlier attempts to create animated portrayals of Middle-earth like *The Hobbit* (1977) and the incomplete *The Lord of the Rings* (1978), produced by Rankin/Bass and Ralph Bakshi, respectively, which have had little impact on the popular consciousness. Since one of the main claims of this book has been how Tolkien uses his legendarium to challenge the hegemonic beliefs of many of his readers, this final part of the book examines whether these adaptations are faithful to the books' messages or undermine the books' original philosophies and what this might suggest about how well Tolkien's works can continue to challenge and inspire new audiences.

The early twenty-first century has been a golden age for commercially successful adaptations based on J.R.R. Tolkien's legendarium, the most significant being Peter Jackson's films based on *The Lord of the Rings* (2001, 2002, and 2003) and *The Hobbit* (2012, 2013, and 2014). Using Tolkien's most famous books, Jackson has produced two movie trilogies that have generated hundreds of millions of dollars in revenue. Because of the profitability of these films, it seems likely that parts of *The Silmarillion* will also end up becoming movies and/or television projects in the future. This success has not been confined to films. Almost from the start of video game technology, there have been video games based on Tolkien's legendarium, such as Melbourne House's *The Lord of the Rings* and *The Hobbit* in 1982. Still, much of these early video games were so crude that they hardly had any sort of narrative attached to them. But as video game technology has become more immersive and increased in complexity, the narrative possibilities for games based on Tolkien's legendarium have also grown. Now many gamers feel that they are part of a story as well as playing a game.

To a certain extent, part of this explosion in Tolkien film and video game adaptations comes from recent technological advances that for the first time have made it possible to create a visually believable Middle-earth. In the past, several directors, including visionaries like Stanley Kubrick, turned down chances to make *The Lord of the Rings* because they believed it was "unfilmable" based on the technology available at the time. Similarly, advances in computer technology have allowed video game graphics to become ever more detailed and the worlds generated more viscerally immersive. Therefore, these new visual technologies have allowed both film and video game makers the opportunity to create characters and settings that match the grandeur of Tolkien's vision. Still, these new capabilities in films and video games are not always used to realize Tolkien's moral vision, and the adaptations vary in faithfulness to Tolkien's work.

Part of the differences between these adaptations and Tolkien's original works reflects the necessary transition that occurs when a work of art moves from one artistic medium to another. In Peter Jackson's movie trilogy *The Lord of the Rings,* the most obvious changes were the elimination of the character Tom Bombadil, and of the passage that includes the Barrow-wights in *The Fellowship of the Ring* movie. In the third film, *The Return of the King,* Jackson excises the entire chapter about the Scouring of the Shire. From a film making standpoint, these decisions make a lot of sense. All three passages detract from what the filmmakers saw as the central conflict of the movies: the struggle between the free and good peoples of Middle-earth against the evil forces of Mordor. They are also, not coincidentally, on a smaller scale and less visually interesting than other parts of *The Lord of the Rings.* Part of the compression reflects the necessary shortening that happens in almost all adaptations of novels to film. Even in movies as long as Jackson's *The Lord of the Rings,* some abridging of the narrative is inevitable to make runtimes practical for theatergoers who do not have many hours to spend watching a movie. Even the extended DVD versions of the movie run into limits on runtimes and cannot encompass every passage from the books.

Still, these changes do alter Tolkien's artistic vision. While these passages might not seem important cinematically, they are especially important for the moral complexity of the novel. Therefore, the decision to eliminate them changes the overall meaning of the narrative. Tolkien includes these passages that involve forces of good and evil that are outside the central struggle between free peoples of Middle-earth and the slavery of Mordor because they reflect his views about the relationship between good and evil. Tolkien deliberately includes characters like Tom Bombadil that are "good" but not part of the struggle against Mordor because Tolkien wants his readers to understand that goodness does not require everyone to sign up for an identical political program. A perennial temptation in modern politics is to leave no social space for nonpolitical people to exist outside the accepted political framework, and to create a world of total political compliance. Tolkien creates Tom Bombadil to be a character who transcends rather than resists evil, and he allows him to *not* join the fight. We can see this transcendence when Frodo gives the Ring of Power to Tom Bombadil; it has no effect on him—it neither makes him invisible nor tempts him with its power. Therefore, Tom Bombadil does not need to fight this evil because it is literally nonexistent for him. Tolkien allows a place for quietists, through characters like Tom Bombadil, something that our conformist society sometimes resists. Similarly, the Barrow-wights of the Barrowdowns are evil, but also outside the struggle between the free peoples of Middle-earth and Sauron. Their evil agenda has nothing to do with Sauron's attempts to control Middle-earth. Even when describing evil, Tolkien resists the totalizing that characterizes our modern approach to politics, one that assumes all questions can be boiled down to a good and a bad side.[2] Finally, the scouring of the Shire shows that even after the defeat of Sauron, evil was not banished from the world. Tolkien's Middle-earth is still a fallen world even without Sauron. The elimination of the scouring in the film gives the false impression that evil can be defeated through a victory in an external struggle. All these purged elements from the movies reduce some of the moral complexity of the films compared to the books. Tolkien, like Solzhenitsyn, believed both that "the dividing line between good and evil cuts through the heart of every human being" and that great political evil was possible. In this sense, neither the "good guys" nor the "bad guys" can ever be completely defeated by destroying some outside enemy. If evil can exist in the Shire even after the defeat of Sauron, it can exist anywhere and at any time.

Despite the way the movies simplify the moral environment of Middle-earth, they add other elements that complicate the characters and make them more morally ambiguous. For example, the movies exaggerate Sam's jealousy of Frodo's relationship with Gollum. In the book *The Two Towers*, Frodo does not explicitly reject Sam on the Stairs of Cirith Ungol and tell Sam to go home, as he does in the movie. Other characters are darkened in a similar fashion. Faramir, in a scene from the movie that is not in the book, decides to take Frodo and the Ring of Power to his father, Denethor, in Osgiliath. The movie does this to intensify the sibling rivalry between Faramir and Boromir that is mostly absent from the books. Eventually, Faramir relents and allows Sam and Frodo to go free, but only after Frodo is nearly captured by a Nazgûl in Osgiliath. This added scene makes the movie Faramir of the movie a more confused and less noble character than the Faramir of the books. Another telling example of this phenomenon is when in the extended edition of *The Return of the King*, Aragorn lops off the head of the Mouth of Sauron before the Battle of the Black Gate—an action added for the movie that was not in the book. Of course, the violence of this scene is gratuitous, but so is the moral nihilism that is so out of character for the Aragorn we know in the book.[3] So while the movies often make the societies depicted morally better than the books, the movies often make individuals morally worse.

I think that this darkening of individual characters in the movie version of *The Lord of the Rings* reflects many moderns' discomfort with heroes. Certainly, Tolkien has morally complex heroes like Frodo, but he has others like Sam, Faramir, and Aragorn who are less so. The need to make heroes more flawed, and therefore vulnerable, is a predictable effect of many contemporary people's desire to have heroes who don't morally challenge them too much. Therefore, they are more comfortable with an Aragorn who doubts himself, a Frodo who chooses Gollum over Sam, and a Faramir who puts his family relationships over the common good. While these characters remain heroic in Jackson's films, they also exhibit more characteristics of the type of antihero many contemporary audiences find more morally comfortable.

Despite the differences between the book series *The Lord of the Rings* and the movie adaptations, Peter Jackson's work remains relatively close to the novels (especially in his extended, uncut movie versions). Jackson's movie trilogy of *The Hobbit*, however, differs much more substantially from the original book—no doubt most of the reason for this difference is financial. In order to create three movies using Tolkien's *The Hobbit* (which is a fraction of the size of *The Lord of the Rings*) Jackson had to use parts of Tolkien's appendices from *The Lord of the Rings* and invent whole new scenes and characters to pad the narrative. The result is a movie trilogy that does not resemble, in action or tone, the book at all. Jackson creates rivalries between Thorin and the orc Azog; he invents a romance between the dwarf Kili and the elf Tauriel (a character created for the movie); and he expands characters barely mentioned in the book, like the wizard Radagast, and makes them central to the plot. Maybe even more significantly, Jackson takes *The Hobbit*, a gentle, mildly frightening but exciting children's adventure story, and gives it some of the characteristics of an epic, like *The Lord of the Rings*. Even so, this transformation of *The Hobbit* into an epic is only partial, and many of the other elements of the movies more resemble a typical action-adventure movie. Therefore, Jackson adds the rather unlikely romance between an elf and a dwarf to provide the romantic subplot that is a common feature of most contemporary action-adventure movies. Tolkien's love affairs in his narratives, on the other hand, tend to be a much smaller part of the plot (no doubt much to the annoyance of his movie adaptors, who like their romances more explicit and obvious). Even worse for modern filmmakers, love affairs in *The Lord of the Rings* are even "off-stage," so to speak, like Aragorn and Arwen's relationship, which only appears in Tolkien's appendices. Similarly, the hyped hero–villain rivalry between Thorin and Azog follows the predictable pattern of most Hollywood blockbusters, complete with a final combat scene, where the "bad guy" is dispatched in a spectacular fashion after an overblown, ridiculously long combat scene. In *The Hobbit* novel, on the other hand, Tolkien plays down the violence in the Battle of the Five Armies, as one would expect in a children's book. The movies, however, provide many minutes of spectacular CGI battle scenes. Unsuprisingly, as the source material drifts from Tolkien in terms of approach and even actual plot, the many elements from Tolkien's approach to his legendarium that make his stories unique also occur less frequently.

Even though the Peter Jackson movies strayed farther away from Tolkien's source material as time has passed, his movies are more faithful to Tolkien's vision than other projects based on Tolkien's work—especially video games. Part of the change is just due to the nature of video games. Most video games require that players constantly receive external rewards through some sort of token system (i.e., money, health) in a way that counteracts the selflessness that is central to Tolkien's legendarium. Not surprisingly, most video games center on action and battles so these features figure much more prominently in the games than they do in the books. A central part of the appeal of Tolkien's legendarium is the sense of wonder that he creates, but this wonder does not always translate well to gaming. Many players on a mission are less likely to slow down and appreciate this sense of wonder no matter how high the quality of the game graphics or how spectacular the setting. Finally, video games are "games" after all. The focus of most of them and for many gamers is not to experience a story (even if experiencing the story is part of the appeal) but to win a game.[4] Once again, since Tolkien's narratives are often about abnegation, the opposite of "winning," this gaming convention often works at cross-purposes to many of Tolkien's narrative objectives.[5]

Even with these caveats, video games vary widely in how faithfully they reflect the letter and the spirit of Tolkien's books. Some of the video games, like *The Lord of the Rings* official games that are licensed by Tolkien Enterprises, are more faithful to the plots of the books than the movies. Other *The Lord of the Rings* games are licensed by New Line Cinema, the films' producers, so they follow the plots of the movies, including Peter Jackson's insertions and deletions, rather than the books.

Of course, there are also video games that are only tangentially related to any source material from Tolkien. The recent video game *Middle-earth: Shadow of Mordor* abandons all pretense that it is faithful to either the letter or the spirit of Tolkien's legendarium. The plot of the video game involves a character, Talion, invented for the game, who is murdered but comes back from the dead after being bonded with a ringwraith. Talion is also aided by the spirit of Celebrimbor, the elf who fashioned the three magic rings worn by elves. Throughout the game, Talion seeks to avenge himself on Sauron through gaining more and more power. By the end of the game, it becomes apparent that Talion intends to forge his own Ring of Power with the help of Celebrimbor and become the new Dark Lord of Middle-earth. As this synopsis suggests, Talion is an antihero, yet one whom the game presents in a sympathetic manner and with whom the player is expected to identify. This sort of character is very different from anything Tolkien created. He was very capable of creating flawed heroes (like Túrin) but he did not create antiheroes. He also was careful to show (and I hope I demonstrated throughout the book) how gaining power through evil means was self-defeating because evil means replacing the greater with the lesser.

An even more unlikely Tolkienesque character in *Middle-earth: Shadow of Mordor* is the elf spirit (or ghost?) Celebrimbor. There are disembodied spirits in Middle-earth, but they are universally evil.[6] This is true because mortality, properly understood, was a gift, so to remain trapped in the mortal realm after death is a curse. Therefore Celebrimbor's very existence after death suggests his evil,[7] yet nothing in the brief biography of Celebrimbor suggests that he was evil. This also calls into question whether, spirit or not, he would agree to help a power-hungry character like Talion. What seems especially ridiculous is that Celebrimbor would help him forge a new Ring of Power. Celebrimbor chose to die rather than cooperate with Sauron's attempt to corrupt the three rings of the elves, so why would he voluntarily create another Ring of Power?

I think it is clear that a pattern emerges based on this multimedia sampling that has implications about the relationship between most contemporary people's beliefs about the route to a good society and Tolkien's very different beliefs. The moral conflicts in the narratives are simplified and the moral natures of the characters are made more complex in the sense that they are made less good. This drift from Tolkien's original philosophical axioms suggests that these new creations are predictably replacing his moral axioms with morality closer to most contemporary people's beliefs. The most important substitution is that of Tolkien's essentially tragic view of humanity that sees the most perfect world coming from accepting our limitations with the ever popular contemporary view that we can make a more perfect world for ourselves through self-fashioning and breaking out of restrictions. In Tolkien's books, good societies come about, however fleetingly, when people willingly abnegate power, like when Faramir accepts Aragorn as the legitimate king of Gondor or when the hobbit Shirriffs agree to be reduced to their original number after the defeat of Saruman. Thus, benevolent societies, for the anarchist Tolkien, come from people willingly limiting their power. The implication of Tolkien's good societies is also that evil is both an external and an internal threat. In contrast, the implication in *The Lord of the Rings* and *The Hobbit* movies is that evil comes from a mostly external evil threat, that is, from Sauron, Smaug, the goblin Azog, that can be destroyed and defeated. The internal dimension of evil is played down. This fits in with a more conventional view of utopia that assumes utopias appear out of the correct political arrangement (i.e., removing some bad "others") rather than seeing evil as a constant temptation that must be resisted by all, even people who start off as good. At the most extreme end, video games like *The Shadow of Mordor* celebrate the acquiring of power rather than the abnegation of it. This power becomes a way of removing limits, which is a perennial theme of the current zeitgeist; the way to happiness comes from removing the barriers that inhibit us from achieving our desires. Obviously, this message of personal fulfillment through shattering limits is as opposed to the underlying philosophy of Tolkien's legendarium as one could imagine.

In the same way, these derivative works of art show a pattern of drifting away from Tolkien's beliefs about dystopian societies as well. For example, Tolkien was careful to avoid making his evil characters of a particular class (one is often surprised at the good grammar of many orcs in Tolkien's books, though not his trolls). In many of the movies and video games, however, the evil characters speak with an obvious "lower-class" cockney accent. This is part of the tendency to "externalize" evil that we see in popular adaptations of Tolkien's works. If evil is a certain type of person, maybe with certain characteristics (like lack of education) they (the characteristics) can somehow be eliminated, or even more troubling, maybe the evil persons could be eliminated. These Tolkien adaptations also often "humanize" evil characters in such a way as to make them more appealing. Sometimes this is done quite explicitly, like when Shelob, who is only described as a monstrous, repulsive spider in *The Lord of the Rings* books, is transformed from a spider to a beautiful woman in the video game *Middle-earth: Shadow of Mordor*. There are even more obvious ways that evil is humanized, or even glorified, in the video games. The most extreme example comes from video games where one can choose to *be* Sauron rather than just identify with him. Approaches like this are part of the general contemporary tendency to glamorize evil, a tendency that Tolkien never shared in his legendarium.

Lurking in the background of edgier adaptations of Tolkien's works is the influence of a fantasy series that does seem to glamorize evil and the quest for power. George R. R. Martin's *A Song of Ice and Fire* and the TV series *Game of Thrones*, based on Martin's novels, have some superficial similarities to Tolkien's work. Both Martin and Tolkien base their works on medieval and ancient societies, both have mythological characters like dragons, and both have a sweeping, complex narrative that includes hundreds of characters and vast geography. Even so, differences in the two series are obvious as well. Martin's series contains a much more existentialist message than Tolkien's and almost all of Martin's characters are antiheroes to a degree. Martin has argued that his series is an attempt to make a more "realistic" fantasy novel that depicts the depravity of medieval warlordism and political intrigue. Thus, he bases at least part of his plot on the War of the Roses, a complex fifteenth-century civil war in England. I put "realistic" in quotes earlier because deciding whether a fantasy novel (or any work of fiction) reflects real situations and real people is fraught with all kinds of difficulties beyond the obvious problem of describing a work with dragons and zombies as "realistic." The shocking level of depravity of some of the characters, like Ramsay Bolton in *A Song of Fire and Ice*, makes them too cruel in ways that mirror some critics' complaints that Tolkien's characters like Aragorn or Gandalf in *The Lord of the Rings* are too good.[8] In the real world, there are people as depraved as Bolton and as good as Aragorn, but they are vanishingly rare. The unspoken assumption in Martin's assessment of what makes a story realistic is that the realism involves depravity and violence. Even based on this criterion, a broader view of Tolkien's other works, such as *The Silmarillion*, *The Children of Húrin*, and *The Book of Lost Tales*, shows plenty of violence and depravity, including massacres, mutilations, and incest (though Tolkien does not describe them graphically). More important than the amount or graphic nature of the sex and violence in Martin's work compared to Tolkien's novels is the philosophical underpinnings of the works. I have spent several hundred pages describing how unique Tolkien's beliefs are. In contrast, Martin's philosophy is likely familiar to many Western readers. Martin describes himself as a lapsed Catholic and an agnostic. His politics are conventionally liberal (in the American sense of the word). Not surprisingly, despite the dragons and white walkers, the world Martin creates feels much less enchanted and much more "modern" than Tolkien's Middle-earth. There is magic in Westeros, but not enchantment. The atmosphere and action resemble the political intrigue of *House of Cards* more than the epic narrative of *The Lord of the Rings* or *The Silmarillion*. Finally, Martin replaces Tolkien's sense of meaning with existential nihilism: the idea that our choices do not matter morally or, most of the time, even practically. Heroes are snuffed out quickly, evil characters prosper because of their bad deeds, and even the briefly moral characters become compromised. Unlike in Middle-earth, good does not come out of evil because events have no moral weight in the "game" of thrones.

In the end, the difference between *Game of Thrones* and Tolkien's legendarium is not that too many bad events and bad people exist in Westeros and too many good events and good people exist in Middle-earth. Indeed, like *Game of Thrones,* one could argue that Tolkien's legendarium is a litany of terrible disasters broken by a few respites represented by his societies' golden ages. Still, because of the sense of Providence that Tolkien realistically creates in Middle-earth, his world's evils are tragic rather than pointless.[9] This makes the goodness and badness of characters matter morally in Middle-earth in ways they do not in Westeros.

I do not think, in the end, that Tolkien's works could be made into a work as safe for our contemporary sensibilities as *Game of Thrones.* Despite the propensity of our popular culture to distort and tame Tolkien's message, I also do not think that in the long run Tolkien's legacy will be completely absorbed by the current zeitgeist. One of the reasons for Tolkien's continued popularity throughout the past several decades was that his legendarium answered a need that most other art did not. While many movies and video games will leverage the general "feel" of Middle-earth without its philosophical substance, the adaptations that are more faithful will be able to tap into the same desires that have kept Tolkien's works popular for more than half a century. Of course, Tolkien's original works will always be available and perhaps become even more suffused with their original power in our increasingly spiritually desiccated postmodern world. In those works, readers will continue to find utopian hopes and dystopian warnings in their original form through the varied societies of Middle-earth described in Tolkien's own words.

NOTES

1. Imagine the chances of an incomplete (or complete!) epic poem, written entirely in alliterative verse, being published by any author other than Tolkien in the twenty-first century. The only other example I can think of is Seamus Heaney's translation of *Beowulf,* but of course that is a translation rather than an original work.

2. In Jackson's defense, he does allow characters who, at least at times, seem outside this binary. Treebeard, Shelob, and Gollum are not always clearly aligned with one side or another.

3. This is especially true in the context in which the violence happened. Aragorn killed someone before a battle under the auspices of a truce. Violence under these conditions would be the last thing that Aragorn would do as an exemplar of medieval chivalry. That the spokesman for Sauron was evil and treacherous does not matter one bit. Aragorn's killing someone under a white flag would dishonor *Aragorn*. The fact that these types of distinctions are lost on most modern audiences shows the moral distance between the book and the movies.

4. There are, of course, more story-oriented video games, such as *The Last of Us* and *Fallout 4*. It is interesting that many of these games have apocalyptic themes.

5. I have not played these games, but my children are of the opinion that the games based on the movies are superior to the "official" games based on the books. I suppose this should not be surprising. Sometimes less faithful adaptations are "better"

than more faithful ones in the sense of being more fun. For example, many people consider Stanley Kubrick's *The Shining* "better" than the Stephen King novel by that name. Still, I think that the movie and the book also convey a very different message (that was certainly King's opinion).

6. Perhaps the Army of the Dead that Aragorn leads from the Paths of the Dead to defeat the Corsairs complicates this assertion a bit. These specters do a virtuous deed in the end by fulfilling their oaths to Aragorn as the heir of Isildur. Still, before they fulfill their oaths they were both evil and cursed. It is only by acting as they should have when they were alive that they were freed. Note that freedom also means losing their spectral immortality.

7. One could argue that Gandalf's return from the dead after his combat with the Balrog weakens this point. Still, there are significant differences between Gandalf's return after his "death" and Celebrimbor's ghost. First, Gandalf is not disembodied, but comes back in a material form. Second, Gandalf makes clear that he was sent back (presumably by Eru), not at his own request to complete his mission.

8. Bolton's outrages are so disturbing in Martin's book that they were actually played down for the television series *The Game of Thrones*, which in itself is controversial for its routine depictions of rape and torture.

9. In places in *The Silmarillion*, Tolkien's tone appears more pagan than Providential. Still, even in the stories where Tolkien is most pagan, like *The Children of Húrin*, his characters are never nihilistic. Even though Túrin's situation is hopeless, his struggle against Morgoth is not. His virtues, and his vices, are morally significant, despite his tragedy. Indeed, the moral significance makes Túrin's fall tragic.

Bibliography

Auden, W. H. "The Quest Hero." In *Tolkien and the Critics,* edited by N. D. Isaacs and Rose Abdulnoor Zimbardo, 40–61. South Bend: University of Notre Dame Press, 1969.

Bentham, Jeremy. *The Works.* Vol. 10, *Memoirs Part 1 and Correspondence. Online Liberty Library,* edited by John Bowring. Edinburgh: William Tait, 1838–1843. 11 vols. https://oll.libertyfund.org/titles/.

Berry, Wendell. "Conservation Is Good Work." *Sex, Economy, Freedom & Community.* New York: Pantheon Books, 1993.

Black, Kevin. "The Battle against Modernity in J. R. R. Tolkien's *The Lord of the Rings.*" Senior Thesis, Princeton University, 1995.

Booker, M. Keith. *Dystopian Literature: A Theory and Research Guide.* Santa Barbara: Greenwood, 1994.

Campbell, Joseph. *Pathways to Bliss: Mythology and Personal Transformation.* Novato: New World Library, 2004.

Campbell, Liam. *Ecological Augury in the Works of J.R.R. Tolkien.* Zollikofen: Walking Tree, 2011.

Carr, Nicholas. "Utopia Is Creepy." *Utopia Is Creepy and Other Provocations.* New York: W. W. Norton, 2016.

Chesterton, G. K. "The Ethics of Elfland." *Orthodoxy.* Page By Page Books, 2004, 1–13. https://www.pagebypagebooks.com/Gilbert_K_Chesterton/Orthodoxy/The_Ethics_of_Elfland_p.

Croft, Janet Brennan. *War in the Works of J.R.R. Tolkien.* Santa Barbara: Praeger, 2004.

Curran, Giorel. *21st Century Dissent: Anarchism, Anti-Globalization, and Environmentalism.* London: Palgrave Macmillan, 2006.

Denton, Melinda Lundquist, and Christian Smith. *Soul Searching: The Religious and Spiritual Lives of American Teenagers.* Oxford: Oxford University Press, 2009.

Dickerson, Matthew, and Jonathan Evans. *Ents, Elves, and Eriador: The Environmental Visions of J. R. R. Tolkien.* Lexington: University Press of Kentucky, 2011.

Donovan, Leslie A. *Approaches to Teaching Tolkien's The Lord of the Rings and Other Works.* New York: Modern Language Association of America, 2015.

Evans, Robley. *J.R.R. Tolkien (Writers for the 1970s).* New York: Ty Crowell, 1976.

Fiegler, Verilyn. *Splintered Light: Logos and Language in Tolkien's World.* Kent: Kent State University Press, 2002.

Fimi, Dmitra. *Tolkien, Race, and Cultural History: From Fairies to Hobbits.* New York: Palgrave Macmillan, 2009.

Francis I. *Laudato Si': On Care for Our Common Home: Encyclical Letter.* June 18, 2015. http://w2.vatican.va/content/francesco/en/encyclicals/documents/papa-francesco_20150524_enciclica-laudato-si.html.

Gallant, Richard Z. "Original Sin in Heorot and Valinor." *Tolkien Studies* 11 (2014): 109–29.

Gasque, Thomas J. "Tolkien: The Monster and the Critters." In *Tolkien and the Critics,* edited by N. D. Isaacs and Rose Abdulnoor Zimbardo, 159–63. South Bend: University of Notre Dame Press, 1969

Garth, John. *Tolkien and the Great War: The Threshold of Middle Earth.* Wilmington: Mariner Books, 2005.

Graber, Doris. *Verbal Behavior in Politics.* Champaign: University of Illinois Press, 1976.

Grant, Sterling. "The Consolation of Bilbo: Providence and Free Will in Middle Earth." In *The Hobbit and Philosophy*, edited by Gregory Bassom and Eric Bronson, 206–17. Hoboken: John Wiley and Sons, 2012.

Greer, Germaine. "The Book of the Century." *W: The Waterstone's Magazine*, Winter–Spring 1997.

Guardini, Roman. *The End of the Modern World*. Wilmington: ISI Books, 2001.

Helms, Randall. *Tolkien's World*. Boston: Houghton Mifflin, 1974.

Holmes, John. "'Like Heathen Kings': Religion as Palimpsest in Tolkien's Fiction." In *The Ring and The Cross: Christianity and* The Lord of the Rings, edited by Paul E. Kerry, 119–44. Madison: Fairleigh Dickinson University Press, 2013.

Jarvis, Stephen. "Live Long and Die Out." *The Independent* (London, UK), 23 April 1994.

John Paul II. "Address on the World Day of Peace." Papal Address. Vatican Website. January 1, 1990. http://w2.vatican.va/content/john-paul-ii/en/messages/peace/documents/hf_jp-ii_mes_19891208_xxiii-world-day-for-peace.html.

Kolakowski, Leszek. "The Death of Utopia Reconsidered." Lecture, Tanner Lectures on Human Values. Australian National University. June 22, 1982. Canberra, Australia. *The Semantic Scholar*. pdfs.semanticscholar.org/1eb5/cce5c90d57415355b2c60 2b2d381fec0b615.pdf.

Knepper, B. G. "The Coming Race: Hell? Or Paradise Foretasted?" *No Place Else: Explorations in Utopian and Dystopian Fiction*, edited by Eric S. Rabkin, Martin H. Greenberg, et al., 11–32. Carbondale: Southern Illinois University Press, 1983.

Kumar, Krishan. "The Ends of Utopia." *New Literary History*. 31, no. 3 (2010): 549–69. Accessed 3 June 2017. www.jstor.org/stable/40983884.

Kuznets, Lois R. "The Hobbit Is Rooted in the Tradition of Classic British Children's Novels." *Readings in J. R. R. Tolkien*, edited by Katie de Koster. Farmington Hills: Greenhaven Press, 2000.

Leo XIII. *Rerum Novarum: Encyclical Letter*. May 15, 1891. http://w2.vatican.va/content/leo-xiii/en/encyclicals/documents/hf_l-xiii_enc_15051891_rerum-novarum.html.

Lobdell, Jared. *The World of the Rings: Language, Religion, and Adventure in Tolkien*. Chicago: Open Court, 2004.

Mitchell, Philip Irving. "Conceptions of the Pastoral in *The Fellowship of the Ring*." In *Approaches to Teaching Tolkien's* Lord of the Rings *and Other Works*, edited by Leslie A. Donovan, 108–13. New York: Modern Language Association of America, 2015.

Moylan, Tom. *Scraps of the Untainted Sky: Utopia, Dystopia (Cultural Studies)*. Boulder: Westview Press, 2000.

Pearce, Joseph. "Tolkien vs. Belloc on Distributionism: A Response to Joseph Pearce. *Imaginative Conservative*. Accessed 12 March 2017. http://www.theimaginativeconservative.org/2014/11/response-joseph-pearces-distributism-shire.html.

Pius XI. *Quadragesimo Anno: Encyclical Letter*. May 15, 1931. http://w2.vatican.va/content/pius-xi/en/encyclicals/documents/hf_p-xi_enc_19310515_quadragesimo-anno.html.

Richards, Jay, and Jonathan Witt. *The Hobbit Party: The Vision of Freedom That Tolkien Got and the West Forgot*. San Francisco: Ignatius Press, 2014.

Rosebury, Brian. *Tolkien: A Cultural Phenomenon*. London: Palgrave Macmillan, 2003.

Sale, Roger. "Tolkien and Frodo Baggins." In *Tolkien and the Critics*, edited by Neil David Isaacs and Rose A. Zimbardo. South Bend: University of Notre Dame Press, 1968.

Sergeant, Lyman Tower. "A Problem with 'Flawed Utopia': A Note of the Cost of Eutopia." In *Dark Horizons*, edited by Raffaella Baccolini and Tom Moylan, 225–32. London: Routledge, 2003.

Shippey, Tom. *J.R.R. Tolkien: Author of the Century*. London: HarperCollins, 2000.

Simpson, Eleanor R. "The Evolution of J.R.R. Tolkien's Portrayal of Nature: Foreshadowing Anti-Speciesism." *Tolkien Studies* 14 (2017): 71–89.

Strachan, Hew. *The First World War*. London: Penguin Books, 2005.

Suvin, Darko. *Metamorphoses of Science Fiction: On the Poetics and History of a Literary Genre*. Edited by Gerry Canavan. Pieterlen: Peter Lang, 2016.
Synder, Christopher. *The Making of Middle Earth: A New Look Inside the World of J. R. R. Tolkien*. New York: Sterling, 2013.
Testi, Claudio A. "Tolkien's Work: Is It Christian or Pagan? A Proposal for a 'Synthetic' Approach." *Tolkien Studies* 10 (2013): 1–47.
Tolkien, J.R.R. "Beowulf: The Monsters and the Critics." Sir Israel Gollancz Lecture. British Academy. November 25, 1936. London, United Kingdom. Accessed November 14, 2017. jenniferjsnow.files.wordpress.com/2011/01/11790039-jrr-tolkien-beowulf-the-monsters-and-the-critics.pdf.
———. *The Book of Lost Tales*. London: Ballantine Books, 1992.
———. *The Fellowship of the Rings*. London: Ballantine Books, 1994.
———. *The Hobbit*. Wilmington: Mariner Books, 2012.
———. *Leaf by Niggle*. New York: HarperCollins, 2001.
———. *The Letters of J.R.R. Tolkien*. Wilmington: Mariner Books, 2000.
———. "On Fairy Stories." In *Tolkien on Fairy-Stories Expanded Edition, with Commentary and Notes*, edited by Verilyn Fliegler and Douglas A. Anderson, 27–79. London: HarperCollins, 2008.
———. *Return of the King*. London: Ballantine Books, 1994.
———. "The Sea Bell." *The Adventures of Tom Bombadil and Other Verses from the Red Book*. Boston: Houghton Mifflin, 1963.
———. *The Silmarillion*, edited by Christopher Tolkien. London: Ballantine Books, 1999.
———. *The Two Towers*. London: Ballantine Books, 1994.
Wilkin, Peter. *The Strange Case of Tory Anarchism*. Faringdon: Libri Publishing, 2010
Wilson, Edmund. "Oo, Those Awful Orcs." In *The Bit between My Teeth: The Literary Chronicle of 1950 to 1965*. New York: Farrar, Straus and Giroux, 1965, pp. 326–32.
Witzel, E. J. Michael. *The Origin of the World Mythologies*. Oxford: Oxford University Press, 2013.

Index

1984 (Orwell), 2, 11, 12, 17, 25, 30
2312 (Robinson), 13

anarchism, 6, 19, 137, 141–143; communal versus individual, 142; definition, 141–143; left versus right, 142
anti-utopia, 40n4
Aragorn, 46–47, 178; 2-dimensional, 57; leadership, 29, 60, 68–69, 162, 168–170, 177, 181, 183n3; orphan, 130
Auden, W. H., 25, 35

Barfield, Owen. *See Splintered Light*
Bauman, Zygmunt, 46
Brave New World (Huxley), 2, 12, 16, 17, 25, 29, 30
Beowulf, 20, 29, 49
Belloc, Hilaire, 139, 140, 155
Bentham, Jeremy, 58
Beregond, 164–166, 169
Beren and Lúthien, 29, 57, 119
Berry, Wendell, 82–83
Black, Kevin, 67–68
Blake, William, 82
Boromir, 35, 62, 163, 178
Brecht, Bertolt, 11
Byronic hero, 61–62

Carlyle, Thomas, 60; *Past and Present*, 54, 59; *Sartor Resartus*, 59
Campbell, Liam, 78
Campbell, Joseph, 113, 114, 120
Carpenter, Humphrey, 107
Celebrimbor, 18
Chateau general, 68–69, 75n46
Chesterton, G. K., 139, 140; "The Ethics of Elfland," 18; *Outline of Sanity*, 140

Christianity, 45, 48–49, 72n3, 72n11, 73n18
Conrad, Joseph, 63, 64
critical utopia, 40n4
Croft, Janet Brennan, 65–66, 67–68
Curran, Giorel, 41n18, 141–142

Denethor, 163, 164–165
distributionism, 6, 138–141, 155
Day After Tomorrow, The, 99
Dispossessed, The (Le Guin), 13
Divine Comedy, The, 47, 88, 105n13, 165
Dr. Jekyll and Mr. Hyde (Stevenson), 14
"Dream of the Rood," 45
dwarves, 74n31, 87, 89, 95, 104n5, 105n19, 148–150
dystopia: definition, 2, 4, 10–11, 12, 17, 25, 29–30, 38, 40n7, 158; increased frequency of, 15
Drúedian, 28

Elves, 134n8; conservatism, 21–22, 23; as chosen people, 129; creation of, 84; as environmentalists, 14, 83, 96; fall of, 34; immortality, 21, 22; magic, 161; mating with men, 14; *mono no aware*, 22; relationship with the past, 18; xenophobia, 22
ents, 44, 85
Ents, Elves and Eriador (Dickerson and Edwards), 78
environmental movement, 5, 79–82
Eliot, T.S., 63, 64
Erewhon (Butler), 12
Erlich, Paul, 81
Eru Ilúvatar, 14, 26, 44, 89, 98
eucatastrophe, 35
evil, 11

fairyland, 117–118

fan behavior, 123
Faramir, 165
Fëanor, 18, 20, 57, 61, 163
Fimi, Dimitra, 129
Freudian desires, 130–131
Frodo, 29, 47, 77, 119, 120, 167, 177–178; 3-dimensional character, as, 57; adventurer, as, 18; folk hero, as, 125; leadership, 169; master of Sam, as, 46; Modern hero, as, 63–64, 70; orphan, as, 130

Gallant, Richard Z., 34
Game of Thrones (Martin), 181–183
Gandalf, 164, 166–167, 181, 184n7; as clergy, 143; as father figure, 130; ethics, 173n46, 174n48; leadership, 163, 168–169; magic, 161
Garth, John, 57
Gasque, Thomas, 36
Garth, John, 57, 67
Goldberry, 45, 95
Gollum, 25, 41n23, 57, 64–65, 128, 157, 167–168, 169, 177
Gondolin, 9, 12, 17, 23, 38, 83, 93, 125
Gorbag, 156–157, 165
Greer, Germaine, 3
Gríma Wormthougue, 30, 35, 168
Guardini, Roman, 46, 70, 92
Gulliver's Travels (Swift), 11, 13, 145

Hazony, Yoram, 172n10
Helms, Randall, 111–112
Hobbes, Thomas, 82
hobbits, 3, 14, 18, 62, 86, 146–147, 151, 163, 168; as children, 41n19; classes, 143; as environmentalists, 83, 93; as distributionists, 139; as mythical creatures, 124–125; faults, 22; as modern people, 63; nonviolence, 23; as Victorian gentlemen, 21, 62, 70; vulnerabilities, 24
Hobbit, The (movie Bakshi), 175
Hobbit, The (movie Jackson), 175, 178
Hobbit Party, The (Richards and Witt), 41n17, 146–148, 155
Holmes, John, 50
Hopkins, Gerard Manley, 52

Inferno, The (Dante). *See Divine Comedy*
Inconvenient Truth, An, 99
industrialization, 150–151, 154

Joan of Arc, 47, 51
John Paul II, 92
Jung, Carl, 114, 121–123, 130

Kalevala, 45, 135n25
Kolakowski, Lezek, 15, 18
Knepper, B.G., 10
Kubrick, Stanley, 176
Kumar, Krishan, 15
Kuznets, Lois, 41n19

Laudato Si, 92–94
leadership, 6
legendarium, 1, 10; chosen peoples in, 129; class in, 46; popularity, 1; original sin, 34; race in, 14, 129–130; religion in, 15; reception, 3; sacramental quality, 37; sources, 5
"La Belle Sans Merci" (Keats), 118
Latour, Bruno, 72n6
Limits of Growth, The, 81
liquid modernity. *See* Bauman, Zygmunt
Lewis, C.S., 15, 65, 115, 120
Lobdell, Jared, 57
Locke, John, 82
Looking Backward (Bellamy), 10, 12
Lord of the Rings, The (movie Bakshi), 175
Lord of the Rings, The (movie Jackson), 175, 176–178

Madison, James, 10
Maeglin, 23
Madsen, Catherine, 73n18
magic, 22, 152, 161; embalming, relation to, 161; machines, compared to, 153; magia versus goeteia, 153, 173n34
magic realism, 134n15
Manichaeism, 34
Marx, Karl, 17, 72n4, 140
Matrix, 16
Manwë, 44, 98
medievalism, 43–51

men: ambivalence about nature, 84; fall of, 34
Mere Wife, A (Headley), 74n24
Merry, 24, 46, 51, 65, 169
Moralistic Therapeutic Deism, 116–117, 120–122; in relation to fan behavior, 117
Mordor, 24, 28, 30, 58, 70; creatures one-dimensional, 27; damage done to leaders, 24; environment, relation to, 77, 81, 92, 93, 94, 99; economy, 25–27, 27; fleeting nature, 37; industrialization, compared to, 60; leadership, 137, 155, 156, 157, 158–160, 161–162, 168; Modernism, relation to, 61, 63, 67–68, 70, 74n28; underworld, as a, 132; utopia, relation to, 33
Morgoth, 4, 24, 155; centralization of power, 28; chateau general, 67, 68; environment, relation to, 77, 86–87, 93, 98, 104n5; devolution, 14, 28; division of will, 28, 155, 161; greed for silimarils, 33; intellectual sin, 88, 94; power over Middle-earth, 29; rebellion against Eru, 61, 130
Morris, William, 11, 13, 19, 52, 54, 59–60
Modernism, 5, 61, 62–70
myth, 5, 50, 57, 86, 104n6, 134n5, 134n13, 134n18; anachronisms, 127–128; atmosphere, 126–129; creation, 126; compared to pop culture, 110; definition, 108, 133n1; journey to the underworld, 132; family romance, 130–131; negative effects, 132; of Middle-earth, 109; property of peoples, 142; relation to religion, 109; relation to supernaturalism, 128–129

nature/civilization binary, 85–86
Newman, John Henry, 52, 53, 54
News from Nowhere (Morris), 11, 13, 19, 101
Norse mythology, 29, 44, 45, 132
northern courage, 29, 124
Númenóreans 3n3: ban on, 89; chosen people, 129; "elvish" characteristics, 34; destruction of nature, 98–99; fall of, 34; "man-like" characteristics, 34

oaths, 46, 72n8, 165, 169, 184n6
Odysseus. See *Inferno, The*
Old Man Willow, 44, 79, 95
O'Neill, Timothy, 134n13
orcs, 27, 65, 67, 104n5; breeds, 158, 160; cannibalism, 32; class, relation to, 181; compatibility with Christian theology, 31; creation, 30; elves, relation to, 130; environment, relation to, 28, 84, 85; family, 33; greed, 33; free will, 29, 30–33, 105n8, 123, 158, 165, 173n44; leadership style, 156–160, 165; species, relation to, 14; sense of justice, 32; as uncontrollable, 30, 162
Orwell, George, 3, 12, 40n4, 144–145
Oxford Movement, 53–54
Owen, Wilfrid, 66

paganism, 29, 45, 47–48, 49–50, 72n3, 72n10, 72n11, 73n14, 97, 100, 132, 184n9
Pippin, 24, 25, 31, 35, 47, 66, 163–166
Postmodernism, 5, 8n6, 61, 121
Princess and the Goblin, The (MacDonald), 55
Providence, 33, 36–37, 84, 91, 183
Pusey, Edward, 55

Quadragesimo Anno, 90–91, 138

Rank, Otto, 130
Red Fairy Book, The (Lang), 55
Rerum Novarum, 90–91, 138
Remarque, Erich, 66
Republic (Plato), 2, 10, 17, 19, 22, 33, 39
Ring of Nibelung, 45
Roman Catholicism, 5, 49, 53, 72n10, 114, 170; limits in, 88–89, 90; relation to *The Lord of the Rings*, 94; syncretism in, 47
romance novels, 56
Romanticism, 5, 46, 51–52, 57, 61–62, 73n20; and environmentalism, 55, 77, 78–79, 82, 86
Rosebury, Brian, 24–25, 26, 57

Ruskin, John, 59–60

sacrifice of Abraham, 87
Sale, Roger, 63
Sam, 29, 37, 80, 95, 119, 123, 126, 128, 132, 177, 178; changing class, 139; folk hero, as, 125; modeled after World War I soldiers, 65
Saruman, 21, 24, 25, 30, 33, 35, 67, 147, 150, 161, 167–168; environment, relation to, 81; as a "modern" character, 27–28, 58
Sauron, 4, 24, 57, 67–68, 94, 155, 158; Anti-Christ, 132; centralization of will, 28; chateau general, 68–69; devolution of, 28, 41n23, 99, 161; division of power, 28, 29, 159; paranoia, 58, 60, 168; weaknesses of, 25, 28, 30, 35
Sergent, Lyman Tower, 11, 12
Shagrat, 156–157, 164–165
She (Haggard), 56
Shelob, 85, 181, 183n2
Shippey, Tom, 21, 27, 28, 57, 94
Shroeder, Sharin, 65
Silent Spring (Carson), 78
Silvestris, Bernadus, 50
Simpson, Eleanor, 86
Sir Gawain and the Green Knight, 45
Smeagol. *See* Gollum
Small Is Beautiful (Schumacher), 103n2
Solzhenitsyn, Aleksandr, 177
Splintered Light (Fiegler), 100
Sterling, Grant, 42n42
Strachin, Hew, 66
Strange Case of Tory Anarchism (Wilkin), 144–145
Sturlson, Snurri, 73n15
subcreation, 26, 86, 87, 93, 102
Suvin, Darko, 11
Swift, Jonathan, 10, 11, 144, 145
Synder, Christopher, 72n1

Tea Club and Barrovian Society, 67
teleology, 44, 46, 51, 84
Testi, Claudio A., 49
Thangorodrim, 2, 12, 14, 137, 155, 159, 163; centralized, 28; chaotic, 30; creatures, one dimensional, 27; damage done to masters, 24; destruction of, 98; environment, relation to, 27, 81, 93, 94, 99; Modernism, relation to, 61, 67; specialization in, 160, 161–162; underworld, as a, 132; utopias, resemblance to, 33
Thomas Aquinas, 53
Tolkien, Christopher, 151, 175
Tolkien, J.R.R., 3; anti-Semitism, 130; anti-socialism, 147; authority, relationship with, 19, 125, 137, 143, 169; *Book of Lost Tales, The*, 57, 65, 109; conservatism, 145, 146; electoral politics, relationship with, 143–144; *Hobbit, The*, 1, 3, 19–20, 41n19, 62, 70–71, 75n48, 86, 109, 111, 124, 127, 130, 134n5, 147–150, 151; "Kôr: In a City Lost and Dead," 57; "Leaf by Niggle," 101; *Lord of the Rings, The*, 1, 3, 9, 12, 15, 22, 29, 31, 36, 43, 44, 48–49, 51, 57–59, 60, 62–65, 70–71, 73n18, 75n48, 77, 78, 83, 86, 94, 101, 105n8, 109, 111, 119, 124, 127–128, 130, 132, 134n5, 145, 146–147, 150–151, 156–161, 164–169, 170, 174n55, 176–178, 181; "On Fairy-Stories," 6, 21, 48, 112–113, 152; machines, attitude toward, 151–155, 160–161, 171, 173n34; "Monsters and the Critics, The," 114; mythology for England, 109; pronatalism, 80; *Sea Bell, The*, 117, 119; *Silmarillion, The*, 1, 3, 9, 12, 14–15, 18, 20, 26, 28, 29, 31, 34, 36–37, 44, 45, 48, 49, 57, 59, 60, 61–62, 65, 71, 75n47, 75n48, 77, 78, 83–88, 97, 98, 100, 102, 105n8, 109, 125, 128–129, 130, 132, 145, 148, 181, 184n9; trees, relationship with, 96–98, 102
Tolkien, Mabel, 52
Tom Bombadil, 45, 79, 95, 176–177
transhumanism, 111
Trolls, 27, 181; creation, 31, 104n5, 162; greed of, 33; nature, relationship with, 85
Trollope, Anthony, 55, 56
Tory anarchism, 144

Toryism, 6
Tractarianism. *See* Oxford Movement
Tuor, 23, 57, 130
Túrin, 44, 57, 163
Turgon, 23
Trouble in Triton (Delany), 13

Ulmo, 23, 44, 99, 130
Uruk-hai, 14, 30, 32, 35, 99, 157
utilitarianism, 4, 29, 58, 59, 60, 70, 74n28, 89–90, 105n16, 105n17, 166–167, 171, 173n46, 173n47
utopia, 15, 38, 101, 180; authoritarian tendencies in, 19; distributionist, 140; creepiness, 16–17; definition, 2, 4, 5, 10–15, 40n1; rigidity, 17; resemblance to Tolkien's evil societies, 33; revolution, relation to, 18; wealth redistribution, 19
Utopia (More), 2, 10, 17, 19, 39
"Utopia is Creepy" (Carr), 16

Valar, 23, 28, 42n43, 49, 89, 104n5; creation of Middle-earth, 83, 84–85; forces of nature, 44, 93; guardians of nature, 98; remaking Middle-earth, 98; pagan pantheon, 44, 93, 128

Verbal Behavior in Politics (Graber), 97
video games, 179; *Hobbit, The* (Melbourne House), 176, 179; *Lord of the Rings, The* (Melbourne House), 176; *Lord of the Rings, The* (New Line Cinema), 179; *Middle-earth: Shadow of Mordor* (Monolith Productions), 180–181
Victorian medieval, 5, 43, 52–60, 69–70, 73n22; distributionism, relation to, 141

Ward-Perkins, Bryan, 104n3
Waugh, Evelyn, 144–145
Weisman, Alan, 78
Wormtogue. *See* Gríma Wormtongue
We (Zamyatin), 30, 40n4
whig view of history, 58, 100, 132
Wilson, Edmund, 3
Witch-king, 47, 51, 58, 157, 166
Witzel, Michael, 133n1
World War I, 65–70, 75n46
wyrd, 29

Yavanna, 85

About the Author

Mark Doyle is a professor of English and Chair of the Humanities Department at Marion Military Institute. He earned a BA in English from the Virginia Military Institute, an MBA in Finance from the College of William and Mary, an MA in English from the College of Saint Rose, and a PhD in English from Indiana University. Before teaching at MMI, he was a financial analyst for General Electric and served as a United States Marine Corps officer. He enjoys spending his free time with his wife and five children.

www.ingramcontent.com/pod-product-compliance
Lightning Source LLC
Chambersburg PA
CBHW050906300426
44111CB00010B/1404